THE POLICING MIND

Developing Trauma Resilience for a New Era

Jessica K. Miller

With a foreword by John Sutherland

T0313508

P

First published in Great Britain in 2022 by

Policy Press, an imprint of
Bristol University Press
University of Bristol
1-9 Old Park Hill
Bristol
BS2 8BB
UK
t: +44 (0)117 954 5940
e: bup-info@bristol.ac.uk

Details of international sales and distribution partners are available at
policy.bristoluniversitypress.co.uk

© Bristol University Press 2022

British Library Cataloguing in Publication Data
A catalogue record for this book is available from the British Library

ISBN 978-1-4473-6190-9 paperback
ISBN 978-1-4473-6191-6 ePub
ISBN 978-1-4473-6192-3 ePdf

The right of Jessica K. Miller to be identified as author of this work has been asserted
by her in accordance with the Copyright, Designs and Patents Act 1988.

All rights reserved: no part of this publication may be reproduced, stored in a
retrieval system, or transmitted in any form or by any means, electronic, mechanical,
photocopying, recording, or otherwise without the prior permission of Bristol
University Press.

Every reasonable effort has been made to obtain permission to reproduce copyrighted
material. If, however, anyone knows of an oversight, please contact the publisher.

The statements and opinions contained within this publication are solely those of the
author and not of the University of Bristol or Bristol University Press. The University
of Bristol and Bristol University Press disclaim responsibility for any injury to persons
or property resulting from any material published in this publication.

Bristol University Press and Policy Press work to counter discrimination on grounds
of gender, race, disability, age and sexuality.

Cover design: Lyn Davies Design
Front cover image: Zoonar GmbH / Alamy Stock Photo
Bristol University Press and Policy Press use environmentally
responsible print partners.
Printed and bound by CPI Group (UK) Ltd,
Croydon, CR0 4YY

This book is dedicated to all those who, at times, may have felt drenched in human suffering. The world is waiting for you. (And it's a beautiful world.)

Contents

List of figures and tables

Figures

Tables

Glossary

CPTSD	Complex post-traumatic stress disorder
CSE	Child sexual exploitation
DNA	Deoxyribonucleic acid
EMDR	Eye-Movement desensitisation and reprocessing
fMRI	Functional magnetic resonance imaging
GDPR	General data protection regulation
HMICFRS	Her Majesty's Inspectorate of Constabulary and Fire and Rescue Services
MRI	Magnetic resonance imaging
MTA	Marauding terror attack
NCA	National Crime Agency
NHS	National Health Service
PCSO	Police community support officer
PFEW	Police Federation of England and Wales
PFNI	Police Federation of Northern Ireland
PSNI	Police Service of Northern Ireland
PTSD	Post-traumatic stress disorder
TJTL	*Policing: The Job and the Life Survey*
UK	United Kingdom
US	United States

About the author

Jessica K. Miller is Principal Investigator for the Trauma Resilience in UK Policing project at the University of Cambridge, consultant for the Royal Foundation of The Duke and Duchess of Cambridge and Director of Research for Surfwell. She was also Director of Research at Police Care UK for 7 years and now works across other high-risk professions including the RNLI, the military, journalism and construction in the UK and abroad delivering training, advice and guidance on cognitive resilience, specialising in trauma.

Acknowledgements

My first thanks go to the thousands of police, military, NHS patients and civilians who have given their time and shared their darkest times with the research I've been privileged to conduct over the last ten years. My second, to the driver who hit me with their car in November 2009 and the officers from Dorset Police, including in particular Les Fry who took the time to notice in me that something wasn't quite right in the weeks and months that followed. You set me on a personal voyage of discovery into trauma impact, which enabled me to enquire of myself and to fall in love with the human brain and bring that respect home to the people who deserve it most, those who risk their lives to serve on the front line. To Cheryl Pinner, Alan Page and Simon Megicks who watched and supported my progress from awkward Critical Incident Personal Support Team recruit and Traveller Liaison Officer to police trainer 18 years later – thank you. A fulsome thank you to Brendan Burchell who took me back in under his wing after my epic fail as a young academic going through a very hard time, and for giving me my first First as an MPhil student, despite never really understanding how I managed to get into Cambridge! For the inspiration from day one of reading what on earth PTSD was, my *alma pater*, Chris Brewin – you have shown more patience and offered such firm but discrete rigour to my journey as a budding neuropsychologist than I could ever have imagined. Thanks to Jan Wiener, who urged me to pursue the PhD despite my hesitancy and bore witness to so many ideas, their gestations and, at times, their graceful diminishing – often against a backdrop of the sea. An attitude of gratitude to Jem Shackleford for his professional assistance but also his support in my ambitions to bring a touch of Zen to all things blue and uniformed. Huge gratitude to Gill Scott-Moore – without you, none of this would have come to fruition – thank you for your trust, your sponsorship and your laughter. Chè Donald, you're the naughty cousin I always wanted and Lee Jackson – what can I say, the brother I don't think I deserve. You are family. (Fact). Kevin Maddick, thank you for your introduction to Lee, for your relentless smile and your shared fancy for all things neurological. Alex Peart, your companionship from *Cerne Vegas* to Greater Manchester will never be forgotten and will always raise in me a cheeky smile. To James Mallows and the whole Surfwell team – thank you for accepting me on board (eventually, standing up!) and for having the bravery to extend mental health beyond tired offices back into nature where resilience surely and truly belongs. For those pioneers of trauma resilience, those who teach, listen and champion honest talk about what it means to police in the UK: Alan Fairclough who heard my vulnerability and went on to help me establish a formidable programme, Phil Spencer for the wellbeing fire in his belly and, more recently, Mark Chambers, my professional wing man and resident poet who helps us find words against all odds. A big thanks too to the wonderful Daniel and Sharon of Police Care UK for their input on the techniques. Mary Elliott-Davies and Magdalena Soffia, your sisterhood while trying to make sense of thousands of descriptions of horrific trauma exposure will stay with me – I couldn't have done it without your tenderness, tenacity and humour. S.J. Lennie and Fi Meechan, thank you for wearing your heart on your sleeves and looking out for mine and trusting in compassion on the front line. John Sutherland, thank you for teaching me how to stand up and share with honour. Neil Basu, thank you for your continued faith and leadership in telling it how it is and being the human leader we all need. I'd like also to thank Karen Hodgson for her inclusive approach to all things trauma resilience and for offering me the privilege of supporting the work of an incredible organisation that has the capacity to change our future in the UK. To Ash Alexander-Cooper, thank you for giving me permission to buzz and thrive in an ambition to make a difference despite (and perhaps because of) early life challenges. A profound Thank You to Rick Hanson: as you are probably well aware from our interactions, you have changed my life since I first heard a neuropsychologist who specialised in trauma see the value of the human heart and the wonder of the human brain. That you feature throughout the book, alongside Tara Brach is nothing less than mind-blowing and beautiful. To Nick Cave, thank you for being the most *surprising* 'thank you' a neurogeek could imagine – thank you for articulating so tenderly the way that our brain plays with time in our greatest pain, borne out of our deepest love. To my grandmother, who at 97 years old offers me her insight into counselling policing minds and who this year finally retires. And finally, to the family I thought I would never have: to my companions, my reasons for being where I am *and as happy as I am* and as *grateful* as I am for being in this world at all, *just as it is*: Den, Null and Void.

Foreword

John Sutherland, author and former police officer

I joined the police service in 1992 and served as an officer for more than 25 years. I loved my job with every single fibre of my being: it was my duty and my joy. But, in 2013, I suffered a massive nervous breakdown – caused in significant part by the pressures and strains of work – and it led to my eventual medical retirement from policing.

I have learned any number of powerful lessons since the early days of my illness, but perhaps the most significant of them is this: that it would be impossible to do the job of a police officer for any length of time and to remain untouched – unaffected – by the things you see and the things you do. The painful privilege of policing is to venture repeatedly into life's hurting places – at the scenes of crimes and car crashes and every other kind of catastrophe – and to find yourself face-to-face with every possible kind of human trauma and suffering. Every police officer has stories to tell of people and places they will never forget.

But, for the overwhelming majority of my career, no one in policing was talking about those things – about the entirely unavoidable physical, emotional and psychological consequences of a life lived in blue. It was just the job, and we all got on with it.

Fortunately, times are changing. We are beginning to have a much more open and compassionate conversation about mental health in policing. We are starting to develop a much better understanding of the endlessly demanding realities of the job and their impact on the women and men who serve.

Dr Jess Miller understands the policing mind better than anyone else I know. In this timely and important book, she explains how the brain functions and, in particular, how it is impacted by the unique rigours of police work. Most importantly, she suggests a series of practical tools and techniques to help officers improve their mental resilience and wellbeing.

It is no overstatement to suggest that it might just be a book that saves lives.

Preface

Policing in the 2020s has taken a hit. Raw from austerity measures, propelled into a global pandemic, reeling from a backlash from unrest in the US, contending with an increased terror threat and accepting shocking figures on the impact of trauma on policing, the service also faces the prospect of training thousands of new recruits.

That policing is under pressure is perhaps nothing new. What *is* new, is a power surge of resilience in the world of neuroscience – as yet untapped by the front line.

As forces across the UK and the world forage to procure or recycle interventions to try and meet the needs of their force, there is a resource that lies dormant. That resource is one of understanding the policing brain.

Understanding the common experience of trauma exposure and burnout.

Understanding that whatever experiences are inevitable on the job, damage from them is not.

Understanding that however many individuals make up a team, a network, a force or an institution, each of those individuals has something in common – the ability to work better with their brains.

So long as policing sees the answer to its mental health challenges as being under the invisible cloak of its culture, at the discretion of a hierarchy of wellbeing decision-makers or in the hands of a tireless third sector, then it will never grasp its own resilience.

This book takes a fresh look at the world of policing through the lens of the human brain. In doing so, it radically challenges notions of police culture and empowers the individual to embrace the reality of their experience in the service. The book encourages officers and staff on the front line and in high-risk roles to understand the neural mechanisms already at play every day on the job. It introduces practical cognitive techniques police can apply on their own or with others in the service to help make sense of their experiences and stay well.

Many officers adopt the approach of mimicking the resilience of those who *don't* report adversity within policing. When we do this, we risk getting in our own way. If we compare ourselves to others who are not like us (those who are seemingly and somewhat unrealistically unaffected by anything), there is a tendency for us to dissociate from and suppress our genuine response to what is going on around us. This limits our chances of doing something about the lives we *actually* lead.

Our approach is to take an honest, down-to-earth and pragmatic look at the life lessons and inherent strengths that lie beneath the negative states and experiences of contemporary policing. Our experience of working with thousands of voices in policing and our understanding of the scientific evidence tells us that those who accept that they experience adversity are those most likely to see the benefit from thinking more clearly about it. The benefits of working with how you think can revolutionise your inner life, your interactions and your sense of what it means to do what you do.

If there is one thing you can do for public service, it's to befriend your own brain.

Why the need to be resilient? How it feels to be a police officer in the UK and why

Introduction

This exploration into the policing brain begins with taking stock of the world in which we find ourselves in the 2020s. As there are calls on everyone's resilience, so are there calls on the resilience of emergency responders, police officers, police staff and those who share their lives with them. Some challenges we all share, and some are unique to our own jobs and the ways we have adapted to them. The opening chapter looks at the obvious environmental influences on contemporary policing from the wider social and political sphere of criminality and social care. Crucial findings from socio-psychological research show how we interpret these wider influences and how they translate into our perceptions of everyday policing – and how the emerging discipline of 'police wellbeing' addresses them. Finally, we introduce some initial glimpses of what makes a 'policing mind', supported by the latest developments in neuroscience. In doing so we open to a new way of perceiving police resilience – from the inside, out.

The times we are in

The 2020s began with a year when the phrase 'unprecedented times' tripped off the tongue of every social and political commentator, and the police service was not immune to the infectious sense of instability that COVID-19 brought with it. The nation's latent anxiety was palpable, intensified by months of disparate attempts by governments and scientists the world over to gain any grip on what was needed to keep the public safe.

So, what might this have meant for the policing brain? At home in the UK, serving police had their own version of events. Increases in domestic violence[1] and attendance to sudden deaths[2] brought with them relentless exposure to the suffering of the vulnerable, worsened by forces feeling under-resourced and ill-prepared and in addition to officers' personal worries of contaminating their family's safe space at home. Resilience specialists have highlighted that some individuals may be more vulnerable to the impact of the pandemic than others due to their underlying issues and professional histories.[3] Areas of concern included those with experience of other contagion-related incidents (such as the Salisbury poisoning) and those waiting for HIV tests from public assaults. In this book, we will explore similar themes to these (that is, the nature of anxiety, threat perception and retriggering of trauma impact) in the broader context of the policing brain. Then, in July 2021, news from the University of Oxford relayed worrying neuroscience data suggesting that in just mild cases of COVID-19, the virus attacked a key part of the brain on which we rely for trauma resilience – findings that raised alarm throughout the scientific and emergency response community.[4]

The start to the 2020s was awash with unknowns and no snapshot of contemporary policing can avoid at least *some* mention of the nation's withdrawal from the European Union as one of those. The immediate demands that Brexit exerts on policing in the main may never be fully quantifiable. Yet it is reasonable to expect that there will be demands on local policing that may develop over time as the nation beds into its new separateness and internal divisions. Many argue that policing culture has long left behind its 'statist' perspective (a term coined by Rowe[5]) as our localities, our policies, our forces and our social lives have become increasingly culturally diverse. But now what? What pressure on law enforcement and public protection will build with fear of economic decline, civil unrest and the fracturing of community cohesion? The time will come when the ramifications of Brexit (be they big, small, negative or positive) will be less about a chronic, tired political rhetoric and simply about the very real lived experience of life in the UK. In our exploration of the policing brain, we will look at what some of these themes of uncertainty, a sense of 'other' and social connectedness mean for mental resilience on the job.

The decade also began with more overt manifestations of public discontent, including the disruptive campaigning of the Extinction Rebellion and the reigniting of the Black Lives Matter movement. The repercussions of the latter showed how politicisation of crime dynamics can complicate police resilience. One incident stands out as a remarkable testimony to the complexity of 2020s uneasiness. On 13 June 2020, far-right protestors gathered in central London to 'protect statues' (in response to statues commemorating the work of slave traders having been vandalised in the UK, in association with Black Lives Matter contesting police brutality in the US).[6] A right-wing extremist activist urinated on the memorial of PC Keith Palmer, who was murdered on 22 March 2017 defending the public at Westminster from a terror attack by Khalid Masood. The insult of the defilement boggled the minds and aggrieved the hearts of citizens across the UK. For the policing mind, the cut was deep. How does an officer make sense of a member of their nation's public defiling the memory of their colleagues (a public protector) as part of a counter-protest against grievances by law enforcement in an entirely different nation? Again, in March 2021, 20 officers were injured in a violent attack in Bristol in response to a policing bill introducing COVID-related restrictions on the right to protest.[7] This book will explore how the policing brain might deal better with these notions of contradiction, of public sympathy, of humiliation and of situations where expressions of discontent seek a common enemy.

> There's no other job that comes close in terms of the scrutiny that police officers are subject to: from politicians, from the media, from the Independent Office for Police Conduct, from the public we come

into contact with and from *anyone with an armchair and an opinion.*[8]

The 2020s also brought with them unique pressures on the public purse. As echoes from the 2010s spending review still resounded, austerity measures withdrew facilities such as the police bar, canteens and gyms, compromising opportunities for police to regroup in between jobs and shifts and reducing basic spaces for on-the-job decompression. While 'canteen culture' may have once been condemned for being a subversive hot bed of discontent and social intolerance, its virtues for enabling peers in a unique job role to align, connect and mutually support have not been forgotten.[9] The human cost to officer *mental health* of removing modest, natural places to facilitate vital cognitive functions such as trauma processing was either ignored or misunderstood.

Perhaps the hardest blow struck by cuts to public sector funding has been the lack of sufficient numbers of officers on the ground. Beneath the increasingly clichèd mainstream parlance of there being fewer 'bobbies on the beat', there is the brutal reality of single crewing. Research by the Police Federation of England and Wales (PFEW) in 2016 revealed that verbal abuse and physical attacks requiring medical attention were significantly elevated in those who were often or always single-crewed.[10] In the 2018 PFEW *Demand, Capacity and Welfare Survey*, the proportion of respondents from front-line roles reporting that they were often or always single-crewed over the previous 12-month period was 76.1 per cent.[11] Such research highlights how single crewing robs officers of peer support, physical backup, shared decision-making, debrief and opportunities to reflect, boost morale and make sense. This book seeks to offer some insight into how officers can cultivate a sense of being resourced, feeling connected, and being backed up by others to fill the gap that single crewing has left behind in contemporary police resilience.

There have been considerable challenges to police resilience emanating from some extraordinary circumstances in the dawning of the 2020s. So, how have these challenges been managed by those *responsible* for developing the wellbeing of serving UK officers and staff? The culture of police wellbeing is something to welcome and to comprehend – but still, one to query. From 'guarding the guards' to more contemporary explorations of 'policing the police' and modern-day accountability[12] an alternative discourse emerged in 2018 of 'protecting the protectors'. With more of a focus on understanding the impact of harm to individuals on the job, initiatives such as the PFEW's *Protect the Protectors* campaign[13] have contributed to (an arguably overdue) public acknowledgement that police officers and staff share with wider society very human vulnerabilities to physical and mental harm. The first decades of the millennium saw the emergence of highly respected business models for managing wellbeing responsibly and effectively within forces[14] as well as the development of the online platform Oscar Kilo, 'home to the National Police Wellbeing Service' launched in 2018[15] alongside promises for governmental reform with the Police Covenant in 2020.

However, there is still progress to be made. We suggest that much can be achieved with the help of neuroscience. Neuroscience is a way of looking at life which deals with the functions, structure and chemicals of the human brain and this can help us understand how to get underneath a *felt sense* of what it means to police in the UK. With that understanding, we will be in a better position to make policy and operational changes from which policing brains are likely to benefit most.

There are already signs of hope. Understanding the inner workings of the policing mind are being acknowledged with sensitivity and respect in pioneering wellbeing work, such as that on 'emotional labour'. Emotional labour is the notion that a job (in our case, policing) requires individuals to make a deliberate effort to manage their expression of the stress, fear, grief or empathy that resonates from the territory of human distress in which the job operates. That effort, Lennie[16] argues, requires scrutiny and support:

> There are rules around how our police officers are permitted to experience and express their emotions. ... Worse still, these 'rules' do not just govern our officer's emotional experiences within

the organisational setting (on the street or back in the station) but they also stretch out into their family homes and social relationships. What we find is that police officers have nowhere to turn to experience, express and process their emotions without fear of judgement or recrimination.

Managing what it means to make a difference, to help those who are in challenging situations (on either side of the law) may be intrinsic to the job. But are those implicit human skills definable or learnable? New discourses in the world of police wellbeing suggest they are – or, at least, they are becoming so. The National Forum for Health and Wellbeing at Work[17] offers emotional labour a helping hand with the Compassion at Work Tool Kit, given that 'there is increasing research evidence to show that empathy and compassion in the workplace are related to a number of positive outcomes related to improved employee wellbeing, increased productivity and reduced cost to the business'.

This book will show that the way that our brain has evolved to perform at its highest level is contingent on our ability to manage compassion – and, what is more, that this is perhaps one of the most critical factors to improve resilience on the job.

What this more *intuitive* understanding of stress resilience and humans' inner emotional might mean for operational policing is still fairly new territory. Nonetheless, some are breaking boundaries with tangible results. 'Trauma informed supervision'[18] is an intervention with Camden and Islington NHS Trust which piloted novel supervision of Metropolitan Police officers – supervision which explored the influence of their repeated exposure on their wellbeing and behaviour, especially when dealing with serious youth violence and conflict. Results indicate that looking at trauma impact square in the face at an operational level can improve officer resilience and performance, delivering real change in relations with offenders and wider communities in which police serve. This book will demonstrate more broadly how encouraging the brain to be proactive in the face of trauma exposure, rather than avoidant, can revitalise individuals' resilience and bring newfound confidence in communicating about life's knocks – communication that can improve peer support, personal relationships and even how we deal with conflict on the job.

Changing crimes and changing minds

We have briefly considered some broad environmental, political and social influences on police resilience and how wellbeing and trauma-informed initiatives are gaining new ground. For us to stand secure in resilience, though, we should acknowledge that the world of crime and public service is continually shifting. Key shifts are changes in the nature of criminal acts (including those related to technology and to terrorism) and the demand on policing inherited from a depleted public sector (particularly regarding mental health and adult social care).

As the social world becomes increasingly digitised, criminal acts become so too. As they play out on screen, digital scenarios provide far less accurate information about when and where incidents happened location-based incidents do, and this makes a difference. Space and time are two very concrete components that are critical for our ability to make sense of experiences, especially those which are traumatic.[19] Without the date stamp and pinned location of 'this happened then and there', a traumatic incident can linger uncategorised in memory, potentially trespassing into what we consider to be the here and now. What is more, in digital depictions of traumatic incidents, a victim's suffering is separated from us physically (because it is on screen) and our brains cannot call on our bodily resources to reach out and 'do something'. Much of resilience is known to emanate from how we use our body (consciously and subconsciously) to understand another's predicament and to take action.[20] The perils of losing our connection with our body, with what is going on around us and of managing the sense of helplessness that can come with that, will all feature as key components of policing resilience in this book.

Perhaps the most toxic disadvantage of cybercrime is related to the ever more common phenomenon of online Child Sexual Exploitation.[21] CSE challenges our most basic human worldviews: evolutionary principles of protecting the sanctity of childhood innocence, sensuality and family. We know from established trauma literature that incidents that contradict our world view and which violate our beliefs and goals can constitute a 'moral injury' from our work[22] and are strongly associated with Post-Traumatic Stress Disorder (PTSD). We will look more closely at how those in public protection cope with these violations and explore how we might use the brain to mitigate against the inevitable damage that these crimes cause to the wellbeing of those who fight them.

Terrorism is another area of policing that brings with it unique challenges – not just in terms of what it is to be a social animal but also what it is to have a culture, religion or ideology. It has also changed over recent times. As terrorism is defined, redefined, conceptualised and reconceptualised according to change in political discourse, technological advancements and even in response to the pandemic,[23] operational policing has a job to do on the ground that it needs to get on with. This job is not always just about fighting crime, but arguably it is about sustaining social cohesion. UK policing has sustained a response to terrorist activity that has morphed and fluctuated greatly over the past 40 years. From the home-grown, political, targeted attacks of 'The Troubles' (peaking in the 1980s and 1990s), to the mass critical incidents deriving from Libya and Iran (including the Lockerbie disaster in 1988); from the large-scale assaults of 9/11 in the US (2001) and the UK's first coordinated suicide attack by Islamic terrorists on commuters on 7 July 2005 to the Manchester Arena attack on children and families in 2017; and the spate of Marauding Terror Attacks (MTAs) from 2017 through to the 2020 s by the British right wing, including the murder of MP Jo Cox in 2016, we can see that terrorism is a very diverse phenomenon, with which the policing brain has to keep up. Richards[24] asserts that the essence of terrorism 'lies in its intent to generate a psychological impact beyond the immediate victims' to non-civilians and combatants. The psychological impact of terrorism is well recognised,[25] and this book will explore what this means for police's resilience in investigative, response and family liaison roles. We will examine what unique challenges contemporary terrorism can bring to the policing brain and will learn from officers themselves about what it means to adapt their resilience to fit those challenges.

Our brief tour of the changing nature of the demands on UK policing concludes with recognition of the impact that the 'broken' adult social care and mental health system[26] has on operational policing. The strain on the allocation of police resources to meet public sector shortfall elsewhere has not gone unnoticed by the media. In 2020, two fifths of people in England waiting for NHS support called emergency or crisis services,[27] and in 2019, the Police Service of Northern Ireland (PSNI) stated that 'one in five people in Northern Ireland will have a mental health issue at some point during their life, and each month there are around 1,600 calls made to police that have a mental health component'.[28] For call handlers, dispatchers and response teams, the cost of the emotional labour conveyed by these calls needs to be fully understood before it can be met with resilience, as echoed by the National Police Chiefs' Council (NPCC):

> We know from understanding those tragic incidents gone awry that police officers are not a substitute for professional mental health care, even where officers are acting with compassion and attempting to ensure the dignity and safety of those detained. We recognise the role of the police service as one of society's 'safety-nets' but remind everyone that this has natural limitations.[29]

There has been a long appreciation that policing is about people – regardless of which side of law and order they affiliate with at any one time. Bayley[30] poignantly described police patrol officers as 'tour guides in the museum of human frailty'. This book acknowledges the frailty that front line policing works with on a day-to-day basis and does not avoid the uncomfortable reality that human frailty is just as much a feature for police officers and staff as it is non-police. The question is how can we work with that frailty to mitigate against it?

What officers and staff tell us themselves

As we explore the world of trauma exposure and resilience in UK policing, we explore personal experiences – either through voices expressed in national surveys or in-depth studies. We will also listen to single voices who narrate their own human story of policing. Before doing that we will familiarise ourselves with the headline news and take-home messages from recent research, ranging from long-established inspection reports to the latest studies following a year-in-the-life of new recruits.

Inspections into the activities and service delivery of the territorial forces of England and Wales date back to 1868. In 2019, Her Majesty's Inspectorate of Constabulary (HMIC)[31] stated, 'high levels of public service motivation – even to the detriment of individual wellbeing – are in the police's DNA'. In the same year, a wellbeing survey conducted by the Chief Police Officers' Staff Association reported that 10 per cent of chief officers registered high anxiety scores with 'an absence of appropriate support for them in their own force'. Wellbeing is being recognised as an issue at the higher echelons of the institution, as evidenced by the National Wellbeing Service, launched in April 2019.[32] The programme delivered its first national survey with the University of Durham in 2020.[33] Using an undisclosed 'civilian' screen, the report told us that 67.1 per cent of 18,066 officers and staff from the 43 territorial forces of England and Wales met the threshold for PTSD. The project also reported on anxiety[34] and factors synonymous with resilience, such as a sense of being valued among coworkers, the public and their own force, and a sense of 'relatedness' to others.

One of the most comprehensive and consistent acumens into police wellbeing comes from the PFEW series of surveys into demand, capacity and welfare in 2016, 2018 and 2020. Tracking year on year changes was complicated by the extraordinary conditions of 2020, making trend analysis a little less straightforward than what may have been possible had COVID not struck. Since 2016, there have been some positive signs of progress: for example, in 2016, 63 per cent of officers that had sought professional help for their mental health and wellbeing had disclosed this information to their line manager, rising to 70 per cent in 2018 and again to 71 per cent in 2020. In addition, in 2016, 54 per cent of those that disclosed seeking help to their line manager also reported that they were subsequently treated with empathy, increasing to 59 per cent in 2018 and 2020. Attitudes towards mental health and wellbeing seemed to improve over the same period with the proportion of officers reporting that they would feel confident in disclosing mental health difficulties to their line managers rising from 28 per cent in 2016 to 39 per cent in 2018 and again to 43 per cent in 2020. Force openness on talking about mental health doubled from 22 per cent in 2016 to 45 per cent in 2018 and increased further to 55 per cent in 2020. Nonetheless, between 2016 and 2018 three quarters of officers were being single-crewed too often in front-line roles (such as neighbourhood, response, roads policing, operational support and investigations) and 52 per cent of officers were never (or rarely) able to take their entitled rest breaks. In 2020, the PFEW collected worrying evidence that the COVID-19 virus brought a new challenge: it was being weaponised by the public, with almost one in four officers reporting that a member of the public, believed to be carrying COVID-19, had deliberately attempted to breathe or cough on them at least once over the last six months, contributing to a significantly negative relationship between the nature of the job and officer wellbeing. A further 28 per cent of officers indicated that they had been performing specific COVID-19 duties, including those that could place them in direct contact with the virus itself, predominantly including attending sudden deaths.

PTSD is now a prominent marker of mental health in policing roles that incorporate trauma exposure. PTSD is an anxiety disorder emanating from exposure to traumatic events and includes symptoms of re-experiencing, avoidance and a sense of threat. Complex PTSD (CPTSD) is where chronic unprocessed trauma has a detrimental effect on sense of self (feelings of worthlessness or of being a failure), emotion regulation (the ability to calm down after getting upset) and relationships (becoming distant and cut off, for example). A key fact about PTSD (that is arguably underreported in society) is that as well as unpleasant personal symptoms, there are symptoms that can disturb and deplete areas of cognitive function that are integral to practical policing, including threat perception, situational awareness and memory[35] (to be discussed more in Chapter 2).

In 2018, understanding the experience of mental health and wellbeing in the UK police forces broke new ground. The

University of Cambridge, funded by the charity Police Care UK (then The Police Dependants' Trust)[36] surveyed 18,185 officers and staff of all ranks in England, Wales, Scotland and Northern Ireland on wellbeing and working conditions in a study called, *Policing: The Job and the Life* (TJTL). Critically, for the first time in history, UK police were screened for probable levels of PTSD and, for the first time in the world, a professional population was being screened for probable levels of CPTSD. The game-changing findings were that one in five UK police were likely to have clinical levels of PTSD and that the most common form of PTSD was CPTSD.[37] These figures made headline news in 2019 and raised questions in the House of Commons immediately on their release, and again 18 months later.[38]

Since the TJTL survey, a global systematic review of mental health problems in police personnel revealed[39] an overall pooled point prevalence rate of 14.2 per cent for PTSD (exceeding twice the figure previously reported in emergency responder studies). The strongest risk factors for PTSD were higher occupational stress and avoidant coping strategies, and its protective factor was higher levels of peer support. Subsequent research published as part of a national study into the use of communications hardware in the UK[40] suggested a UK police PTSD prevalence rate of 27 per cent (although this was limited to a population who reported trauma exposure only within the last six months). Whatever the calculation from whichever study, the unavoidable truth is now obvious: unprocessed police trauma is an issue and regularly leads to disorder and undisclosed distress.

Part of the impact of the TJTL findings was that PTSD aside, *the nature of the job* alone is rendering individuals vulnerable to trauma impact. This shift in literature away from individuals' unique characteristics and personal histories towards professions and livelihoods signals a new era in our understanding of trauma resilience.[41] The TJTL revealed that 90 per cent of the serving UK policing population was trauma-exposed that 53 per cent of trauma-exposed officers and staff self-reported overall fatigue, 48 per cent anxiety and 51 per cent daily or weekly sleep disturbance (51 per cent). Worryingly, of the 71 per cent of officers who shared that they had had a psychological issue as a direct result of police work, nearly all (93 per cent) said they would simply go to work as usual. Furthermore, 72 per cent of officers or staff who met the criteria for some form of PTSD said they had never even been diagnosed and only 27 per cent of those who reported a mental health issue to do with work had accessed any help whatsoever.

New indicators for PTSD in policing were also identified, and there were surprises. Inevitably, exposure to incidents at work contributed most to police developing PTSD and CPTSD. Yet, contrary to previous civilian and clinical research, PTSD and CPTSD were more common in males.[42] Being of lower rank and longer in service also predicted PTSD. Another revelation was that exposure to humiliating behaviours and sexual harassment by colleagues and the public (but not to verbal abuse, threats, or physical violence by the public) contributed to the development of CPTSD. A likely explanation for this is that over time, police acclimatise to everyday abuse and threats on the job – but being vulnerable to forms of humiliation may be the final straw for many. The notion of shame and humiliation is integral to resilience and will be discussed further later in the book.

On the back of the TJTL study, academics from Police Care UK, the University of Cambridge and the PFEW[43] went on to dissect and define what a 'traumatic incident' *meant* in UK policing. When asked about which types of trauma exposure made up more than half of their time at work: 41 per cent of respondents selected exposure to traumatic incidents (such as those involving fatalities and serious injury). A further 32 per cent selected indecent or explicit visual material (from child sexual exploitation to terrorist propaganda) and 22 per cent selected auditory trauma (such as hearing jobs being called in over the radio and taking emergency calls.).[44] Of the 1,531 traumatic work experiences described by officers and staff, the most common reference points were incidents involving children (such as abuse, fatalities and injury), sudden or unnatural deaths (and the viewing of bodies) and incidents involving serious injuries (to the public, themselves or their colleagues).[45]

Different policing roles inevitably involve different trauma exposures and are associated with different psychological risks. Role-specific studies on the impact of trauma exposure on police wellbeing tend to fall into two categories: those that deal with secondary trauma (or vicarious trauma)[46] and those that look at specific types of incidents. Regarding secondary trauma, roles involving exposure to child abuse[47] and auditory exposure through call handling and dispatch roles are widely recognised as high risk.[48] Regarding specific incidents, response policing and critical incidents (in particular, terrorist attacks) feature heavily, alongside some studies on the viewing of human remains and shooting incidents.[49] As our exploration into police resilience deepens, we will look at how different trauma exposures are perceived and processed in the brain and what this might mean for different job roles.

Our final visit to the world of research is perhaps one of the most eye-opening for our understanding of what makes being in the police so unique. While repeated survey work might help to track the ebb and flow of life in general on the thin blue line, tracking life as a *new recruit* helps us to engage in that critical phase of when the thin blue line between civilian life and the job is being crossed for the very first time. In those life-changing months, new recruits are in a prime position to narrate how expectations meet reality, how a 'culture' shows itself and through whom, how exposure to human suffering on peoples' worst days morphs from novel to being the 'new normal' and – most importantly for our exploration – how seeds of resilience are planted.

The qualitative study *Becoming Blue*[50] gave voice to a new generation (coining the phrase #newbreed) and the hope of a certain 'cultural plasticity' in contemporary UK policing – plasticity in which, we will argue, true resilience lies. Several perceptions stand out in the study. When asked about what they deemed the most important of five characteristics of being a police officer, new recruits ranked communication and empathy the highest, with empathy becoming more valuable to recruits over their first four years. During the same period, authority and power declined, suspiciousness increased, physical strength remained the lowest priority and gut instinct and adaptability were valued learning tools. How to orient the mind to make the most of these qualities will feature in our exploration of the policing brain.

Insights into police wellbeing from all these studies are unquestionably valuable. However, how far can presenting these findings back to officers and staff in the form of numbers and words go? How does this help steer a person with a heart, brain and soul to go out, do this work and come home again in one piece?

In this book, we argue that it's up to us.

We need to develop a more powerful relationship with the voice in our head that narrates our every move – in moments of danger, in our moments of distraction, and in our moments of connection with those who ask us how our day went. In this book, we learn what type of techniques might be useful to practice, so that we can do this for ourselves, without waiting for extra resources, or new management, or a change in culture or that one special person – and without waiting for retirement before we can see clearer and feel better.

How neuroscience gives a voice to the policing brain

At this point, we are going to take a step back from the whirl of research studies, survey data, wellbeing initiatives and cultural shifts, and peek into where our experiences of policing are ultimately constructed, sustained and lived out – the human brain.

We have learned more about the thinking brain in the last 10–15 years than in all of human history.[51]

Arguably, the biggest revelation in neuroscience to date is that brains can be rewired and restructured based on how we choose to use them – what scientists call *self-directed neuroplasticity*.[52] Thanks to the technology (such as fMRI),[53] we are able to watch images of brain activation and adaptation according to the demands placed on them, including demands from professions such as policing. Since 2000, there have been a plethora of police neuroscience studies looking at thinking styles (such as avoidance, distortions, emotional control and compassion management), memory processes, autonomic functions (such as heart rate and breathing) and structural or activation changes (after trauma, brain injury and stress, for resilience, in response to treatment, during special operations, in simulation training and even monitoring Russian legislation!). Critical performance risks from anxiety have also been identified (including shooting inappropriately in simulated critical incidents).[54] All the studies briefly reviewed here had one component in common: *managing threat*.[55]

Neuroscience in policing gives credence to the known, felt and raw certainty that policing is tough and we need to adapt mentally to maintain resilience. The question is, are we adapting in the best ways we can? In this book, we will learn about 'self-directed neuroplasticity' (rewiring our brains) and tried and tested cognitive practices to apply in the everyday world of operational policing. We will do this with the help of voices and stories of officers and staff who have shared what it is like to find out the hard way about staying resilient in a job like no other.

What's so different for policing?

'A job like no other' sums up policing for many officers and their families. However, there are other jobs out there that one might argue are not too dissimilar from policing, such as paramedics, those in the fire service, search and rescue and the military. One way to support policing brains is to acknowledge that inner mental experiences and adaptations to one job might have much in common with those required in another. The common ground and unique qualities that unify and differentiate our emergency responders is a territory that deserves to be reconnoitred and is being done so by inspiring initiatives such as the global charity the UNSUNG Foundation[56] and the UK's Royal Foundation. The 2020 report 'Assessing the mental health and wellbeing of the Emergency Responder community in the UK'[57] (undertaken by the Open University and King's Centre for Military Health Research and commissioned by the Royal Foundation) expressed the need to maximise the incredible progress underway in the sector in establishing evidence-based approaches to mental health support in blue light services. Key highlights included *overcoming barriers* to implementation (including a mismatch between corporate vision and individual needs) and engagement (including concerns regarding stigma/masculine culture, confidentiality and career advancement) as well as *maximising on facilitators* of implementation (including a culture of openness and buy-in from leadership/management) and engagement (including the presence of emotionally intelligent managers and allowing self-referrals to services). The acute relevance of these themes is validated by the personal words and statistics running through this book's exploration of contemporary policing. Encouraging constabularies to reflect the individual needs of officers in policy, to acknowledge the increasing limitations of an outdated 'stiff upper lip' culture, to call on police leaders to share their authentic, honest stories of life on the job and to inspire individuals to put their hand up for support when they need it is all part of this collective endeavour to improve the experience of UK policing.

Conclusion

With a start to the 2020s being infused with latent global health anxiety from COVID, national economic insecurity from Brexit, wildly vacillating public sympathy for the police and wavering government commitment to the police wellbeing agenda, the chances of psychological resilience being readily accessible to UK police are questionable. Dealing with mental health crises in members of the public may come second nature to many officers but what about detecting the needs of their peers or the vulnerabilities of their inner world? With fewer resources come more single crewing, more shifts ending solo and no place to go for meaningful contact with others, no space for transition before going home and trying to sleep before starting it all over again. Listening to, watching or being with others who are suffering or in trouble accumulates in memory. Without clarity on what happened where and when, the brain can struggle to differentiate one experience from another and to make sense of what one's role was in those experiences, the difference made because of our actions. A natural consequence is to shut off our experiences rather than learning from and feeling resourced by them as we brace for whatever threat or problem is going to come next. As our minds contract in this way, our quality of life can slowly slip out of reach, and a mentality of deferring happiness and open-mindedness until retirement can subtly creep in. Yet, it doesn't need to be like this. New evidence from science and new generations of officers with fresh perceptions of what it can mean to police in the 2020s are bringing untold opportunities to learn resilience for the policing brain like never before. We hope those opportunities can start here.

Chapter 1 snapshot

- The COVID pandemic has changed the way we organise and prioritise work, how we communicate and interact and even how we think in UK policing not only on a national level but also personally. (What is more, mild symptoms of COVID have been associated with damage to key parts of the brain required to make sense of traumatic incidents.)
- Genuine political and public understanding of trauma exposure on the front line has a lot to be desired, despite the issue being raised by the national press and in Parliament.
- Officers and staff are becoming more proficient in sharing their experiences of trauma exposure through many channels (be it in national surveys, social media or professional platforms). Nonetheless, the Home Office is yet to mandate that forces monitor the impact of trauma on the front line. The refusal to commit to asking their workforces about trauma impact damages the integrity of any efforts that forces profess to make to address the issue and support their people.
- New initiatives and cohorts of new recruits offer hope for more trauma-informed and open-minded approaches to living with trauma exposure on the front line, yet these approaches lack cohesion.
- In the simplest terms, officers and staff need to make sense of their *own* trauma exposures in the same way that their job calls for them to do regarding the *public's* experience of crime and disorder. Police need to interrogate, contextualise and file cases and crimes on a daily basis. So too do they need to interrogate, contextualise and file their own experiences in their mind's eye.
- Neuroscience has been very busy getting to grips with how the brain processes trauma exposure and maintains resilience, and it is long overdue that officers and staff benefit from this in the everyday life of their service. This book is a fresh opportunity

for all of those in emergency response (and those who support them) to know the 'policing mind' and *befriend it*.

Checklist

☐ How has the pandemic changed how I think about my actual job, the way I do it, the way I relate to others and have I noticed any change in my own everyday resilience? *Would it help to acknowledge this with someone at work or home?*

☐ How do people's opinions of policing affect how I feel about the job? *Is there anything I can do, say or privately think in response to that to help me when opinions do affect me?*

☐ Have I been able to verbalise or flag my experience of trauma exposure (or that of others) in my force or through other channels? *Can I do more with others to build on opportunities to do this?*

☐ How do I typically respond to traumatic jobs when they come my way? Am I aware that I am making sense of them before moving on to the next? *Could I do with finding more out about how to do this more effectively when I'm on the go at work? What about how I deal with them at home?*

☐ Do I ever stop to think about '*how* I think'? How comfortable is it for me to do that? Have I avoided doing that before? *Am I open to learning to do that in ways that would help me feel more resilient?*

2

Risks to resilience in operational policing: from trauma to compassion fatigue

Introduction

Policing can be as exciting and rewarding as it is challenging. It can give us aptitudes, experiences and mindsets that can nourish and uplift us as well as deplete us. The essence of resilience is to be able to differentiate between the states we find ourselves in and to invest in ways to develop beneficial traits from them. Chapter 1 set the scene for why resilience is needed in contemporary UK policing. In Chapter 2, we hear from individuals about how challenging experiences of policing manifest in common habits of thought, perceptions and the messages we tell ourselves about our potential resilience. Courtesy of Police Care UK, we hear from officers and staff who, among nearly 18,000 others, took part in the 2018 survey *TJTL*.[1]

Crossing the thin blue line

Rhetoric about stress – be it from sociologists, commentators, influencers or barstool philosophers – describe the highs and lows in the life course such as relationships, house moves, having children, losing parents and changing jobs. Policing is different. For those transitioning from being a civilian to a new recruit, it soon becomes clear that there is a line that is crossed when you join up – and on the other side of that line, the bar of stress tolerance is set higher. There is a logical explanation for this: the police service deals with collective stress, other peoples' worst days (let's face it, police rarely show up in someone's life simply to help them celebrate something that is going well). The demand to deal with life problems is also a continual one – this is the day job. Each new case or incident will require a stress response stronger than the last to get our attention. The escalating stress response to repeated exposure may be barely perceivable over time. This 'normalisation' of distress (and the coping mechanisms that accompany it) is a maladaptation to the job and can lead to burnout.

Figure 2.1 illustrates how the bar of policing stress can be set higher than average lifespan civilian stress, due to the relentless exposure (upward arrows) of police to that civilian stress. The police stress response (upward chevrons) needs to be continually reset (downward chevrons) to avoid burnout.

> In order to be able to deal effectively with the myriad of bizarre and extreme circumstances … you develop your own coping methods. … In order to work like this, it does something weird to your brain and you adapt in order to survive. (Male, late 30s, constable in investigations, 11 years in service, *TJTL* Police Care UK, 2018)

Figure 2.1: Escalating stress in policing compared to civilian baseline and the need to reset stress

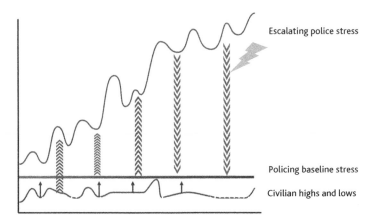

> I don't think we actually realise what effect constantly
> dealing with other people's problems and traumatic
> scenes has on our mental health ... [but] many of us
> would probably see doing something less traumatic
> within a policing setting as 'less important' and
> a demotion. Catch 22 really. (Female, mid-40s,
> constable in investigations, 22 years in service, *TJTL*
> Police Care UK, 2018)

These officers voice an uncomfortable reality: that while we 'get' that we need to (and choose to) adapt to the job, we don't necessarily understand how this happens or if it is genuinely working out for us.

The following chapters offer a new way forward by answering:

- What if we could learn to reset the stress response in between jobs?
- What if we could periodically 'wake up', reacclimatise to the wider world around us (that isn't only about people's worst days) and not feel that we had taken our eye off the ball?
- What if we could upgrade our awareness of how we are responding to the job so we can rectify our thinking just when we needed to?

Survival of the fittest

> I can't explain it better than that – you become hard
> and insensitive for personal health survival. (Male,
> late 40s, constable in incident response with 19 years
> in service, *TJTL* Police Care UK, 2018)

'Surviving' sounds heroic and yet also suggests sacrifice, going without or missing out on the lighter side of existence. Media depictions of 'burned out' police officers are abundant in contemporary film and television drama and give a veil of social acceptability (if not glamour or romanticism) to the trajectory of personal decline in the job. Through series such as *The Sweeney* (1975–1978), *Inspector Morse* (1987–2000) and *Rebus* (2000–2007) – to name but a few – the entertainment industry sanctions offering one's life to public service to the detriment of our sense of self as we watch our relationships unravel, develop unhealthy dependencies on alcoholism or workaholism, and 'numb out' to things that once made us happy. Series such as *The Wire*[2] capture the policing survival conundrum well, narrating the stories of officers at points in their career, where they reflect on who they were before it all started and where it seems to be going. The distinction between surviving and thriving has not gone unnoticed in the police wellbeing arena with it being the focus of the Police Superintendents' Association of England and Wales in 2016.[3] So what does it mean to survive? The Darwinian adage of 'survival of the fittest'[4] is more helpful for police resilience than one might think. The phrase does not refer to survival being the prize of those who are toughest but rather describes the natural outcome of those who *adapt* and 'wise up' to what is going on around them. Ironically, survival denotes the quality of being sensitive (a trait that doesn't always go down well with many keen to keep their head down and 'tough it out'). True survival in policing may come down to being sensitive to what is already happening and how we are responding and adapting to it.

States of the policing mind

How do we know what good adaptation to the job looks like? States of mind, moods and emotions are said to have evolved to help us adapt to fundamental and recurrent life tasks.[5] We survive and evolve *because* of our emotions, not despite them. Core emotions in generic social psychology comprise anger, disgust, fear, happiness, sadness and surprise[6] with an additional 23 emotions having been identified in relation to facial expression and language.[7] States of mind that feature prominently in policing discourse include over focussing on the job, managing threats and trauma exposure, developing cynicism or mistrusting, managing compassion, feeling separate from people, not talking as much as we used to, treating our bodies differently, putting off fun and accepting the status quo. Figure 2.2 shows how these common states can overlap with each other as we adapt to the job. How we manage those is fundamental to our resilience.

Figure 2.2: Common states of mind in policing that come with the challenges of the job and that are interrelated

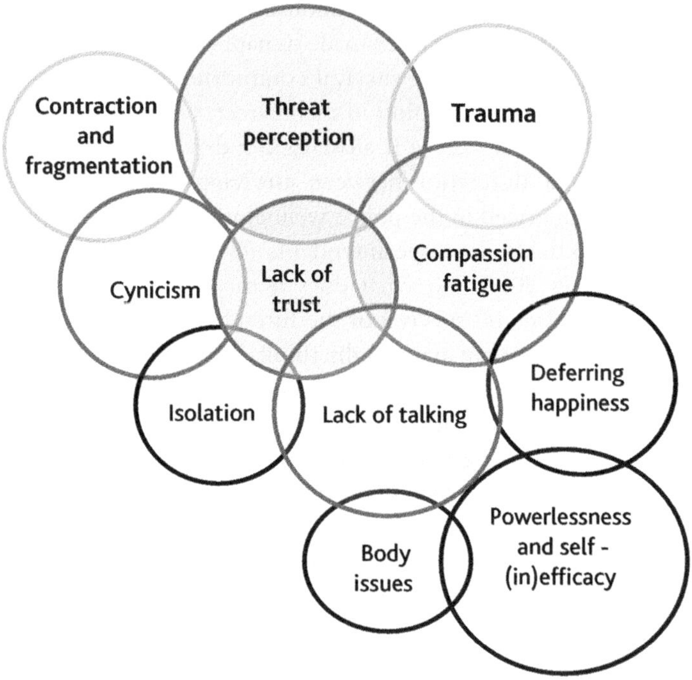

Contraction and fragmentation

We begin with what happens when we focus on the job: contraction. It is instinctive for a mind to focus on a problem to solve, but that focus needs to relax when we don't need it. In policing, there is no natural cue to relax the grip on the job, as problems to solve are often extreme and incessant. A once healthy 'focus on the job' can subtly pervade our inner life, gradually shutting us off from what *else* was important to us before we joined up. This can prevent us from putting what we are doing in perspective. It's soon easy for our life to seem somewhat separate and fragmented from those around us as we develop a sense of division between work and privacy.[8]

My family life has taken a massive hit for being in this job. I hate the job for what it has done to my family, but don't want to leave it because I love the job. (Male, mid-30s, inspector in investigations, nine years in service, *TJTL* Police Care UK, 2018)

With fragmentation can come a lack of central coherence, an anchor point holding it all (and us) together. People can have different ways of describing this and the sensation can be very destabilising and frustrating when things don't turn out well.

I feel as though I have 'sold my soul' to a way of life that has ultimately betrayed me. (Male, mid-30s, sergeant in investigations, 15 years in service, *TJTL* Police Care UK, 2018)

That said, research in policing has shown that strong peer support and line management can be an effective buffer against this sense of separation and being divided.[9]

The following chapters offer a new way forward by answering:

- What if verbalising the predicament of feeling divided (between policing and life outside) naturally relaxes the tension that divide generates without us actually having to do that much about it?
- What if feeling separated can be eased just by being more open with those we know who may be experiencing similar mind states?
- What if this kind of non-intrusive communication could help bridge other divides within our work, neighbourhood, social circles, and even help us feel connected to other (non-police) emergency response workers?

Threat perception

Contracting around a job that continually sounds an alarm when something isn't right and needs addressing is never going to be comfortable. But does anyone spell that out when you join up? In roles that require a response to a dire or urgent need, the dominant mind state will become threat perception – perception of threat to others' safety and our own – because it has to be.

Yet, if left to sound (without being reset), the incessant alarm can permeate the space we have between thoughts, between tasks, between jobs, between work and home, and even around our sense of self.

> I worry daily for my family and friends and myself should they encounter some of these people in daily life. Terrorist threat is another concern that affects work and private life severely. (Male, early 40s, constable in neighbourhood policing, 13 years in service, *TJTL* Police Care UK, 2018)

> I now actively avoid social situations, crowds, public celebrations. I am hyper-aware/alert and constantly feel responsible for everyone around me. Before working for the police, I was extremely sociable and outgoing, now I am far more reclusive. (Female, early 40s, constable, local policing, nine years in service, *TJTL* Police Care UK, 2018)

When we learn from experience to brace for repeated threats, our minds will predict negative scenarios, to make sure we have all bases covered. In a recent policing survey[10] nearly a third (27 per cent) of respondents were 'moderately' to 'extremely' affected by re-experiencing traumatic incidents, 28 per cent reported a moderate to extreme level of avoidance and 43 per cent reported a moderate to extreme sense of threat. Yet none of these individuals showed clinical levels of trauma disorder.

- What if we were able to gain more immediate control of threat perception without feeling that we were lowering our guard?
- What if we could – in an instant – get a taste of *other* states of mind and body that make our jobs and our lives as a whole more enjoyable, light-hearted and satisfying?

Trauma

When the brain senses a threat, it is not likely to passively file that incident to memory as something that is over until we have been able to render the situation safe. Some situations are harder to render safe in the mind's eye if they are particularly traumatic, extreme, conflict with our world view or don't make sense to us. There are other job-related situational factors that can aggravate trauma impact, such as feeling vulnerable, being under-resourced, or being first on the scene.[11] As traumatic experiences accumulate on the job, they need to be filed as being over, or else the brain will retain a sense of them in the present as situations unresolved, even though we know the moment has passed. This can become very uncomfortable. Dealing with trauma exposure is part of life in policing, affecting over 90 per cent of officers and staff in the UK, but 63 per cent of all police who had had a work-related experience that troubled also report having flashbacks and another 57 per cent nightmares, both of which are symptoms of trauma processing disorder.[12]

> Being a response officer you do not have the luxury to simply reflect on the traumatic incident you have attended. The next call is only minutes away and you attend with the previous job you have just dealt with in your mind. You try and suppress this but in reality, it feels as though these traumatic incidents build up until you become absolutely insensitive and numb. (Male, late 40s, constable in incident response with 19 years in service, *TJTL* Police Care, UK 2018)

Not ever making time to process or make sense of the traumatic impact of any incident is common and problematic. Over half (55 per cent) of 16,857 UK police have reported that they hardly ever had time to process the impact of one job before heading on to the next.[13]

> In a response role, there is no luxury of being able to avoid the places that remind you of the incident (you go where you are sent and have to deal with what's there) or even of being able to take time out to recover from it as there are just not the resources. ... Flashbacks to scenes can come out of nowhere ...

and don't need to have any stimulus. (Male, early 30s, constable in incident response, 11 years in service, *TJTL* Police Care UK, 2018)

There are other impacts of trauma exposure on healthy brains that are less well known. Evidence is growing of functional and practical impairments of trauma exposure on simple faculties, including knowing where we are, our situational awareness.[14] Long-term memory is also affected,[15] as this officer expresses:

I have not disclosed my poor long term memory diagnosis. My medical notes state 'significant impairment to long-term memory [and] moderate impairment to working memory from long term repeated exposure to work traumas'. I just wish I could have known the hidden impact of what our brains are asked to process from the age of 18 in the police. (Male, late 30s, sergeant in investigations, 19 years in service, *TJTL* Police Care UK, 2018)

A slightly more subtle symptom of unprocessed trauma, of being compulsively pulled back to the emotive intensity of past events, is impairment in mental flexibility or 'failure of imagination' and the ability to see things afresh.[16] Singer-songwriter Nick Cave articulated this from his perspective of the tragic loss of his teenage son, Arthur:

We all hope for this dramatic event in our life that we can write about, but this trauma, it was very damaging to the creative process. ... Time is elastic. We can go away from the event but at some point the elastic snaps and we always come back to it. (*Nick Cave* from *One More Time With Feeling*)[17]

In policing, dealing with others' loss, suffering and distress is commonplace, as is dealing with our own experiences of horror, helplessness and threat to life. It is natural that we can be pulled back to memories of extreme and dramatic jobs as the brain is keen to mark those experiences as something to watch out for. Unfortunately, if this slows our brain's agility or reduces its flexibility then this is likely to have implications for our resilience. This is why improving the brain's natural elasticity and plasticity is so critical in policing.

- What if making sense of a traumatic incident didn't have to be a weighty, emotional conversation but a practical task we could do anytime, anywhere?
- What if we could train our brain to file experiences better, to protect our situational awareness and cognitive agility and to prevent past events from intruding in the job we just want to be able to get on with?

Lack of trust

Tightening and contracting around the job, managing threats and dealing with trauma all contribute to a sense of guarding one's wellbeing – and with this, may come a degree of mistrust of others.

> In my time in the police they have tainted my view on the world and my trust in people. (Male, later 40s, officer in major crime investigations, 19 years in service, *TJTL* Police Care UK, 2018)

Who constitutes 'others' means something to us. If mistrust is functioning to keep us safe on the job, it is plausible that we may begin to associate generating and securing safety with the policing function more than anything else, subconsciously devaluing support and safety we could also gain from other areas of our life, community, friendship groups and family.

> My service in The Met has gone quickly. I've sacrificed friends, family, and relationships in favour of being successful at work. I regret it now. The job has made me short tempered, bigoted, angry and distrusting of anyone outside the Police. (Male, mid-20s, constable in investigations, 14 years in service, *TJTL* Police Care UK, 2018)

To reduce mistrust to simply being the fault of joining the police is probably not that helpful. How trust is experienced in the job is very likely to be influenced by earlier or other life experiences too.

> Since working for the police I have noticed my sense of paranoia has grown and which I know has greatly impacted on trust issues within friendships with colleagues – this hasn't been solely caused as a result from working in the job and could be as a result of childhood bullying issues, however, I think that exposure to crime does leave you feeling more vulnerable as a result. (Female, nearly 30, staff in investigative support, four years in service, *TJTL* Police Care UK, 2018)

If we bring our own trust issues to the job already, how trust then plays out in the workplace is perhaps even more important to figure out. Trust in the policing environment seems to have its own complexities. Fear of doing wrong at work is thought to have contributed to a 'blue code of silence' within policing – a code of secrecy to protect fellow officers from repercussions of suspected wrongdoing.[18] This notion is uncomfortable to grapple with. It suggests that officers (party A) are coerced by peers (party B) into being 'trustworthy', by renegading on the trust that others (party C) may have had in them (party A) to tell the truth, all because the coercers (party B) have an inherent mistrust in the decision-making of others (party D). Fortunately, there may be more simple times ahead. Charman's research suggests that this blue code is on its way out, with new recruits unanimously and strongly disagreeing with its principles by the fourth year of their induction into the job. Notwithstanding, there is some evidence from the third sector that lack of trust within forces can still resonate for those accessing psychological support. Nearly one in ten requests made to a prominent police charity were related to a lack of trust and privacy concerns within the applicants' forces.[19] So if we can't expect unanimous trust in force support for our mental health, this makes proactively taking responsibility for resilience all the more valuable and empowering.

The following chapters offer a new way forward by answering:

- What if we were able to train our brains to trust our senses and our clarity of thought better?
- What if there were means of practising 'fresh eyes' on each case or job so that we can assess risk more reliably?
- What if we could learn to place our trust in others more wisely so that we might reap the benefits of genuine social support without feeling naïve or vulnerable?

Cynicism

Cynicism is defined as a 'pessimistic and suspicious outlook' in policing and can come hand-in-hand with mistrust.[20] When we contract around the job and become familiar with typical patterns of how situations, people and the dynamics within them pan out, we can begin to expect and predict how things will be. We have acknowledged a certain negative bias to police work (that is, policing tasks usually address something going wrong in someone's life, rather than going well) and so it is not surprising that cynicism creeps in alongside threat perception. Our brains become primed to expect the worst – and in some roles, to expect the worst of human nature.

> It's holistically dealing day in day out with child abuse. It wears you down. It gets on top of you. It numbs you. You feel yourself getting more miserable, more cynical, more detached from the outside world; nothing shocks you anymore. (Male, mid-40s, constable in investigations, 12 years in service, *TJTL* Police Care UK, 2018)

> Attending domestics is often the most traumatic in the long term. It is the attendance of these over and over that I find very hard. To listen to and have to advise others on their relationships. (Male, 52 years old, constable in response, 25 years in service, *TJTL* Police Care UK, 2018)

However, cynicism isn't always about what the job inevitably 'does *to* us'. Individual characteristics, such as our gender, race and personality type also can affect how cynical we become on the job.[21] A New Jersey study by an ex-police officer offered a very personal reanalysis of his journals, self-critiquing the development of his own cynical policing mind.[22] His conclusions were mixed. Caplan justified cynicism as a valuable tool for threat perception, all the while admitting that cynicism created a barrier between the public and himself which was 'antithetical to the very reasons he had for wanting to become an officer in the first place,' to 'have a close and mutually respective relationship with the public'.[23] So, giving oneself over to cynicism in the hope it keeps us safe may not be as empowering in policing as we may think – especially if tinged with apathy.

> What's the point? The Police service will continue to be slowly choked to death by the Government. Most of us are resigned to this. Nobody listens. Nothing changes. (Gender 'prefer not to say', late 30s, constable in investigations, 15 years in service, *TJTL* Police Care UK, 2018)

The following chapters offer a new way forward by answering:

- What if we could proactively decide to be cynical only when we know it suits our purpose (to instigate threat perception or to inject humour into a tense situation, for example)?
- What if we could also learn to tone it down when we need to open up to new possibilities, see value in the job or take pride in it?

The C-word – and getting tired of it

As alluded to in our introductory chapter, compassion (and our fatigue of it) features heavily in the world of police wellbeing. Relentless trauma exposure can lead us to feel weary and 'spent', and a cynical lack of trust can prevent us from reaching out to others and refuelling our faith in human nature. Compassion is a contradictory, complex and contentious state of mind in police work; as with trauma, many in service may recoil from the word in conversation because it is either too uncomfortable to feel or too uncomfortable to admit one can't seem to feel it anymore.

> My compassion and empathy has been slowly eroded in a direct correlation with the amount of death and destruction I have been faced with in 22 years as a police officer. (Male, mid-40s, sergeant in incident response, 22 years in service, *TJTL* Police Care UK, 2018)

Prevalence rates of compassion fatigue in policing can range between 10 per cent and 20 per cent.[24] Perhaps more important than knowing the precise number of those who self-report, compassion fatigue is grasping how it plays out on the job. From listening to those who choose to raise the subject, it seems that compassion can emerge in many different ways in policing: for others (typically victims of crime), from management, reciprocally with the public and for self.

> Poor leadership without any compassion or empathy or understanding. (Male, early 50s, sergeant in incident response, 28 years in service, *TJTL* Police Care UK, 2018)

> I was once told by a supervisor I wasn't mentally strong enough because I cried at a couple of jobs like giving a death message to a family when the person that died was my age. The family thought I was being compassionate and didn't mind at all. (Female, late 20s, officer in investigations, five years in service, *TJTL* Police Care UK, 2018)

As with cynicism, compassion fatigue has been associated with personality factors (namely, low neuroticism and high conscientiousness), and self-care is thought to mitigate against it.[25] Interventions to improve self-care (self-compassion) can reduce levels of burnout in palliative care teams,[26] but there is much yet to understand about its implications for policing. Another interesting dynamic to note is that compassion fatigue and compassion *satisfaction* can coexist in policing; it is plausible to be simultaneously satisfied with acting compassionately but exhausted from doing so.[27] In other research, the more fatigued participants were by being compassionate, the less satisfaction they gained from being so.[28]

The following chapters offer a new way forward by answering:

- What if (regardless of our personality) we could *all* learn to work more smartly with compassion?
- What if we could give compassion credit and space to be there when it's helpful but to be wisely cautious with it when we've taken on too much?
- What if doing *this* was the ultimate act of self-compassion?
- What if that sharing this skill with peers and managers could inspire compassionate leadership?

Isolation

As we contract around our job, focus on its immediate tasks, habituate to seeing what we see, we can become isolated. Integration in a busy, people-focussed job like policing can disguise this. In his bestselling book *Sapiens* (2015), Yuval Harari explains that it 'takes a tribe to raise a human' and that evolution favoured those more capable of forming strong social ties. Police officers and staff are not just part of a police tribe; they may well be part of other tribes, they may be parents, siblings, neighbours, childhood friends and like-minded hobbyists. Translate this into the 'tribes' *within* policing and we might ask – does it take a team, a unit, a peer group or a force to raise an officer? Do those who form strong social bonds with the 'tribe' at work do better than those who don't? There is much evidence that peer support can mitigate against a host of psychological issues in policing, as it can in other areas of emergency response and the military.[29] One of the factors most likely to have a positive impact upon police respondents' morale is said to be their relationship with colleagues.[30] What is more, recent research with an English police force has differentiated between *actual* received peer support and 'perceived' peer support, with both predicting psychological wellbeing.[31] This suggests that even the *idea* of being supported at work (of not being isolated) can be enough to improve our resilience.

> [The job] makes you become closed off from people, pushing your partners or friends away as you don't want to show that you are at breaking point ... and more importantly it drives you to seek comfort elsewhere. ... Colleagues look out for each other, more so now more than ever before. (Female, 30 years old, constable, seven years in service, *TJTL* Police Care UK, 2018)

The balance between isolation and connectedness becomes more complicated when we accept that sometimes being a member of one tribe infers *not* being part of another. This may explain why it is common for those in service to establish (new or extramarital) personal relationships at work, with nearly one third of officers and staff reporting having partners or spouses on (or formerly on) the job.[32] The division between the police and the wider community is thought to derive from underlying anxiety that performance is impeded if officers are socially close to those on whom they enforce the law.[33] The contemporary machinations of police work also determine opportunities for officers and staff to feel connected to the tribe.

> People act and work in a more isolated manner. ... Senior managers [have] dismantled the structures that allowed decompression within teams ... that social element to dealing with issues. (Male, early 50s, local policing sergeant, 26 years in service, *TJTL* Police Care UK, 2018)

What about developing connections with others alongside you, because of the kind of job you're doing? One might reasonably expect that working in high-risk, specialist roles dealing with extreme trauma exposure (that might separate individuals from the wider world) could be the perfect opportunity for peers to galvanise mutual support over time, to hunker down in their unique experience. However, this doesn't necessarily work out as quickly or as naturally as some may really need it to.

> I find it difficult to share with the team that I have been negatively affected by some of the material as I am new and keen to fit in with them and not be seen as a problem. As a result, I stay quiet at work and internalise the feelings. I take myself away for a quiet cry at the other end of the building where no one is around and then return to the office. (Female, mid-30s, staff in investigative support in child sexual exploitation, nine years in service, *TJTL* Police Care UK, 2018)

Yet, it can and does happen. When the conditions are right, sharing experiences with peers can help transform what feels like an intensely challenging personal situation into something more manageable. According to research, police work colleagues boost our psychological wellbeing by providing 'experientially salient information that allows an individual to foster a sense of control'.[34] In other words, how we behave in our roles and how we share that experience with others can have a powerful effect on their resilience as well as our own. Author John Sutherland talks in his police memoirs of a phrase from forensic science that denotes that 'every contact leaves a trace'.[35] Sutherland deftly applies this to the notion of human contact on the job – that there is a human exchange and a trace from that human contact that we leave behind in people's lives. As we progress our exploration into the policing brain, we will take this a little further and look at the impressions that we make on each other's neural pathways – what that contact physically leaves behind inside us. We will see that there is an interconnection between us, not just in what we say and do but one that takes place in our very brain cells.

The following chapters offer a new way forward by answering:

- What if we could learn to tap into our connection with others whenever we needed to without waiting for the conditions or the company to be just right?
- What if we could feel resourced and supported in the most challenging moments, even when single-crewed or first on the scene?

- What would it be like to know that we could leave behind something valuable to others, regardless of how well the job did or didn't go?

Lack of talking

Contracting around the job, mistrust and managing compassion may constitute everyday life in policing, but these mind states are not necessarily conducive to casual conversation or meaningful chats at work or home. Neuroscience explains why. What might come as a relief to all of us who find talking when stressed difficult is that there are biological, physiological, *bodily* reasons why this is. When we are under threat, our cognitive resources are preoccupied with taking action and the areas of our brain which facilitate conversation (our language centres) 'drop out' because they are essentially redundant in crisis mode.[36] The irony is that these language centres help us to contextualise fear responses and threat perception: they help us makes sense of the very stress that is stopping us from using them. When we use language, we regulate our emotions.[37] The contradiction between it being 'good to talk' and it being hard to find words might explain why some people benefit and others struggle with trauma interventions that are designed to spark conversation. For example, trauma risk management (TRiM) interventions and talking therapies may be perfect opportunities for some to help them make sense of that which has so far gone unspoken. For others, the prospect of talking goes against every fibre of their body in that particular moment. There are some ways around this – ways of almost talking, almost sharing the 'un-sharable'. Police humour (or dark humour) is one such method.

> Most police officers are affected by what they see and deal with but lock it inside and develop that 'police humour'. Everyone has a story to tell; supervisors have never been proactive in bringing that to the front because it would be like opening a can of worms. (Female, mid–30s, constable in investigations, 13 years in service, *TJTL* Police Care UK, 2018)

Another 'get around' is the cover story – a version of events that we feel able to articulate on demand. A cover story gives the listener just enough information to satisfy their need to hear about how difficult something was for us, without the speaker giving away too much, triggering their stress response or attracting unwanted attention. Hearing how mandatory annual psychological assessments are experienced in some high-risk roles suggests that cover stories are often an attractive decoy for those not ready or willing to open up. However appealing, a cover story may well be counterproductive, giving us an escape route from the very path that might help us make sense of that we essentially need to.

> We are far better than we used to be around helping staff that have experienced trauma. There is also some responsibility on individuals to seek help when needed. I suppose we need to be more open about it and that starts with being comfortable talking about it. (Male, early 40s, inspector in incident response, 18 years in service, *TJTL* Police Care UK, 2018)

The following chapters offer a new way forward by answering:

- What if we didn't have to go out of our way to avoid awkward conversations?
- What if we also had the means to make sense of traumatic incidents without having to talk about emotions at all?
- What if we could learn to open up and really maximise opportunities when they are right for us?
- What if we could use language to help process incidents without having to find the right people to talk to?

The body

Sustaining threat perception and holding chronic stress response can have a pervasive physical effect on us, including gastrointestinal distress (irritable bowel syndrome, food intolerances), raised blood pressure, heart arrhythmias and problems with shoulders, jaws and backs from containing muscle tension.[38] It can also be more subtle. Sometimes, we can start to relate to our bodies differently, wanting to cut off or distract ourselves from how we're feeling in response to the situations we are in.[39]

> I attended a suicide on the train line and physically bagged up the remains of a deceased person. ... My body and clothes smelt like that incident until I was able to go home that evening to shower and change. I do not feel officers are given chance to recover mentally from what they have just dealt with and very much feel that day will haunt me for the rest of my life. (Female, early 30s, constable in investigations, 11 years in service, *TJTL* Police Care UK, 2018)

The majority of 'coping mechanisms' we develop change the chemicals coursing through our veins. Habits familiar to those feeling the pressure of contemporary policing include drinking, comfort eating, extreme sports, physical exercise, gambling and even sex addiction. Qualitative research with those in high-risk roles revealed that manipulating bodily sensations by engaging in extreme physical activity (such as cold water swimming or long-distance running) had limited success because it failed to address the source of the distress: the mind.

> Being functional with your body should be so healthy, but the most valuable tool is your brain, and if you fuck that up, you fuck up everything else. (CSE staff, female, 30s, 15 years in service, unpublished data, courtesy of Police Care UK, 2018)

Other officers shared the relief of breaking free from unhealthy relationships with food:

> I am feeling healthier than I've done for years after having a gastric sleeve and am losing weight. I have comfort eaten, gaining weight over the last 8 years or so but am now losing it and feeling happier and healthier. (Female, nearly 50, control room sergeant, 22 years in service, *TJTL* Police Care UK, 2018)

When we have a coping mechanism, we become dependent on it to distract us from the source of our distress (what we are coping *with*). We contort ourselves in all sorts of uncomfortable ways, creating daily rhythms of physical distractions, rules, targets and conditions that become part of our routine. Some may be as innocuous as over-training at the gym, others can result in escalating alcohol tolerance in a desperate bid to get to sleep quickly before the onslaught of the next day. Over time, reliance on these patterns can escalate, destabilising our relationships as well as our bodies. Not only can the impact escalate, but its hold on us can deepen. This is because by reinforcing the 'coping mechanism' we are hardwiring the idea in our brain that there is something that we need to hide from, divert our attention from, fear or be in conflict with in our experience. We are repeating to ourselves over and over again that there is a problem the more ferociously we try to disguise it. It is very common for this to happen to those with trauma exposure. Author of *The Body Keeps the Score,* Van der Kolk, reassures us that there is a better way forward; that we can transform the physical imprints with which past experiences leave us: 'Agency starts with what scientists call interoception, our awareness of subtle sensory, body-based feelings: the greater the awareness, the greater our potential to control our lives'.[40]

Many of those long in service reflect that there once was a time when there were opportunities and spaces on the job where officers and staff could physically engage and release tension as part of the wind-down after a working day – but that these times are long gone.

> The police service used to have social activities to allow staff to socialise and let off steam. Since police clubs have closed and sports teams and activities have been reduced as have the opportunities to do them, the social cohesion amongst all the people who work for the police has reduced. (Male, mid-40s, inspector in criminal justice arrangements, 22 years service, *TJTL* Police Care UK, 2018)

Finding new ways to contradict and overwrite the imprints of stress on our bodies is something that police in the UK are already engaging with and thriving from. One example is the Surfwell initiative. Supported by a wealth of neurophysiological evidence on the embodiment of connection with others,[41] Surfwell demonstrates that being on the open water, overcoming a physical challenge and learning new skills with peers who understand the realities of the day job and its impact on the mind can bring about transformational improvements in resilience. Results are powerful and a report by the University of Exeter relayed extensive, statistically significant post-intervention improvements in participants' personal wellbeing as well as their commitment to and advocacy for the job itself.[42]

The following chapters offer a new way forward by answering:

- What if we could reconnect with the policing body and manage accumulating stress rather than trying to numb out?
- What if could tune in to it to relax the body when it needs it, invigorate it and enjoy its rewards?
- What if we could maximise our physical presence as a healthy source of connectivity between each other?

Powerlessness or reduced self-efficacy beliefs

As we near the end of our brief tour of challenging mind states in contemporary policing, we take a frank look at the concept of being able to *do anything about all of this*. Part of the reason things don't change for us is that we are too busy getting on with what we need to do. In the immediacy of the job, feeling empowered to deal with the task at hand often comes down to the physical resources available to us. A recent survey on pay and morale revealed that over a third of police officers in England and Wales thought personal protective equipment was insufficient for their role and, longer-term, 62 per cent didn't think that their force would have enough tutor constables to induct new recruits.[43] Being seen as powerless by the public seems to intensify a sense of being physically under-resourced on the job.

The feeling of being powerless in your daily duty, limited PPE [personal protective equipment]. The feeling that support should you need back up could be a number of minutes away, this has a massive effect on how involved you get or be reluctance to attend for fear of your own safety ... the criminal community do not see us as force; we are often sent to jobs were more than 10 people may be causing problems, often you are alone. (Male 50s, local policing PCSO, 12 years in service, *TJTL* Police Care UK, 2018)

Feeling ineffective (either because we are drained or under-resourced) can build up and become quite personal. In the 2018 survey,[44] the dominant symptom for nearly half of respondents with CPTSD was feeling like a failure and feeling worthless (which was over double the frequency of other symptoms such as not being able to calm down after getting upset and issues relating to others). Moreover, powerlessness wasn't just the domain of those with clinical trauma disorder.

Every serious/fatal collision takes a little piece out of you which can't be replaced.

As does each assault, threat to your family, and each time you are shot at. (Male, early 50s, constable in traffic, 29 years in service, *TJTL* Police Care UK, 2018)

It's just groundhog day ... the apathy ... it's the same people, the same offenders, the same paperwork, some, it doesn't even make sense the reports you have to put through, the bureaucracy, the futility of the paper work. ... You just don't get the rewards. (Firearms trainee, 20s, unpublished data, courtesy of Police Care UK, 2018)

In cases where individuals proactively made decisions to do things differently, the sense of empowerment was palpable.

[Firearms] has reignited my passion. ... I'm chomping at the bit: I have 7 days off now and I just don't want it! I don't mind being treated like the Newbie, it's an opportunity for learning and for becoming better, a better police officer, a better kind. (Firearms trainee, 20s, unpublished data, courtesy of Police Care UK, 2018)

Not everyone in policing will be able to or want to transfer into an armed response to reignite a sense of self-efficacy on the job, granted. The good news is that research into professional efficacy and emotional labour has shown that there are those among us who genuinely thrive on dealing with people and the emotional demands that come with it, as well as those who burn out.[45] One explanation from evolutionary psychology is that when we are less powerful and more dependent on our social group, we will benefit from forming rewarding relationships with others.[46]

The following chapters offer a new way forward by answering:

- What if in policing we could learn to feel effective alongside our connection with and compassion for others, rather than feeling depleted by it?
- What if we could prevent the build-up of inefficacy and apathy by acknowledging the small rewards and wins we have every day on the job?
- What if we could enjoy a sense of purpose and reward that didn't depend on others' opinions or views on the relative successes of one job to the next?
- What if we could attune our brain to the satisfaction of novelty, of the unknown, without feeling that we weren't in control?

Deferment of happiness

There is a contentious idea in resilience that, unwittingly, many of us may be *our own* worst enemy – that we ourselves might actually be getting *in our own way*. For those clocking up years in policing, the 'way' towards happiness is often inextricably linked to the countdown towards retirement. Often accompanied by a wry smile, these tongue-in-cheek references to living a life after the police can mask real discomfort with the investment we have made in the job. What meanings police attach to retirement isn't wholly understood,[47] but research does tell us that when matters are taken out of our hands or we don't have alternatives on offer when we transition out of service, this makes things a lot harder.[48]

> Having had my goalposts moved to the tune of 11 years by pension reforms, I would ask, how could I – or anyone else for that matter – be expected to complete 41 years in service, and either survive it, or at least come out the other end with any sanity? (Male, near 40 years old, constable in investigations, *TJTL*, Police Care UK, 2018)

The following chapters offer a new way forward by answering:

- What if the golden watch of retirement, of long-awaited satisfaction, was actually a clock that is already ticking?
- What if, still on the job, we could open up to and galvanise all we've learned from policing to bring satisfaction closer to home, closer to the here and now?
- What if there was no need to wait?
- What if all it takes is a little cognitive up-skilling and a 'why not?' attitude?

Who do we think we are?

Who is to say any of us can do this? Who is to say that any one person reading this has a chance of changing the trajectory of their policing life or their life working with police or in other emergency response roles? The true impact of the time you have taken to get this far reading this book depends only on one thing: how much credit you give your brain for being able to change. We all have a tendency to say 'that's just the way I am'.

Psychological profiling has been a very seductive force in criminology that has seeped into the world of police wellbeing under the guide of psychological screening, seemingly with few questions being asked until recently. Concerns have been raised among policing and military professions that psychological screening is ineffective at identifying those most vulnerable or resilient to trauma impact and that its approach of labelling individuals in such a static way can be psychologically damaging.[49] This damage is three-fold. Intrusive screening can trigger a sense of inadequacy or shame in being affected by our experiences. This can then lead to individuals distancing themselves from how they genuinely respond to life (tempting them to hide their inner experiences and dissociate). Together, these responses to the screening can inhibit an individual's sense that they *can* go on to successfully adapt to the challenges of the job they have committed to and the personal challenges that life outside of the job also brings. Essentially, the notion of categorising vulnerability or resilience in such as static way goes against everything that the last 20 years of neuroscience shows us about the brain's innate plasticity.

Concepts of personality (such as the Big Five personality model[50] by Costa and McCrae[51]) can be useful in identifying states of mind that predict wellbeing – yet their usefulness is limited if we perceive them as being permanent features person X or person Y either has or hasn't when they are screened. Traits of thinking may be hardwired into the brain but only because we repeatedly think in those ways. If we choose to repeatedly practise thinking in *other* ways, *those* ways can become our hardwiring, our traits and – over time – our 'personality'.

What determines our ability to change is our ability to see clearly how and why we think and behave as we do. This can be challenging as human brains will use as little energy as possible to stay efficient. Diverting habits of thought requires deliberate effort and it's not always immediately obvious to us how we might even go about starting to think differently.

This split between that which we are aware of and that which we are *not* aware of is often represented by the image of an iceberg (what we see on the surface and that which lurks below). In psychology, terms such as conscious or subconscious thinking, implicit or explicit actions describe that same divide. Figure 2.3[52] represents the division between how we may respond outwardly to the world around us (above the line) and that which drives much of this going on underneath (below the line).

The left-hand image derives from one said to be the inspiration for George Lucas' *Star Wars* trilogy,[53] the Hero's Journey. It depicts the hero's story: someone who embarks on an ordeal, leaving the ordinary world (above the line) for another world (below the line). In doing so, they face mortality, discover truths, find allies, new insights and rewards, and then return to the ordinary world, resurrected and enthused, helping others to find a new future. This book does not intend to turn contemporary policing into a blockbuster adventure movie. It does aim to show the reader that while we may not all be heroes, in the words of Tara Brach,[54] we are 'response-able'; we have the capacity to *choose to respond* to the demands placed on us. We can do this by getting to know how our minds work (below the line), then returning to everyday policing with practical insights and rewards to enrich our lives and better support others on the job. Chapter 3 shows us how we can cross that line by understanding more about how the human brain gets to work in policing.

Chapter 2 snapshot

- The nature of stress in policing is different to that in civilian life. It's not only made up of all the bad experiences, misdemeanours and suffering that civilians experience in crime and disorder (on either side of the law), but this relentless exposure to stress builds over time.
- When officers and staff join the police service, there is an adjustment to life on the job. This adjustment can be informed by those who go before us, by subtle cultural messages

Figure 2.3: The policing brain circle: a variation on the Hero's Journey by Joseph Campbell

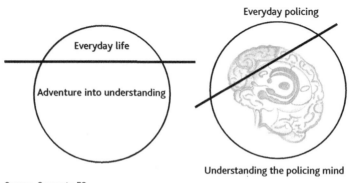

Source: See note 53

and expectations about policing or can be quite explicit in training. However, being informed about trauma exposure on the job is not a guaranteed part of our induction. That's left down to us.

- 'Survival of the fittest' doesn't mean what many people assume it does. The notion refers to the resilience that comes to those who accept and adapt to what is really going on around them – that is, the extent to which they can fit into their circumstances. Fitting to circumstances doesn't mean denying that there are difficulties. It's quite the opposite. Survival means working with adversity and the feelings and states of mind that come with it.

- In policing, there are various ways in which the brain tries to manage what it experiences. Some ways of coping are more constructive than others.

- If we regularly default to specific ways of thinking or behaving in response to challenges, these states can become traits that we identify with – and this can be detected in some psychological assessments such as personality profiling. While it can be useful to notice habitual patterns, telling ourselves (or being told by others) that 'this is the way [we] are' can be limiting, even damaging, and hold us back from working better with our very malleable brains.

- States of mind that many people identify with in policing include over focussing on the job, managing threats and trauma exposure, developing cynicism or mistrusting, managing compassion, feeling separate from people, not talking as much as we used to, treating our bodies differently, putting off fun and accepting the status quo.

- Together, these states can hardwire into longer-term traits. Yet the policing mind needn't be confined to this wiring. We can observe, interact with and change how our mind responds to the job. We can learn to rewire it so that more helpful states of mind and qualities of thinking can become our new default. This increases our ability to get more out of the here and now and helps us build greater resilience for the future.

- Exploring those states of mind by stepping back and seeing how and why the brain does what it does on the job is an adventure in its own right. If we can take a bit of time to do this, we can refresh and rejuvenate our inner experience of policing – and help others to do the same.

Checklist

- ☐ Thinking about the time before I joined the police service, what traits have I developed since then that have helped me for the better? *Are there any ways of thinking that I enjoyed before I signed up which I wish I could tap into again? Are there positive states of mind that the job has given me which I could practise more?*
- ☐ Can I relate to over-committing to the job, to trying to not think or talk about traumatic experiences? Do I talk cynically about the job? Do I trust people in the same ways I used to? Can I cope with others' pain better or worse since being in the police? How connected to other people do I feel? What's my body's experience of the impact of the job (do I eat, drink or exercise less or more, do I hold tension in my muscles or have problems with digestion, chest pains or headaches)? *Which more negative states of mind and body do I identify with most? Which ones come and go?*
- ☐ Do I tend to resign myself to (or celebrate) these states of mind, as their being 'who I am' or simply 'part of the job'? What do I expect my family and friends to accept (or enjoy) about my approach to life? *Could it be time to check in with myself? Can I see myself as others might?*
- ☐ How much does it matter to me to have control over how I feel about life? *What time can I give to finding out? Can I recognise that I am worth the effort? If a colleague asked me if it was worth trying to think differently, what would I say to them?*
- ☐ Would understanding more about the human brain help me be more objective about my experiences in policing? Would hearing about how others have worked with their thinking help? *What are my expectations?*

3

What might be happening in the brain? Introducing simple neuroscience for policing

Introduction

In Chapter 2, we took an honest look at the kind of mental states that can develop as we acclimatise to the stress response on the job, as we develop our own coping mechanisms and as we generally absorb 'the way things go' in policing. Here in Chapter 3, we go beneath these mind states to see some of the processes, systems and chemicals that likely formulate them. This prepares us for Chapter 4, where we will make more conscious choices about how we think by learning straightforward techniques to activate specific brain functions. With practice, these new ways of thinking can become second nature over time, slowly building formidable resilience in all areas of life, including our work. For now, though, our intention here is just to get to know the brain a little bit more.

Why is understanding the brain so useful?

We all have a brain, and each one of us, whether we like it or not, is largely governed by our ability to be on friendly terms with it. Having a general appreciation of the 'kit' we have inside our skulls (and why it is the way that it is) enables us to make the most of it and also helps us to understand what's happening when it's not working so well for us or others.

We don't need to be a neuroscientist to grasp this. School biology lessons have long explained that the human brain sets us apart from the animal kingdom, typically through our use of language and complex tools, our potential for spirituality and our capacity to watch our own thought processes (these days called *metacognition*). Our capacity to observe the thought processes of others and to generate conversation about them (or to put it another way, to gossip!) is said to make Homo sapiens who we are today.[1] The scientific revolution of the 17th century was all about observation of the natural world and all its mechanisms, forces and processes.[2] Following that came the 'cognitive revolution'[3] when we started to turn all this observation back onto ourselves by observing how and why we think in the ways that we do. That is what we are doing in this book: we are simply observing ourselves in policing, our processes and coping mechanisms – and next up, we are considering what neural circuitry might be involved underneath it all. Science recognises that brains are plastic, malleable – and now we are turning that to our advantage, learning how to hardwire useful functions to keep us resilient (and to release the less useful mechanisms that don't). Perhaps right here we are even joining a new 'neuroplastic revolution'. More and more people across the world, in all sorts of disciplines and from all sorts of backgrounds, are practising *self-directed* neuroplasticity, physically restructuring the brain to improve resilience purely by practising new thinking styles.[4] All we are doing with this book is applying that capacity to the reality of everyday policing.

And the first thing we need to do to achieve this is to get to know our equipment.

What is a brain?

The average brain is said to weigh just under 1.5 kg (about 3 lbs), have the consistency of tofu (or jelly), be primarily made of fat (about 60 per cent) and powered by electricity, steering itself with chemicals (chemicals we sometimes call feelings) and generating around 70,000 thoughts a day. The brain's actions are determined by genetic coding as well as what is going on around it (environmental conditions). It uses 20 per cent of our calorie consumption, even though its mass is only 2 per cent of our whole body's mass[5]. We use all our brains when conscious and much of it when we are asleep. (It's worth noting that the myth that humans only use 10 per cent [or 90 per cent of it being untapped] is unfounded but may have emerged from 20th-century discussions about efficiency and how the brain uses as little energy as possible. This suggests that without distinct effort we may not be reaching full potential in using it.)

> Everyone is familiar with the phenomenon of feeling more or less alive on different days. ... Compared with what we ought to be, we are only half awake. We are making use of only a small part of our possible mental and physical resources.[6]

Now for the detail. You don't need to understand or learn any of this detail to benefit from the techniques we share with you later, but it helps to set the scene and may be useful for future reference. We are going to take a whistle-stop tour of the brain, pausing along the way to consider certain functions, systems and chemicals that may be particularly relevant to policing (and indeed other areas of emergency response). We will use different maps on the tour, each illustrating brain areas of interest and we might expect to experience from activating them. Feel free to pick up and put down different illustrations (our maps); they are there as a guide only and you can always come back to them.

The basics: your evolutionary brain

Before we start, it's useful for us to take some ownership of what is tucked away inside our skull by imagining it in our hands. Quite literally. Dan Siegel[7] is a psychologist who is really interested in understanding the brain in very hands-on ways (excuse the pun) and has developed the well-known image in Figure 3.1.[8] It shows how the brain developed in its earliest formation in reptiles from the stem up (depicted by the wrist) to then develop a limbic system in mammals (depicted by the thumb and palm) and eventually the prefrontal cortex in primates and humans (depicted by the overlaying fingers of the clenched fist). As we have evolved, we have developed thinking styles and traits that were common

Figure 3.1: 'The brain in your hand' can be a useful way of reminding ourselves to check in with whether we may have slipped into reptilian or mammalian thinking

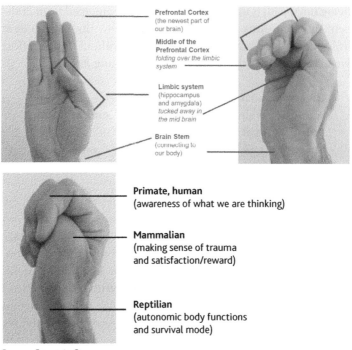

Prefrontal Cortex
(the newest part of
our brain)

Middle of the
Prefrontal Cortex
*folding over the limbic
system*

Limbic system
(hippocampus
and amygdala)
*tucked away in
the mid brain*

Brain Stem
(connecting to
our body)

Primate, human
(awareness of what we are thinking)

Mammalian
(making sense of trauma
and satisfaction/reward)

Reptilian
(autonomic body functions
and survival mode)

Source: See note 8

to those stages of our evolution: reptilian, mammalian and then primate. Those very basic modes of thinking dominate our brain today – but we are not always aware of them. The systems that evolved first tend to dominate our thinking more because they are more established. The newer, more advanced thinking tends to be activated only when conditions are right, and can need a more deliberate nudge for them to kick in. Borrowing Dan's hand analogy, sometimes we need to 'wiggle our fingers', to wake up the smart stuff in the front brain so it keeps in check the more basic systems underneath that keep us alive (but don't necessarily make us happy).

> Our brains evolved to fit our environment, not to make us happy.

So, what do the different stages of the evolved brain mean for us today? The essential functions of the evolutionary brain comprise keeping us alive and safe (reptilian), motivating us to get what we want and need (mammalian) and empowering us to connect with others (primate and human). Our use of the three evolved systems is epitomised by neuropsychologist Rick Hanson as being to 'pet the lizard' for safety, to 'feed the mouse' for satisfaction and to 'hug the human' for connection.[9] A policing analogy might be to 'catch the criminal', 'close the case' and 'check in with colleagues' in order to render a situation safe, apply our resources to get a job done and reconnect with those around us.

We can see from Table 3.1[10] that many of the policing mind states from Chapter 2 can fall into these categories. It's useful to revisit which combination of states is most akin to your own thinking habits – the reptilian, the mammalian or the human (primate). Even being able to label moods and states in this way brings about more self-control and less distress.[11] In Chapter 4, we will learn more about how to balance our reptilian, mammalian and human (primate) brains so that each can support us in the right ways at the right times.

Now we will embark on our more detailed tour of the human brain. We begin with areas of functionality that are relevant to police resilience, then we will consider the habits, zones and modes of thought that the brain can naturally slip into just because we are human. We will finish this chapter by developing

Table 3.1: Rick's evolutionary 'brain zoo' and policing mind states

Safety Pet the lizard (reptilian)		Satisfaction Feed the mouse (mammalian)		Connection Hug the human (primate)	
Negative -	Positive +	Negative -	Positive +	Negative -	Positive +
Pain	At ease	Dissatisfaction	Gratitude	Separation	Being included
Threat	Grit	Boredom	Being resourced	Rejection	Compassion
Anxiety	Resolution	Driven-ness	Capabilities	Shame	Being seen
Hypervigilance	Stand down	Addiction	Accomplishment	Isolation	Assertiveness
Hyperarousal	Relaxation	Dissatisfaction	Resolution	Other-ness	Self-worth

Source: Adapted from material by Rick Hanson, 2017 Neuroscience Summit; see note 10

a more physical understanding of the body-brain connection and how this can help our interactions with others on and off the job.

Brain function for police resilience

So, we begin with areas of functionality that are likely to be relevant to police resilience – functions that reflect some of the mental states we covered in Chapter 2 (Figure 3.2). (There may well be other areas of function that also grab your attention here, so please feel free to home in on whatever you find useful right now, as you can always come back to it). Functions we cover that may be relevant to policing include threat perception, trauma exposure, emotion regulation and communication. These functions also feature in everyday civilian life and may be pertinent to other areas of emergency response and service such as the military.

In policing, either threat perception, trauma exposure, emotion regulation or the requirement for communication may dominate our experience at any one time. Sometimes, all of these may feature in a single experience or incident. For instance, if we perceive a threat, we may experience trauma and emotional impact from that threat, which then affects how much we can talk about the experience and therefore how we connect with others (Figure 3.3). So, given that these areas of function are related, they must work well together.

Figure 3.2: Areas of the evolutionary brain and key areas of the 'policing brain'

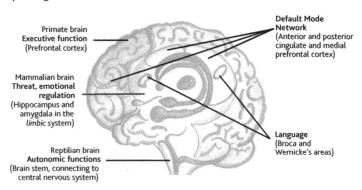

Unfortunately, when these functions are in relentless demand, glitches, hiccups, imbalance and general brain bickering can complicate things:

- Persistent trauma exposure often reduces our ability to regulate our trauma response.
- We have evolved with an inbuilt negativity bias.
- Not talking about trauma reduces our ability to regulate our emotional response to it.

Trauma exposure

When we perceive a threat, our alarm system in the brain activates, alerting us to do something to render the situation safe. Once dealt with, the experience is filed as a memory. This takes place in the *limbic system*. Threat processing involves two key regions: the alarm itself (the *amygdala*, called such because it is shaped like an almond and amygdala is Greek for almond) and its 'reset' button (the *hippocampus*, called such because it is shaped like a seahorse, and hippocampus is Greek for seahorse), which allows the experience to be filed as a memory. In policing, threats come thick and fast due to the nature of the job, so the amygdala and hippocampus need to work well together. Some experiences are more traumatic than others, meaning the alarm has to sound extra loud, which in turn means the hippocampus needs to work extra hard to enable us to put the experience in context and perspective so that we can stand down, file it and move on. Unfortunately, there is a twist. The amygdala's loud alarm signals (stress toxins) damage the hippocampus over time, which then limits its capacity to make sense of the experience, so the alarm isn't turned off (leading to even more damage). As a result, we can feel that the experience is 'still happening' and our body retains stress reactivity. As we try to get used to this, dysfunction can develop discretely, leading to anxiety issues and disorder, and chronic conditions involving our cardiovascular system, our digestion and our immunity.[12] When the hippocampus is compromised in this way, resetting our *emotional* response and calming down after stress, in general, is also harder. Adults with trauma-impaired hippocampi can

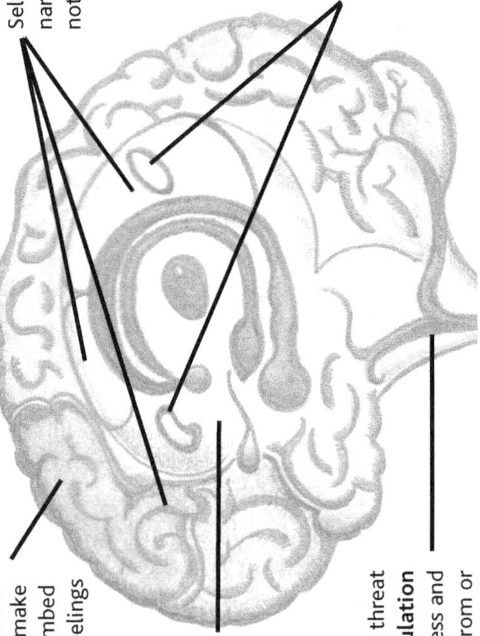

Figure 3.3: Areas of the 'policing brain' and how it feels to use them

Satisfaction vs wanting
Mind wandering
Self-ing, planning,
narrating, comparing,
not in the here and now

Connectivity vs 'otherness'
**Talking & sharing
experiences**
vs not finding words,
inventing cover stories,
avoiding being asked to talk

Connectivity vs 'otherness'
**Being decisive, open-minded,
managing compassion**
vs not wanting to make
decisions, ruminating, numbed
to others' feelings

Safety vs threat
**Threat processing, making
sense of traumatic incidents**
vs hypervigilance, re-
experiencing events and
foreboding future

Safety vs threat
Body ease & regulation
vs chronic stress and
being cut off from or
controlling body

find themselves in a state of agitation and reactivity for longer than they used to after a challenging event. Unrelenting stress signals can also lead to disruption in other functions related to the hippocampus, functions on which performance in policing may rely. Examples of affected functions include:

- a form of perspective-taking called *allocentric processing* (which is indispensable for situational awareness in policing and is now known to be key to our resilience);
- inhibitory control (which is critical for making decisions under stress, such as to shoot or not); and
- exaggerated startle response.[13]

In conditions where the alarm is likely to sound, again and again, we need to train the hippocampus to be able to apply the perspective we need, again and again. Fortunately, there are now tried and tested ways to improve how we make sense of difficult incidents. These involve adding information about what (and who) was where, when, and what was neutral or even positive about the event, and crucially, what wasn't about 'us'.[14] For those incidents where what happened where and when isn't so clear (such as exposure to extreme digital material), the mind needs alternative means of gaining perspective, rather than trying to apply context it doesn't have.[15] We will learn specific techniques to help make sense of different types of trauma impact in Chapter 4. The good news is that the hippocampus is notoriously plastic and for many of us, training it brings about real, effective results.[16]

The negativity bias

Before we start to beat ourselves up for finding threat management and trauma exposure challenging on the job, it's worth a mention that the human brain already has a bias toward looking for the negative (the threat) in a situation, because that is what keeps us alive.[17] Through evolution, we have needed to detect and log what we find threatening so we can respond to it should it arise again in the future. As Rick Hanson says, our brains are like 'Velcro for negative experiences and Teflon for positive experiences'.[18] Our 'need' to detect and log positive experiences when we are in the thick of things (especially in a threat-based environment) are not so strong in us and it's common for us to mistrust moments of positive reflection, brushing them off as fleeting flights of fancy, 'frivolous and inconsequential'.[19] To regulate our stress response when we are biased toward negativity takes more deliberate action.[20] Essentially, we need to feel safe, rather than worrying all the time to feel positive.[21] But we know from police survey data that this being worry-free isn't a hallmark of life on the job: over 40 per cent of UK officers and staff report that they worry all or most of the time about work.[22]

What is more, a negativity bias can also become very personal for those who take on responsibility or shame when things don't work out. Like children of unsafe parents who might prefer to say 'I'm bad' or 'there's something wrong with me' rather than admit they are being put in danger by their caregivers,[23] those in the police may all too easily assume personal fault or weakness, rather than admit that it is simply the nature of the job that is unsafe. Shame is also a driving factor for police developing more complicated, long-lasting trauma issues,[24] likely because we are making traumatisation intensely personal by identifying with it as something that happens because of 'who we are' rather than 'what can happen' on the job. The parallels between a 'blame culture' in the institution of policing mirroring and retriggering such a culture experienced in the family home is worth considering. Drivers to join the police often involve wanting to make a difference and to 'right' wrongs – the possibility for these moral endeavours emanating from a place of shame is something that institutions might address even simply be encouraging more pride in the workforce for committing to the path they have done by signing up. If shame is likely a factor of vulnerability to trauma impact, pride could well be a factor of resilience to the same.

So, we can see that the negativity bias (and the lack of safety, the sense of worry and the unrealistic sense of responsibility or shame that can come with it) is a critical risk to our resilience in policing. At this point, we could well suggest the reader counteract this bias with a PMA ('positive mental attitude') and to 'not worry, be happy' or 'look on the bright side', but, albeit well-intentioned, such quips can be inadvertently toxic.

> It's like papering over the messy reality of being human with a simple yellow smiley face.[25]

Instead, in Chapter 4, we will engage in practical exercises to cultivate the sense of being safe and resourced, to manage the responsibility we take for things that are out of our control and link genuine, real-life experiences of positive outcomes on jobs to diminish the impact of those that have been more challenging.

Talking and not talking

We understand that managing threats and trauma exposure is part of the job, and that negativity bias can make managing threats harder, so how do we respond to how this negativity feels? Do we respond outwardly? Do we do or say anything? For many who are busy getting on with incident after incident, case after case, shout after shout, the idea of stopping to talk about how it feels is at best ambitious and at worst downright ridiculous. The sheer weight of the pressure of the job and the scarcity of opportunities to pause and reflect means that opening up is simply not on the agenda. And yet, the opportunity – if only for a few seconds – to catch the eye of a colleague and acknowledge the impact of what might have just happened could mean so much in the course of an unforgiving day. So what's going on in the brain to explain this?

It turns out that, actually, not feeling inclined to talk about something difficult (when we have a sense that probably that would likely be a healthy thing to do) is likely more neurological than we thought. Rather than it being down to us 'not feeling like it', 'probably not really needing to' or 'not finding the right person at the right time', it may actually be down to the fact that one part of our brain isn't working very well with another. Neuroscience has shown us a few facts that make a lot of sense if we see them in the context of policing. When something happens to provoke a strong threat response (when the amygdala alarm is sounding), an area of the brain responsible for our speech (called Broca's area, named after a French physician in the 19th century) is deactivated – it goes quiet, and so we go quiet, too. This explains the difficulty that trauma patients have in labelling their difficult experiences[26] and may well explain the difficulty that police and staff in the service have done the same. The fact that we can feel better when we do talk is also borne out in somewhat cheeky neuroscience research into swearing. Studies show that swearing can reduce physical pain (such as that from cold water) and emotional pain (such as from feeling ostracised), either by triggering a fight-or-flight response or by distracting the brain from the cause of the pain.[27] Simply saying a conventional 'fuck' increased pain thresholds by a third as well as providing humour and distraction.[28] Writing down experiences is also known to lower our physiological reactivity to them, even if we don't show anyone what we've written.[29] Using language in novel and unique ways to describe intensely stressful experiences is a key feature of some of the more entertaining resilience techniques we will learn in Chapter 4.

Modes and zones of thinking in the brain

So far, we have familiarised ourselves with what is unique about the human brain, how it has evolved through reptilian, mammalian and primate forms (and the circuitry that it leaves us with) and we have introduced ourselves to some areas of function that can be particularly problematic for policing. Next, we will look at the different modes and zones of thinking that the human brain can find itself in:

- mind-wandering vs being aware (the Default Mode Network);
- responding vs reacting (green zone and red zone);
- being vs doing (midline and lateral areas).

Whatever our job roles, our backgrounds or character traits, if we have a brain, we will slip into different modes of thinking and behaving at different times. If we accept this and understand what to look out for, we have more of a chance of steering our minds into states that benefit our resilience when we really need it.

Defaulting to police mode

We all know that our minds can wander. Research suggests we mind-wander 50 per cent of the day.[30] What happens in that wandering matters.

Many of us assume an almost romantic, rosy quality to day-dreaming, as if we are whisked gently off into pleasant fantasies about this or that, giving us a break from the boredom of the immediate situation – or seducing us with ideal scenarios of us, saying whatever or behaving however we've always wanted to with someone. But, there is another side to mind-wandering that is far from pleasant; the kind where repetitive thoughts bug us, where we ruminate over grievances, longings or problems that we can't solve and ping between past and future, reality and delusion until we get so carried off that we can't even remember what it was we were supposed to be thinking about. This is because when we don't have a task to deliberately direct our effort and attention[31] we are more vulnerable to hijack by the lizard and the mouse to focus on what we don't want to happen and what we don't have.

This hijack highlights a critical point: the brain is efficient and will default to modes of thinking that require minimal energy. These modes might keep us physically alive, but they cannot be relied upon to generate or safeguard our happiness (quite the contrary). The Default Mode Network[32] comprises brain areas responsible for fear-mongering (the amygdala) and time travel (the hippocampus). With rumbling activation of these areas with no purpose or task in hand, we can find ourselves sleep-walking into planning and fretting, obsessing about where we stand in relation to everything else. With that comes a comparing mind, ruminating on who thinks what of us and what we have or haven't done, deserve or don't, want or dislike, until our worldview becomes suffocatingly 'egocentric'.[33] We can find ourselves right in the middle of our own drama and the narrative may not be that pleasant or realistic.[34] We can start to contract around our experiences, categorise them, make a 'case' about this or that. We can begin to think that we are the constant amid all of it, that we don't change, that we are one entity and everything and everyone else is separate and moves around us.

Add a bias toward negativity, and this doesn't paint a pleasant or realistic picture of the world from the inside. Thankfully, the reality is that we aren't like that and nor is the wider world; there is change – things are made up of parts and we are all interrelated.[35] What is more, the negative is a statement of fact only as much as the neutral, dull or positive ever is. It's just we don't pay attention to that because we have let the brain coast and wander where it will to save energy and keep us alive.

What might this be like in policing? When thinking naturally defaults to threat perception in the human brain anyway, it is reasonable to expect that this is magnified in those who are working in threat-based environments. With aggravated threat perception, unprocessed trauma and a sense of responsibility from discretionary powers, the territory of mind-wandering for police is likely to be very bumpy. Hyperarousal, being flung between unresolved past jobs and predicting and planning future scenarios, justifying actions, making judgements and comparisons about other individuals and social groups, may all become familiar thought processes that sometimes lead to dead-ends or unnecessary obstacles. There comes a point where, in the words of psychologist Tara Brach, that we simply end up 'getting in our own way'.[36] So, what can we do? Well, we can wise up to the reality that letting the mind wander is not indulgent, fluffy and relaxing. With the smallest amount of effort, we can offer our weary brains a real sense of chilling out, of gaining space, of enjoying what we know makes us happy. All we have to do is fire up the best equipment we have (the primate, prefrontal cortex), which for much of the time is just sitting there, waiting to be used. We do this simply by redirecting our attention to the kind of thinking associated with that area because 'where the attention goes, the energy flows'.[37] This redirection from the ancient lizard and mouse-like areas of the brain to that of our modern-day primate brain is just a question of learning to wake up and get into the right zone.

Seeing red and going green

The best zone is that which meets all the needs of the evolved brain – needs for safety (reptilian), satisfaction (mammalian) and connection (primate). From Rick's menagerie of an analogy (his 'brain zoo'), to be safe we need to avoid what threatens us (like a lizard), to be satisfied, we need to approach what will give us what we want (like a mouse might) and to be connected, we need to attach healthily to others (like a primate can). If we are doing all these things well enough, we are said to be in the 'green zone',[38] responding to life in just the way we need to for our brain to be at its best. Here, our body recovers from stress, conserves our resources and benefits from interaction. In this zone 'wellbeing becomes increasingly unconditional, less based on external conditions with space to choose our response'.[39] For policing, not having to rely on the conditions (the job, the resources or the backup), this independence is priceless.

If we aren't in this zone, we will know about it. We might have a sense of something not being right, of something lacking, of being rattled and needing things to be other than they are. The body burns its resources, agitates its systems, accumulates stress and stops resonating, synchronising and feeling good in company. Our mind states become infiltrated with fear, anger, frustration, a sense of being driven hurt and even aggression. This is the red zone, a reactive mode that may once have helped our species evolve in harsh settings, but that becomes toxic if resided in on a daily basis. As you may have worked out by now, herein lies the risk for the policing brain. Policing can be a harsh setting, an environment laced with threat, avoidance, striving and, increasingly, isolation. It can bring huge challenges which drain the energy of the lizards and the mice in our brain, and yet it offers few opportunities to welcome in the primate, to bring people together and put things right. In Chapter 4 we will train up our inner primate. We will teach it techniques to spot when we're operating in the red zone and how to help us wake up and move towards the green zone when we need it most – on the job, at home or in the transition in between.

Being and doing

Other 'zones' in the brain influence our thinking and behaviour too. It is fairly well known that the two sides of our body are generally steered by the opposite sides of our brain. The left-hand side of the brain is considered to be more logical and formulaic (because this is the side of the brain where language dominates in most right-handed people). Accordingly, the right-hand side is said to be more creative and imaginative. In the next section, we will explain how we can use 'handedness' to our advantage and we'll put that into practice in Chapter 4. Before we do, it is worth noting that the dividing line down between the right and left hemispheres is important in itself for our resilience. Activation of this line (imagining it running from between the eyebrows down to the nape of your neck) can make us feel 'divided' and can agitate us into doing something one way or the other. Being compelled to just 'do something' in a state of reactivity can be risky. This urge is the butt of a Spike Milligan joke, said to be one of the funniest jokes in the world (according to psychologist Richard Wiseman):[40]

> A couple of New Jersey hunters are out in the woods when one of them falls to the ground. He doesn't seem to be breathing, his eyes are rolled back in his head. The other guy whips out his mobile and calls the emergency services. He gasps to the operator: 'My friend is dead! What can I do?' The operator, in a calm soothing voice says: 'Just take it easy. I can help. First, let's make sure he's dead.' There is a silence, then a shot is heard. The guy's voice comes back on the line. He says: 'OK, now what?'

Living on this 'relentless doing' midline can be as uncomfortable as it is risky. In order to feel more balanced, settled and steady, we need energy in the brain to flow laterally, side to side, to even things out. This gives us access to the opposite feelings to relentless doing – sensations of 'just being' with things as they are, as illustrated in Table 3.2.[41] It's pretty obvious that policing, like much work in emergency response, is very much about doing. Imagine the luxury of being able to access the opposite when we need some relief.

Using attention to direct energy laterally can also be helpful to iron out the knots, glitches, ruts and vicious cycles that we can sometimes find ourselves trapped in, especially when

Table 3.2: Clustering of mind states involved in doing and being

'Doing' (midline)	'Being' (lateral)
Focussed on a part of the whole	Aware of the big picture;
Goal-directed	panoramic view
	Nothing to do, nowhere to go
Focussed on past or future	Abiding in here and now
Abstract, conceptual	Concrete, sensory
Much verbal activity	Little verbal activity
Holding firm beliefs	Not knowing, 'seeing newly'
Evaluating, criticising	Non-judgemental, accepting
Lost in thought, attention wandering	Mindfully present
Prominent self-as-object	Minimal or no self-as-object
Sense of craving	Sense of ease
Feeling fragmented	Feeling whole

Source: See note 41

battling with a difficult experience. Many readers may be familiar with the trauma therapy called EMDR,[42] which uses lateral eye movements (or tapping) and may have experienced the energy and clarity this simple exercise can bring to incidents we thought we'd never make sense of. Chapter 4 introduces some more techniques to encourage energy to flow laterally (including using our non-dominant hands and working with eye gaze) so that we can move to the 'being' mode when it is appropriate to do so, to give our brains some relief and to recharge.

So far, we've looked at areas of brain function that are particularly pertinent to policing, as well as some of the zones and modes we can find ourselves in more generally. Next, we look at how we can encourage the brain and body to work better together and how this can help our own resilience and our connection and work with others.

The body-brain connection

Understanding other people's actions and motivations is key in policing. Neuroscience is revealing that some sophisticated networks in the brain may be fertile training ground to improve operational performance and psychological resilience for jobs involving stress, compassion management and interpreting the behaviour and intentions of others. We will briefly look at two of these networks: mirror neurons and the vagus nerve.

> Our awareness of another person's state of mind depends on how well we know our own.[43]

Mirror neurons

The discovery of *mirror neurons* is said to be one of the most important neuroscience discoveries for decades.[44] These brain cells don't only fire with our own physical action, but they also fire when we watch *someone else* undertaking that same action. So when these cells fire, they give us an internal impression of the other person's experience. This can explain why we get thirsty when others drink, and yawn when others yawn.[45] What is more, these neurons can allow us to embody (to feel in our bodies) not just other people's actions but their intentions and their emotional state underneath. This network is a vital source of information – especially in situations when we need to understand someone else's state of mind. However, we can't necessarily delve into compassion and empathy to work it out. One example of how mirror neurons can be useful is that we can train them to activate in response to facial expressions.[46] There are said to be 50 types of smiles we are capable of producing, each giving a slightly different message about what we are thinking.[47] By maintaining eye contact and mimicking someone's expression when we're not quite sure what lies behind it, these neurons can ever-so discretely give us an inkling into their motivations. This may well prove very relevant to roles such as advanced interviewer training, family liaison or tactical firearms training. In Chapter 4 we will learn some basic mirroring techniques to help us raise our game in understanding others.

The vagus nerve

There is another neural mechanism that can achieve similar ends to mirror neurons in terms of understanding others through our bodies. We know from Chapter 2 that getting to grips with psychological stress and how it plays out in the body is key to our resilience. However, we can go further than just talking about it. As scientist Stephen Porges points out, 'language alone can't fix the body-brain relationship'.[48] The relationship between body and brain is complex – but we can work with it very well by training a nerve that manages that relationship.

In gestation, our embryonic cell turns in on itself, creating one line down the middle where all the nerves connect. This later develops into our spine. Nerves remain in all the places from which this cell folded in on itself, providing us with very active neurons in (what later become) our intestines and our hearts. These neurons give us senses of intuition and integrity we may describe as 'gut instinct' or sensing something is 'straight from the heart'. There is a single nerve that runs from the brain and connects neurons in our cardiovascular and gastrointestinal systems and it is called the vagus nerve (Figure 3.4). With the cardiovascular system home to 40,000 neurons[49] and the gastrointestinal system host to another 100 million neurons,[50] a lot is going on for the vagus nerve to manage.

The vagus nerve helps regulate our heart rate and our breathing and its ability to do this is called our 'vagal tone'; the higher the tone, the better we are at regulating our stress

Figure 3.4: The vagus nerve and its connection to the cardiovascular and gastrointestinal systems

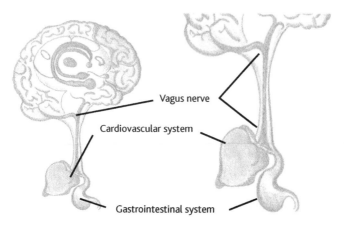

response in our body. This is not only valuable for our resilience in policing but also our performance. In a study using biometric surveillance, higher vagal tone was associated with calming the heart rate and improving shooting accuracy under threat (accuracy which has been shown to diminish from 90 per cent in training to 50 per cent during a real-life threat.[51] The vagus nerve also helps us track a person's voice against background noise,[52] a useful skill in areas of operational policing such as surveillance.

Because of its capacity to help us read others, the vagus nerve is intrinsically related to how we manage compassion for other people's suffering on the job. If we think about it, policing is all about dealing with human suffering – policing and managing those who inflict it on others, tending to and working with those who have been victims of it, and being responsible for our own suffering on the job (because of what we have to see and do every day). Resilience to suffering is integral to being in emergency response work – yet resilience to it does not equate to combatting or fighting suffering: resilience calls for us to accept it just as it is and work with it. Accepting the ugly side of life requires smart compassion: to be there during others' discomfort and acknowledge our own. This plays out at a psychological level and yet it also plays out with physical pain and suffering too.[53] Research has shown that when we imagine the pain of someone we love, we can almost feel it physically – and yet when we imagine the pain of those we don't know, it reaffirms the barriers we think separates us from them.[54] This isn't just relevant to the relationship between the police and the public but to relationships on the job. A study set in a New York Police Department revealed that lack of support at work was associated with reduced vagal tone in female police officers, suggesting that for women, local police culture was affecting their ability to regulate mind and body and to resonate constructively with others.[55]

Studies like these bring home the reality of how the policing brain can be trained better on the job and also how it can be physically affected by its culture. In Chapter 4 we will learn to train the vagus nerve for our resilience, performance and for the wider benefit of those with whom we share our experiences.

The chemical messengers we could call feelings

We finish our tour of the human brain with a brief visit to its chemical laboratory. So far, we can see how influential the electrical impulses in our brain (and running the length of our nervous system) can significantly influence our resilience. Coursing through the mind and body connection are also chemicals, substances that signal to us what our experiences mean and therefore enable us to adapt to our environment.[56] While we ingest many chemicals from food, drink, vitamins and maybe medications and drugs, those chemicals are typically those over which we have some control; we consciously decide to eat the comforting chocolate, drink the relaxing beer and take the pain-killing paracetamol the next morning! It is said in popular psychology that there isn't one emotion that society doesn't spend money on to replicate. Several neurochemicals flow through the brain and body – usually without deliberate direction from us. Table 3.3[57] summarises some of the principle neurochemicals, what stimulates them, how it feels when they are released, and suggests when we might really need them in policing. In Chapter 4 we will learn simple techniques to deliberately release these neurochemicals when we need them, rather than waiting for the perfect conditions for the brain to do so automatically.

What now? Your turn

With our mini tour of the policing brain complete, where does this leave us? Well, as we mentioned at the beginning of this chapter, it may be that we are on the verge of our own 'neuroplastic revolution'. Many professions already harness the capacity to rewire the brain to improve resilience and performance, including training elite athletes and rehabilitating brains after injury. Neuroplasticity practices have also been taken to global organisations such as Google and NASA,[58] so why not policing? As we learned in Chapter 2, one of the most important advances of the last 20 years of neuroscience has been the realisation that individuals can rewire their brains (long into their adulthood) using mental practice alone. This is based on

Table 3.3: Chemicals that flow in the policing mind

Chemical	Feeling	Brain system	Stimulus	Policing...
Dopamine	Reward, satisfaction	Approach Mammalian *Feed the mouse!*	Completing a task, self-care, eating food, celebrating little wins	Sense of getting nowhere in a domestic violence job
Oxytocin	Connection, bonding	Attach Primate *Hug the human!!*	Sharing a secret,* playing with the dog, giving a compliment	Avoiding new people out of suspicion
Serotonin	Mood stabiliser	Approach Mammalian *Feed the mouse!*	Sunshine, walking in nature, running, swimming, meditating	Sense of unease, irritability, up and down at work and at home
Endorphin	Pain killer, soother	Avoid Reptilian *Pet the lizard!*	Laughter, dark chocolate, essential oils, having a good cry	Body aches, stiffness, tightness around a really bad job, upset, loss

Note: * Fredrickson (2013: 49)
Source: See note 57

the fundamental principle that when we repeatedly use brain cells together they will connect (laying down new pathways); 'neurons that fire together wire together'.[59] This phrase is the key that unlocks our potential for improving our resilience using the practices in Chapter 4.

Before we start, it's good to set some ground rules:

- everyone is different;
- only repeat the techniques that will produce long-term change.

This is about you, *others* on the job and those interested in learning how this all plays out in emergency response.

Everyone has the capacity to rewire their brain using regular mental practice. And yet, how easily different practices come to different people will vary for lots of reasons. Some reasons just 'are what they are', and others we can do something about.

Genetics play a big part in how some areas of the brain react to training. For example, there is a gene that is involved in training the hippocampus, the area of the brain from where we gain our spatial perspective and our perspective on past experiences. Research has shown that one in four Caucasians (and slightly more in some Asian populations) will carry a variant of a gene called Brain Derived Neurotrophic Factor, which means it can take a little more effort to notice improvements in practices that target this area.[60] There may be many other genetic differences that may affect (to some degree) how we respond to mental practice. So, it's important to give ourselves the best chance of benefitting from practice by getting the conditions right.

Good conditions for rewiring the brain include: reducing high sugar intake (which can severely damage neural networks), increasing intake of healthy fats (to help protect the new neural connections we lay down with our practice) and even taking regular exercise (which stimulates the growth of neurons in response to many techniques).[61]

There is also a tendency that many of us might have (but to which we may not readily admit) to retreat into thinking 'Well, that's great and everything, but I'm just not that kind of person' – especially when we're tired and faced with something that requires a bit of grit. To label ourselves as not being worthy or able to make a new start in our thinking is a waste and is also scientifically unfounded. Personality profiling and psychological screening (be it in popular psychology or as part of police occupational health) come at a great cost to those deserving the chance to build resilience in ways they never have before. Science demonstrates well how futile and pointless it is to over-identify with a permanent, unchanging sense of having a 'self', which is separate from everything else. There is no location of the notion of 'self' to be found anywhere in the human brain, just an array of systems through which we interpret our experiences.[62] So, do yourself a favour and if you feel inclined to count yourself out of the adventure of a lifetime, *don't*. Give mental practice a try again and again and see what happens.

We can make practising easier by creating the right environment for them and having the right attitude to them. Physically, finding a few minutes and a bit of personal space is crucial. When you start learning the techniques, it's worth allocating a particular time of day or place to get used to them – in a place where you aren't going to be disturbed and where you can jot stuff down or just sit quietly and recognise any difference in your thinking or your body. Once you've spotted the one or two practices that do something for you, make a point of noting what that difference *feels like* and soak it in. Then, make a mental note to match the techniques you like to the kind of situation on the job where you think they might be most useful, and tell yourself that you can come back to them whenever you want.

Finally, it's worth acknowledging from Chapter 2 that the profession you are in has already been proven by neuroscience to be fertile ground for developing some of the most important qualities for human resilience.[63] What is more, when you embark on this, you do so not just for yourself but for your peers and future generations coming up in years to come.

> The best predictor of how you're doing in the present isn't your history of adversity; it's your history of connectedness.[64]

Good luck and enjoy.

Chapter 3 snapshot

- Once we understand how policing might have changed the way we think (in positive as well as negative ways) it's helpful to ask, *how does this happen, why do our brains do this?* The answers are sometimes obvious and sometimes they are more complex (or even not available to us at all). What matters, is realising that we all share a human brain and because we use it in specific ways on the job, we share more about our inner lives with each other than we may have previously thought.
- Neuroscience is doing policing and emergency response a massive favour, it's just we haven't had the opportunity to realise that until now. The game-changing development is science's proof that we can rewire our brains to be more resilient, just by practice alone. We don't need any toxic

cocktail of sophisticated drugs. We don't need to step into a sci-fi movie to simulate it in another dimension, we don't need to be super-intelligent, fast-track geniuses, we don't need to spend hours in training sessions or pass difficult tests. We just need to find ourselves a quiet moment, try a few techniques, choose which ones work for us and enjoy the rewards.

- No one needs to know the ins and outs of why the brain does what it does. Including you, the reader. But if it helps to be more objective about things and to take things a little less personally, then understanding the internal wiring we have inside our heads can be worth it. Even if it's not for our own benefit, understanding that sometimes how we feel is 'just what the brain sometimes does' can help our friends and peers on challenging days. This simple acknowledgement can provide a bit of relief and optimism that there's nothing essentially wrong with us, that we aren't alone in experiencing what we do, and that often it's surprisingly easy to do something about it.

- The part of the brain we have had the longest and that all species share (the reptilian brain) is responsible for reacting to threat. We cannot survive without it. However, we can't just live by that function alone either. If we have a job that requires us to deal with threat and danger on a daily basis, then we need more sophisticated brain functions to kick in. These include being able to make sense of threat and to put it into context (which the mammalian brain does for us), and being able to connect with others and make smart decisions about how to think (which the newest part of our brain, the primate brain, enables us to do).

- There are three things that the human brain needs for resilience: safety, satisfaction and connection. If these needs are met in any context at an individual or organisational level, there will be resilience.

- Four brain functions are vital in policing (and wider emergency response): threat perception, trauma exposure, emotion regulation and communication.

- When we perceive a threat, we need to *act* on it.
  When we repeatedly experience traumatic situations, we need to *process* them.

When we have an emotional response (which are chemical messages about our situation), we need to *feel and listen* to them.

When we experience extreme conditions, the areas of our brain on which we rely to talk about things go 'off-line' and need to restart after the incident to help us *talk and make sense* of them.

- There are brain modes that are helpful to get to know for the 'policing mind': mind-wandering vs being aware, responding vs reacting and being versus doing.
- Everyone is different and yet there are some ways we can all improve our chances of rewiring our thinking by using specific techniques to befriend our brains. These include reducing high sugar intake, increasing intake of healthy fats and taking regular exercise. The biggest chance we can give ourselves, however, is having an open mind and giving ourselves ten minutes a day to practice.

Checklist

☐ To what extent have you thought, until now, that your experience of your inner world is just unique to you? Are you able to acknowledge that others might have developed the quirks and foibles that you have on the job? *How might it feel to realise that having a human brain in the police service, and doing what you do is more of a common experience than you might have thought? That the inner world you take so personally doesn't set you apart from your peers?*

☐ Can you learn to recognise when you are responding from a place of feeling threatened (the lizard brain), from a place of wanting to make sense of experiences, of wanting to feel reward (the mouse brain) or from one of smart decision-making and truly understanding other people (the primate and human brain)? *If you could start to notice these ways of responding to your experiences, how might this change your reactions and responses in your working day? What about your relationships outside of work too?*

☐ How does mind-wandering feel to you? Is it all about daydreaming, indulgent fantasy and distraction about what to eat for dinner? Or does your wandering mind default to assessing what threat might be around the corner, who thinks what of you, what you think of yourself and what you wish was different? *Could you benefit from training your mind to redirect your thinking when it wanders off down dead-ends and blind alleys to more satisfying and constructive ways of responding in the here and now?*

☐ Can you notice feeling safe, satisfied or connected in your everyday experiences? What would it be like to train yourself to pick up on these states? What does it feel like in your body when you feel safe, satisfied with something or in tune with someone else? Is it a feeling in your chest, your tummy or your shoulders? Can you tap into it and remember it? *Can you call up those sensations when you need to? If not, would you like to learn how to?*

☐ How does it feel to be able to sense what others are thinking or what they are about to do on the job? How does it feel to be intuitive like that in your relationships outside of work too? *Would you like to be able to use your own body to help refine these skills? Have you learned the basics already in tactical training and want to know more?*

4

Turning science into action: resilience practices for policing

If you always do what you've always done, you always get what you've always gotten. (Jessie Potter)[1]

Introduction

In Chapter 1 we fully recognised that contemporary policing brings unique challenges to individuals' resilience and in Chapter 2 we recounted states of mind that may be common to the job but potentially unhelpful for resilience. In Chapter 3 we looked at how these mind states play out in the human brain and how they can develop into traits over time. In Chapter 4 we learn ways to use the brain to tweak states of mind to become more useful traits for resilience. It's at this point that understanding turns into pragmatism. The chapter closes with some guidance on how to develop a sense of command and control over the mind for lasting resilience in the job.

We know from our understanding of the policing mind so far that some specific states of mind are more helpful than others. What is more, we have a general idea of the areas of the brain in which these mind states arise. The techniques in this chapter stimulate specific areas to activate more constructive mind states. As we practice, the brain lays down pathways so that when we come to do them again, it becomes easier and more natural. This is the process of rewiring the policing mind for resilience (Figure 4.1).

Figure 4.1: An overview of resilience tools in the policing brain and their areas of function

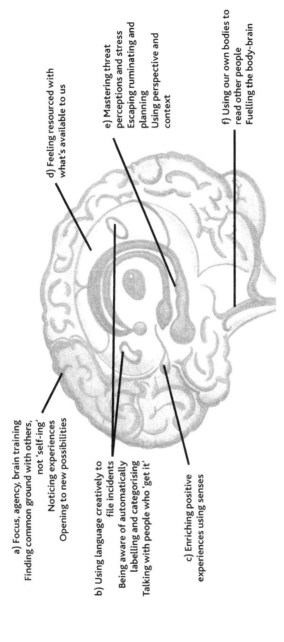

a) Focus, agency, brain training
Finding common ground with others, not 'self-ing'
Noticing experiences
Opening to new possibilities

b) Using language creatively to file incidents
Being aware of automatically labelling and categorising
Talking with people who 'get it'

c) Enriching positive experiences using senses

d) Feeling resourced with what's available to us

e) Mastering threat perceptions and stress
Escaping ruminating and planning
Using perspective and context

f) Using our own bodies to read other people
Fuelling the body-brain

a) PreFrontal Cortex (primate brain, 'attach' system), b) Language centres (Broca's and Wernicke's areas), c) Limbic system, including olfactory bulb for smell d) Mammalian brain ('approach' system), e) Hippocampus and amygdala, f) Vagusnerve and the mind-body connection

It's simple and the rewards are high.

It just requires open-mindedness and practice.

The science is nice, but is this for me?

As discussed in Chapter 3, recent neuroscience has been all about showing how the brain can be rewired, change and adapt if we train it to. Many of the techniques come from disciplines of cognitive training which have had decades of testing, evaluation and (increasingly) neuroscientific research in many different contexts ranging from elite sports performance to stroke recovery.

The reason these techniques are used so prolifically across the globe in so many disciplines is simple: it's because they work.

Yet while the scientific evidence base for the techniques speaks for itself, the proof that they work lies only *with us*. It is only with our own practice that any of us can really see how our minds and bodies benefit from this kind of training. So, it's by slowing down and taking even the smallest bit of time to focus on these new ways of thinking that we give ourselves the chance to *feel* the changes they bring.

This can be a very personal venture. Initially, you might not necessarily be able to describe to other people the changes you feel from applying the techniques – but frankly, who cares? *The practices are for you, no one else.* Some changes might be subtle but immediate, others might be 'slow burners', resulting in profound impacts further down the line. The imperative is to start.

Once your brain becomes more receptive to your practice, you can become more observant of other people's resilient thinking, opening up new opportunities to share and develop policing resilience on a larger scale.

Top tips

You can spend as much time as you like on the techniques – you might start with just two to three minutes, just to gain a sense of them, and then practise for longer on the ones you really 'get into'.

It's likely that you will soon pick up on which of the techniques make the most difference to how you think, and it's those techniques we'd urge you to practise the most.

Many of the techniques suggest you slow your breathing before you start. This helps settle the brain. (This is also referred to as 'tactical breathing' in the military).

You are more likely to be successful if you regularly take time out to practise slowing down your thinking in general so you can increase your command over your own attention.

If we are in more control of our attention, we see more clearly and become smarter decision-makers. We see our thinking more clearly and work smarter (and on friendlier terms) with our brains.

To help you get a sense of what it might be like to try out these practices for yourself, we include a handful of quotes from serving and former police, their families and friends who use the techniques. Some are using them for the first time, and for others, the techniques are part of their everyday life.

There is a full list of all the techniques at the end of this chapter in Table 4.1. We recommend in time that you give each technique a try, just to get to know your brain's natural likes and dislikes if nothing else. Some days, some techniques will be appealing and on other days, others will.

So, how do the techniques work?

Well, it's very straightforward. Each technique is designed to pull the brain in the opposite direction from those unhelpful habits that can cheekily grow roots as we busy ourselves on the job. The techniques relax the grip that unhelpful[2] habits can have over us *just enough* to give us a chance to ask ourselves, 'is this way of doing things useful for me or not?' In that powerful little micro-moment, that tenth of a second, we have agency – a chance to choose what comes next.

Together, the techniques can help to:

- reintegrate brain areas that have not played nicely together for some time;
- revitalise inactive systems that have been deprived of energy and are out of practice;
- redirect energy evenly so the whole brain can get what it needs to do what it needs to.

In doing so, this refreshes our thinking so we can:

- steady ourselves, giving us a bit of time and space to just check in with how things are for us;
- give our thinking a reality check, so we can get more of a grip on our thoughts;
- bring our attention to the here and now (what's *actually* going on) rather than going over old ground or propelling ourselves into the unknown;
- open out our thinking to new possibilities and clearer logic.

Refreshed, we will find it easier to take active steps to:

- feel resourced by what we have already available to us: skills, processes and support;
- reclaim the body as an intuitive source of information about our environment and other people;
- escape unhelpful categories, labels and conditioning by which we limit our thinking and actions;
- find genuinely useful common ground with others about life on the job (and outside of it).

These skills can make big differences to how we live so we can:

- be authentic in all areas of our life as officers, staff, loved ones, citizens and humans;
- befriend our brain to reclaim our natural home base, regardless of what is going on around us.

Getting started

With each technique, we explain what to do to practise it, how it feels when we do, why it works and when it's a good time to apply it on the job. We summarise each technique as we go.

Your personal toolkit: PPE for the brain[3]

The chapter closes with some advice on how to sharpen your tools to get the best out of the techniques. A useful way of thinking about this section is that you have *new kit* on the job with three components: you have tools (your brain functions), instructions on how to use them (the techniques) and a team with whom to practise them (the people you work and share time with). These techniques are likely very relevant to all those working in emergency response, not just those in policing, and may equally be useful for all those supporting those on the front line, including families and friends.

A summary of the techniques

The techniques are grouped under techniques that, with practice, enable all of us to:

- regularly check in throughout the day;
- master threat perception and manage the stress response, knowing when to stand down;
- realise that life and what happens around us is rarely about 'us' at all;
- engage in smart ways with our bodies so they can tell us more about ourselves and other people;
- manage compassion more smartly;
- get a grip on things by being objective, using perspective and context;
- become agents of our own mind, working with what we know (and being fine with what we don't);
- transform the smallest of positive experiences into powerful resources (such as logic and clarity).

Techniques

All techniques are indexed for you to browse at the end of this chapter in Table 4.1, but if you're happy to continue here and flick through what follows until you settle on one that catches your eye, go for it. Each one comes with an easy-read box to practise with, but we recommend you read about each first.

Daily techniques

Starting your day

Morning mindset

Great for feeling resourced, supported, open and inspired for the day ahead.

Our first moments on waking (the first 20 minutes or so) are said to be the most influential for the day ahead. This is for two reasons. First, the brain state with which we wake up involves 'alpha waves' which contribute to creativity. Second, we are better able to set intentions without the disruption from the ego, which accumulates during the day.[4] We can make the most of that time, even just by setting the alarm for getting ready to go to work ten minutes earlier (even if this means ten minutes less sleep, these focussed minutes will likely be far more useful for our mind and body over the subsequent hours than passive sleep). This is a good practice to do before embarking on the day or shift ahead. Simply sit on the edge of the bed or take a moment in the shower or while you're eating, or even in the car.

Take a deep breath in for the count of four and exhale for the count of six, settle your gaze softly in front of you (or close your eyes if you can) and breathe normally.

Make a simple mental note to yourself:

- You're beginning again: this is a new day, full of possibility that will flow on from one moment and opportunity to the next.
- You have what you need: the resources we need to get going (be it a uniform, PPE or transport to get you on your way to work) and the means to do your job when you get there.

- You have a big team: there are thousands of others getting ready for a shift in UK policing and emergency response *right now*, preparing for their respective days, wanting them to go well.
The job means something: policing is there to help others and to protect their core needs of being safe, well and connected. You do that for people, and to do it well you have to do it for yourself too.

Wiggle your fingers and toes, shake out your shoulders, feel your feet on the floor, look up to the horizon and refamiliarise yourself with what is going on around you. If you find repeating this useful, keep the phrases on a sticky note within view of where you get ready for work.

Morning mindset

Practise within 20 minutes of waking. Tell yourself you are beginning again on a new day; you have what you need for the day ahead; you have a team at work and a wider team in emergency response across the world, and that doing this job means something to you. Sense how that feels in your body and remind yourself you can come back to this any time today.

During your day

Checking in

These techniques are great for staying steady in the present, with clarity and perspective on how the day is progressing. As the hours pass on shift, it's natural that the mind will slip into the habits and routines of thought like all brains can do (remember the Default Mode Network in Chapter 3?)[5] What is more, some mindsets are particularly common in policing (as we discussed in Chapter 2) which can push and pull us in different directions as we respond to the demands of the day. These include shifting into 'work mode' (vs home life), dealing with threats, managing compassion, working with responsibility and being effective, having moments of trust and talking (and other moments of cynicism and isolation) and also managing your body's responses to all of that. Being able to just check in with how we are doing in the day for a couple of minutes every few hours can make a huge difference to what your body is 'keeping score of',[6] how you see your day and how *you* are on the inside.

Techniques that help us to 'check in' in this way include the 'body sweep', the breathing space and the eye-gaze expansion.

Body sweep

Remembering that you are actually 'in a body' sounds an odd thing to suggest. But much of the time we become so carried away with thinking and problem solving that we ignore the vehicle that is enabling us to do all these things: a body. The body can hold on to residual stress and tension long after we ever needed it for any action we needed to take at a particular time. This naturally leads to longer-term issues ranging from shoulder problems to heart conditions (as summarised in Chapter 2).[7] Checking in to see if the body is holding unnecessary or redundant tension is vital and yet relatively simple to do – the trick is remembering and making a deliberate effort to do it.

First, take your attention to your feet and feel your toes in your shoes (learn to do this without wiggling them). Even just this first try can feel very weird – some of us just feel nothing at all, just 'blank'. If this is the case, that's fine – just register that you feel 'not much'. Then, gradually move up your legs to see if you can sense your shins. Again, if you feel not much, that's OK, it will come with practice. Just sense what you can as best you can. Then, just keep going – up to your knees, thighs, tummy, chest, both arms, both thumbs, up to your shoulders, your jaw, the top of your cheeks under your eyes, the space behind your eyes, the back of your head, the nape of your neck, your back, your buttocks and back down to your heels. Relax any knots of tension along the way and make a mental note of any pleasant sensations. Whether you are wearing body armour or a suit, see if you can sense the space between the skin you were born in and the clothes you are wearing for your job. This helps to remind you that underneath all this, *you are you* and you need to care for your body because it's always going to be with you – and no one else will do it for you.

Breathing space

There is a well-known phrase that says, 'As long as you are breathing, there's more right with you than wrong with you'. Its source is unknown but the simplicity of it can be very appealing for those times when everything becomes all 'a bit too much'. Realising you still have all the oxygen you need is actually very steadying and can even be quietly empowering.

Pull your shoulders down, open up your chest and soften your belly. Inhale deeply for a count of four and exhale for a count of six. Check to see what your most dominant thought is at that moment, any feelings that are associated with it and any tension in the body. Take another in-breath for a count of four and exhale for a count of six. Steadily be aware of your breathing rhythm for a minute. You can do this with your eyes open as long as you can keep focussed on something still. Feel as many breaths as you can and take some satisfaction in the simple fact that you are being nourished by air, that it's giving your brain, muscles and organs all they need, and, right now, that's a very good thing to know. Keep this in mind as long as you can before you become distracted and enjoy coming back to it each time you remember to do it.

This helps regulate the stress response and reminds you to breathe through whatever comes your way.

Eye-gaze expansion

Being able to see the bigger picture is key to resilience (as discussed in Chapter 3). Using eye gaze is an easy way of waking up the lateral neural networks that generate senses of steadiness, spaciousness, perspective and objectivity in times that feel personal or constricting.

When you are ready, take a few moments to lift your gaze very slowly. Inhale deeply for a count of four and exhale for a count of six. Take a subtle look around you from right to left and back again. If you can, turn around 360 degrees so you can take in the full horizon of where you are. Repeat this once or twice. Then, imagine you could float up above yourself and look down, seeing you amid all that is happening around you. Keep zooming out for as long as you feel comfortable doing so until you can imagine in your mind's eye, seeing yourself as a dot in the building, the street, the neighbourhood, the county, the country ... and let yourself feel the space around you. When you are ready, wiggle your fingers and toes, shake out your shoulders, feel your feet on the floor, look up to the horizon and refamiliarise yourself with what is going on around you.

Tips

You can practise these three techniques separately or you can join them together in one three-minute check-in practice of body, breath and gaze.

On your first go at the 'body sweep', it might be hard to sense the different parts of your body. If you take your attention to a body part and feel absolutely nothing, that's fine – just register it as feeling 'blank' and move on to the next. The more you practise, the more you will feel each time you do it.

Checking in

Find five minutes without distraction. Sweep attention around your body up from your toes to the top of your head, noting when you feel nothing, when you feel temperature, pressure, pleasant sensations or discomfort. Take a deep breath for the count of four and let it go all the way out slowly to the count of six and repeat three times. Rotate 360 degrees if you can and look around you. If you can, close your eyes. Float up above your head and imagine looking down on yourself. Expand out to the wider country and seas until you can just see the planet below you. Stay there as long as you can until you feel more open.

At the end of your day

Sleep debrief

This technique is great for reflecting on being satisfied with the day, connected, in tune with what's important to you, relaxing and getting ready for sleep. Sleep is integral for resilience. Sleep is when the brain gets to consolidate its memories, help manage pain and rejuvenate – and yet, getting to sleep can be very challenging in policing, especially when our circadian rhythms are disrupted by shift work.[8] When the head hits the pillow it's not uncommon for our mind to race from thought to thought – reflecting on the significant experiences or interactions of the day, things that need making sense of and outstanding things we don't want to forget to do the next day. This clearly isn't conducive to sleep. Yet, it's natural, and giving ourselves a hard time about not being able to sleep just makes it harder to relax. Rather than 'trying to sleep', it is often helpful to address the mental states that prevent us from sleeping and then let nature take its course. Then we can more easily enjoy the simple pleasure of being in bed and not doing anything else other than *being in bed*.

Having a 'clocking off' routine before bed helps and all the usual 'sleep hygiene' suggestions we hear about in the wider world apply. If you can, leave your phone to charge on silent mode in another room (and use an alarm clock or watch to wake you up); avoid blue light an hour before bed (so set down devices or if you have to use them, set a blue light filter); choose reading over television for a few minutes before heading to bed; keep a notepad and pen beside the bed to note down any unwelcome tasks that come to mind.

Make yourself comfortable and lie flat and straight if you can. Take a deep breath in for a count of four and exhale for a count of six. Repeat this three times and let your eyes get heavy and close (unless you're writing). Acknowledge that you are in a safe, protected setting, with nothing expected of you. Nowhere to go, nothing to do. Only rest.

Attitude of gratitude

Reflect on the day to the moments when you may have felt pleased about something that happened or someone else's actions that you recognised as being a good thing. If we feel grateful for things, we feel satisfied and our minds are less likely to chase 'settling down' to sleep.

Little wins and giggles

Take a few moments to recognise the small accomplishments you may have had in the day (or bigger ones if there are some real successes to note). They can be as small as managing to clean your shoes before a shift or as significant as closing a case. If you can add a little humour here, that can add to the sense of satisfaction. Noting what brought a smile or chuckle to your day is always going to settle your mind with a sense of contentment that everything is pretty much OK, even if many things aren't.

When you are done, relax your muscles, feel the weight of your body sink with satisfaction and safety down into your bed. Try to let your breathing settle into the pattern you have when you are asleep – one continuous breath in and out, steady and gentle. Let your mind loosen and wander into the state between wakefulness and sleep and relax into the idea of thoughts falling away as you drift off.

Tips

If you are someone who likes to journal, you can add these practices to your journaling. Some might prefer to verbalise this practice or share it with housemate(s), partners or children. You can also increase the number of examples to three, four or more if you enjoy the practice. On difficult days, just finding one example may be enough to help you feel better. Brains love reward and you may find this very satisfying, even if you don't feel like doing it initially because you're tired. It may even help with setting a positive mindset for dreaming.

The 'body sweep' (and later, 'finding your feet') techniques can also be done lying down pre-sleep.

You can also integrate the forthcoming sit-back-and-sigh technique into an end of day wind-down.

Sleep debrief

Prepare for sleep by putting devices away, settling into a lying position, inhaling deeply and slowly exhaling.

Think about three things or people that you were grateful for that day.

Recall three things that you did that made you feel satisfied or proud.

Think back to any moments of lightness, humour or observations that made you smile to yourself.

Let your body sink into the bed and even out your breaths into the rhythm of sleep.

REAL-LIFE EXPERIENCES

Even when I'm really busy at work I make time in the evenings to factor in an attitude of gratitude. I find cooking dinner from fresh ingredients, using nice familiar recipes and then sharing with my loved ones a real way to earth and relax. This active task also helps me process my thoughts. (Trainer in police resilience and peer support lead)

Since leaving the police in Oct 2018, my sleep has improved greatly. I listen to a favourite comedy programme in bed and fall asleep, then leave it playing all night. I know these word for word. When I do awake, the familiarity helps with any 'intrusive thoughts' and I fall asleep again very quickly. (Retired officer)

I have a note pad and keep it by the kettle before bed. So many of the cops I know describe waking at odd hours with that 'something' rattling around in their minds and ask themselves, 'why could I not get it out and get back to sleep?' Write it down. When you see it written down, you see what you need to do. (Serving response officer and TRiM[9] practitioner)

Mastering threat perception

Threat perception (and fear management) is an integral part of policing and presents itself in all sorts of ways across many roles. Whether it's in the immediate acute physical threat of violence in response policing or dealing with protracted cases investigating issues of public protection, the brain is called on to manage the sense of threat for long periods. As discussed in Chapters 2 and 3, this is where evolution's 'negativity bias' can make life very difficult in policing. The innate bias humans have toward the negative and the demand on threat management (from the working conditions in the policing environment) is a complex and potentially toxic combination. It can disrupt our assessment of a threat's likelihood, immediacy, magnitude and severity of its impact.[10] What is more, without managing threat perception, the constant hypervigilance and hyperarousal that comes with it can exacerbate the stress response over time, leading to burnout (as discussed in Chapter 2).

It's therefore helpful to have to hand some simple techniques to allow us to double-check or 'proof' our threat perception so we are clear if we still need to react to a situation or if we can now stand down. The following practices are designed for those moments *when you are not in any immediate danger* (and are not physically under threat), but your mind is behaving disproportionately as if you are. Moments like this can occur after a period of extreme exposure to stress when the brain has yet to settle. They can also occur when we are in a non-threatening situation that has elements to it that remind us of a previous threat, triggering a historic stress reaction.

Sensing threat but needing to get the better of it?

The following details three ways to feel more in command and control of the threat response.

'What's for lunch?'

A simple reality check can be to acknowledge what our reptilian, mammalian and primate brains might be up to and to ask ourselves if we are under threat, needing something or if we are able to connect with others (see Chapter 3).

Sometimes it's useful to ask yourself the question, 'Right now, *am* I lunch, do I *want* lunch or *can I share* my lunch with others?' This can help us get clarity in the moment of whether we are truly under threat here (being someone else's lunch), whether there is something we just want or need (food) or if there is an opportunity to reach out to others (to share our lunch).

If we can move from threat reactivity to a sense of having enough ourselves (so much so that we can start to consider others), we are more likely to feel resilient. Being connected to others feels a lot stronger than feeling threatened by others for no reason.

REAL-LIFE EXPERIENCES

This can be a useful (and a slightly light-hearted) question to ask yourself when you have the sense that you might be feeling a disproportionate sense of threat from someone (when you know in your gut, that you are essentially safe and everything genuinely is OK). It can help us wake up from unnecessary tension that might have 'taken us off' elsewhere when actually, all we probably need to do is get on and connect to those around us.

F.E.A.R. vs T.H.R.E.A.T

These acronyms can help us differentiate between the reactivity of (unnecessary) fear and the more responsive skill of *accurate threat perception*. Recognising the balance in any one moment between legitimate immediate threat and lingering (or residual) fear is vital for our decision-making, performance and wellbeing. Both can be going on, that's OK, but we can choose to engage more proactively and effectively with threat perception and less with a felt sense of fear.

FEAR = **F**alse **E**vidence **A**ppearing **R**eal

THREAT = **T**rustworthy **H**eightened **R**esponse: **E**ffective and **T**actical

REAL-LIFE EXPERIENCES

This technique is similar to *'What's for Lunch?'* but with a slightly more affirmative, tactical approach which can help us focus on the job at hand. It's also good in policing to remember that threat perception is an essential part of the job, and that with that can come fear. Differentiating between the two (with savvy acceptance and without judging ourselves) can remind us that we are both human and fully resourced to do the job we are committed to doing.

So, when you are aware that you are feeling fearful in a situation, simply remind yourself with something like:

'Fear here is a useful flag. I can now get a handle on this threat by trusting myself in this heightened state of alert to be effective and tactical. I don't need to react to this fear sensation, I need to respond to this threat.'

Fear face-off

Face perception is a fascinating area of neuroscience with which policing has engaged for many years, but understanding faces is not just about recognising criminals and lie detection.[11] Science has shown that those who have traits of hypervigilance have stronger fear-based responses to neutral faces that display no signs of threat.[12] This is worth being aware of in policing. Recent research has shown that hypervigilance can be an adaptive *or maladaptive* trait in policing, with 67 per cent of UK police officers reporting a moderate to extreme sense of threat, and therefore being at risk of misperceiving threatening expressions in neutral faces, adding potentially unnecessary stress to non-threatening scenarios.[13]

When feeling threatened by someone's facial expression (in an otherwise non-threatening situation) ask yourself if it is possible that their face is not intentionally aggressive. Even if your answer confirms a sense of threat, at least you have given your brain the chance to help you decide on an appropriate response.

We will learn more about working with faces later in this chapter.

REAL-LIFE EXPERIENCES
This is a technique that can take a fraction of a second. It can be applied in many situations but is best practised when we are sensing an aggressive attitude from someone in a context where we wouldn't expect it, where a situation is otherwise safe. This could be an awkward meeting with a supervisor or colleague or even an online meeting where you're just not quite sure if the aggression you're sensing is something you

need to respond to or maybe something to just 'let be' until you have more information about what is unfolding.

Feeling disproportionately anxious about a harmless interaction? (fear in interpersonal interaction):[14] how to imagine life from someone else's disadvantage

From F-word to C-bomb

We learned in Chapter 3 that the neural circuitry which is activated by fear depletes resources from the area of the brain responsible for compassion and vice versa. So if we are feeling fear, we are less likely to feel compassion and, more importantly, if we are feeling compassion, we are less likely to engage with fear. This is quite handy and arguably one of the sharpest tools in the policing brain's resilience kit when it comes to working with other people. To explain, if we know we are in a situation where our fear of someone is *disproportionate* (or even altogether inappropriate), we can redirect our focus to feeling a degree of compassion (or even pity) for them. This seems to go against our instincts, but *that is precisely the point.* If we don't want to be habituating to feeling fearful (because, rationally we know we don't need to be in that particular moment, and also, it feels horrible) then we can do something about it: pull in the opposite direction. This can be highly effective in a short space of time – even ten seconds, so it is well worth practising.

An example of when this might be useful is when dealing with a neutral or positive issue (that carries no particular threat) that is taking place with someone you're nervous or wary of (perhaps because of past experiences or something you have heard). The technique is useful to apply in the lead up to that moment, during the actual interaction and also in the moments following it. Consider using the following practice for low-level uncomfortable interactions, such as an important meeting with a difficult manager, re-interviewing a passive-aggressive witness or even preparing for a Sunday dinner with the in-laws!

Take a deep breath in for the count of four and exhale for the count of six, settle your gaze softly in front of you (or close your eyes if you can) and breathe normally.

- Recognise the sense of threat and fear you feel in response to the person. See if you can sense that energetic reaction in your body (a tightening chest, bracing in the shoulders or tummy, a clenching of the hands).
- Now bring that person to mind and think about all the influences on them which might explain why they behave and react to life in the way that they do (or you have heard they do) that makes you feel nervous or anxious.
- Think about their social circumstances, their family situation, possible upbringing, how their minds might have developed along the way, how they might have tried to protect themselves from feeling vulnerable.
- You don't have to condone their behaviour, forgive them or care about them in any way. Just recognising their potential inadequacies and challenges can take the sting out of interacting with them. See how that feels for a moment.

Even if this subtle recognition only lowers your reactivity to them just a little, congratulate yourself on your strength of character to do this. (You can even think how grateful you are to not have to wake up being *them*!)

When you are ready, sense your feet on the floor and re-familiarise yourself with what is going on around you. If you are practising in front of them, you could even take this moment of strength to look at them directly in the eye and exhale long and deeply.

F-word and C-bomb

Inhale deeply and exhale slowly. Remind yourself that the brain is wired as such that it's not possible to feel fear and compassion at the same time.

Bring to mind a situation in which you feel mildly threatened by someone and sense how that tension or discomfort feels in your body.

Consider the influences on that person's behaviour, what challenges they might have in their life, what their upbringing may have been like, how they might have responded to vulnerability in their past, what influences there may be on their circumstances that you know nothing about. Ask yourself if someone who behaves in the way they do, without awareness, can really be happy.

Take a moment to be grateful that you are not them. You are you, and you are aware.

REAL-LIFE EXPERIENCES

I really like this, and on reflection where I have handled family arguments badly it's when I have let the F-word emotions run wild and did not let the C-word kick in. (Retired police officer and trainer)

There was this one lady with mental health issues who kept on calling and calling during nightshifts for random reasons and it would provoke a lot of tension. Rather than dreading her calls, I decided to go round and pay her a visit and face whatever it was that was the issue. Turns out all she needed was a lightbulb changing so she could read and settle herself to sleep. That one moment of opening up to her vulnerability saved the team a lot of agro in the long run. (Response officer)

When the day's events are a heavy weight to carry home: create clear boundaries between job and not-job

Boots-at-the-door

A great way of managing threats and fear is to be clear about boundaries: where it is appropriate to be dealing with the challenges of the working day and where it is not. Where you have a safe space and where you take off your uniform is somewhere you can make the clear boundary between you, your body, your job and your home life.

A great technique kindly suggested by a PC and his partner[15] during the COVID-19 crisis was to mark the transition out of 'threat perception mode' by removing his boots at the kitchen door. His partner soon came to realise that if he was sitting down in the living room with his boots still on, that he was still processing the threats and challenges of the day and needed a few minutes space to put them down before engaging with family life.

Boots-at-the-door

After a shift, as you open your front door, ask yourself if you are:

a. ready to relax into engaging with those at home; or
b. still in work mode and need a few minutes.

If the answer is 'a', take your boots off and leave work mode.

If the answer is 'b', keep your boots on until you are ready to put down the day. When you do, really pay attention to taking off the boots, putting them aside and feeling your feet on the floor.

REAL-LIFE EXPERIENCES

This technique is borrowed from another response officer who developed it with his partner as a way of giving himself time to decompress and communicating to her that he needed a few moments before engaging with the family after a tough day.

Constructing a personal story in your mind about an incident?: acknowledging the discomfort and neutralising the narrative in your head

Engaging our language centres in the brain is a good way of regulating the amygdala (our alarm system), which can continue to fire long after a threat has been perceived and effectively managed (as we discussed in Chapter 3). By noting our experiences with words (silently to ourselves or out loud if appropriate), we gain more of a sense of control over what has happened.[16] What is more, if we write down a description of a past threatening experience, this can lower our psychological reactivity to it, even if we show no one and discard what is written.[17] This doesn't have to be emotional or intense. In fact, it's far more useful to be somewhat detached. We can achieve this in two ways: first, by labelling things objectively and second, by getting a little creative. You can choose, one, try both or move from one to the other.

Labelling 'there is...'

Take a deep breath in for the count of four and exhale for the count of six and check in with the most dominant feeling or sense you have about a past threatening experience (either how you felt at the time, how you feel recalling it or both). Swap the words 'I felt' or 'I feel' with the words 'there is' or 'there was'. So, if you feel fearful, say to yourself 'there is anxiety'. If you sense you are sad or melancholic, say to yourself 'there was loss' or 'there is sadness'. This can help us realise that the fearful emotional tone of an event or experience is something that *all humans would have in common* if they too had experienced what you did. Remember, feeling tones are a natural resonance from the environmental conditions we are in. Our bodies and minds are sensitive to them so that we can respond effectively and adapt to what is going on (as we discussed in Chapter 2). It's vital to accept emotions and useful chemical messages to help you understand your environment. It's also good to get into the habit of remembering that these human emotions are there all the time, waiting to be sensed according to what is going on. In a sense they aren't 'ours', but we can tap in and out of them as we need to.

REAL-LIFE EXPERIENCES

This can be helpful when you are aware that you are taking on an emotional response to a situation that is lingering longer than you sense is proportionate or sustainable. For example, when in a family liaison role, a family's sense of loss can linger long after the day has finished, after the case has moved on or even has been closed. There comes a time when it's OK to recognise that a sense of loss is a feeling that happens in the world. This broader space of there being loss 'out there' in the world can bring the smallest sense of relief that this is part of being human and that it can be there and we can feel it as we continue with our lives and our jobs – with that fact just being what it is.

Getting creative (bit weird)

Using language in the mind is a somewhat unique way of 'detoxing' the memory of an uneasy exchange, job or situation. Take a deep breath in for the count of four and exhale for the count of six, and bring to mind the past threatening experience or interaction you would like to take the sting out of in hindsight. Don't think too much at this point but give yourself a 'quick-fire' challenge to come up with a phrase to describe the experience you had by giving it a colour, a texture, a shape, a sound or even a personality. Some people find it can even be helpful to imagine a cartoon voice describing the experience, or 'replaying' it at double speed. Others might imagine a comedic 'double take' in their mind when they think back to what happened. These options seem very abstract and a bit 'out there', but playing with labelling and re-framing experiences in this way can bring detachment and sometimes light relief, especially if we choose to add a little humour and not to take ourselves too seriously when we do it. Even if later, the gravitas hits us once more (as it surely will), we can remind ourselves that *sometimes* we can bring a lighter kind of attention to it and that different ways of viewing an experience are possible at different times.

Tips

This is a very private practice, but we can get a sense of it by exploring conversations with others about abstract thought. A novel conversation might be what colours we think the days of the week have in our mind's eye or what textures we might give certain words.

If you'd like to practise playing with language, a good way to do this is to undertake the Stroop Test[18] which you can easily find online. The test was developed in 1935 and has been used in psychology ever since, in many different ways. It also appears in popular games and home entertainment. The exercise involves seeing how fast you can read the colour of a text, either the colour of the ink in which it is written or the colour that the word spells, for example being shown the word grey written in green ink.

Get creative with language

Inhale deeply and exhale slowly. Check in with how you are feeling about an experience. Take a moment to realise that this feeling is in a wide pot of feelings that everyone dips in and out of sometimes. Rather than thinking 'I feel sad', try saying to yourself, 'yes, there is sadness here right now'. If you sense yourself contracting around an experience as being 'all bad' or something that feels uncomfortable, try describing it with a colour, texture, taste or sound, such as 'spikey and empty cold' or 'thumpy and bland'.

REAL-LIFE EXPERIENCES

I actually started to feel a bit better about a situation by just reading the paragraph/instructions over and over again before doing the 'exercise'. So, when I took the breaths I was already half way there ... it gave me hope of turning a bad situation into an opportunity just to think differently. (TRiM trainer, police mental health champion and TIPT Trainer)[19]

Is your body holding tension and it's starting to be uncomfortable?: reset your body, feel accomplished, at ease and present in the here and now

Shake it out

A really quick and simple way to release the tension of lingering threat perception in the body is to literally shake it out. Making your muscles soft feeds the message back to your brain that now is a time to stand down. Remember from Chapter 3 that when it comes to dealing with threats, the body and brain talk to each other – and the body can quietly hold on to residual tension from trauma and stress unless we learn to (and remember to) deliberately release it as we go. Shaking helps us to do that. As neuropsychologist Lisa Wimberger[20] explains, 'You cannot shake *and* contract and hold your stress and let it linger (which is what most of us do because we're not taught otherwise)'.

Find a space where you can move about and where you're not going to feel self-conscious or send nearby objects flying. Let your arms hang by your sides. Shrug your shoulders up to your ears and then release them heavily. Then shake your shoulders, arms, wrists and fingers, increasing the velocity until your arms feel like warm jelly. You can repeat this with your legs. Swinging your arms as you gently twist at the waist is also a good way of shaking out your torso.

Tips

Use some sticky notes or an alarm on your phone to remind you to have a subtle shake every few hours if you know you are likely to get tense in a certain space at work or have a particularly stressful day ahead.

This can also help release the body of tension from a bad night's sleep or nightmares and can be done on waking before brushing your teeth, for example.

Shake out tension

Find somewhere you won't feel self-conscious moving about in. Inhale deeply and slowly exhale. Shrug your shoulders heavily and move the shrugging down your arms to your fingers. Swing both arms gently in front of you, then increase speed and pace until you're chucking your arms from one side to the other. Bring in a twist at the waist until your arms are flinging round your torso. Keep going until all the tension is released and your shoulders are loose, dropped, floppy and relaxed.

REAL-LIFE EXPERIENCES
Many people feel awkward just THINKING about doing this
(me included) and that's completely understandable when
our 'composure' is typically all about being of stature, steady

and in control, outward-facing, being the epitome of order and regulation. This is precisely why this technique can be an absolute joy and a massive relief for tension accumulated on the job, especially when we are used to being seen and on show. Finding a quiet space to let your body just 'go for it' without anyone looking or having an opinion is incredibly liberating and can feel nicely rebellious.

Feeling your feet

This technique may be very familiar to many readers already and is based on the idea of 'grounding'. The intention is to bring your attention away from frantic head space and back down into the body so we can steady ourselves. It's a very subtle way of tuning into our natural resilience and sensibilities, and 'feeling our feet on the ground'. We can use it in any situation, including those in which we are experiencing (relatively low-level) threat, such as talking through an ongoing or intense negotiation or preparing to engage in a difficult interaction. It can also be used after a threatening event (which may have required a physically active response) at the moment when it is safe and right to stand down. Taking a moment to find your feet after one job can help prepare your mind and body to pick up the next.

You can work in either direction, toes to head or head to toes, or even both. Working from toes to head can help you feel supported by the earth, whereas working from head to toes can help you feel like you are 'coming back down' to earth.

- Take a deep breath in for the count of four and exhale for the count of six.
- To work *toes to head*, feel your feet on the ground first. See if you can sense the underside of your feet in your shoes and the massive weight of the earth rising to meet them.
- Try to sense what it is like to feel the body part you are in 'from the inside' out – the bones, the muscles, the skin, the space between it and the clothes covering it.
- Gradually move your attention up from the soles of your feet to the tops of your feet, ankles, shins, calves, knees, back of the knees, thighs, buttocks, pelvic floor, lower stomach, lower

back, up your torso and down into your upper arms, lower arms to your thumbs and fingers.

- At this point, you can stand straight with your legs together and your spine and chest lifted. This pose is often called 'the mountain' and is more impactful on confidence and resilience than traditional more aggressive 'power poses' (such as standing with your hands on your hips).[21] Hold the position as long as you want to.

When you are ready, take another deep breath in for the count of four, exhale for the count of six, wiggle your toes and fingers and re-engage in what is going on around you.

Figure 4.2 illustrates an example of working from *head to toes*.

Tips

Just as with the 'body sweep', when you first do this, it might be hard to sense the different parts of your body. If you take your attention to a body part and feel absolutely nothing, that's fine – just register it as feeling 'blank' and move on to the next. The more you practise, the more you will feel each time you do it.

The practice can be done at a fair pace or you can take your time over it. If you are short on time, work both sides of the body at the same time and go in one direction. If you have longer, work up one side of the body then up the other side of the body, then down one side of the body and the other side of the body. You can extend this by repeating in both directions.

You can also incorporate this into the sleep debrief practice by doing this lying down and feeling the weight of your body being supported by the bed as you sink into sleep.

REAL-LIFE EXPERIENCES

The sense of grounding in 'feeling your feet' is something I have heard of previously but couldn't engage with, until I read it here. It was when I switched from trying to do it 'head to toes' (which never worked as my head was unable to let me go into my body) to 'toes to head' which made me feel the calmness of the earth beneath me, before I went into my head and that prevented me becoming lost with everything going on in there. (Retired police officer and peer support co-ordinator)

Knowing when to stand down

Is your stress response lingering and not subsiding after an incident?

Get good at standing down, relaxing into safety and reconnecting to the rest of the world again. An important component of

Figure 4.2: Infographic on finding your feet

Source: With thanks to Police Care UK

standing down from a stressful or threatening situation is deliberately noting when it is over. This can be in the moment of closing down the scene of a live incident on return home from work or even much later on after an event. Really establishing in the brain that an experience is over resets the stress response and enables us to file a memory of something difficult as being in the past. This is important as this then permits us to re-engage with the present, telling us it's OK to continue with our lives, other people and the wider world of activity around us. By being able to do this, we are also reminding ourselves of our own resilience, that we survived situations that were challenging or even life-threatening and that we are still intact. Safety cues are also good for counterbalancing the brain's tendency to log threatening events and ignore positive and neutral ones. Cues for safety (or 'fear extinctions') are the responsibility of the hippocampal region in the brain and this is the area of the brain that many of these techniques are designed to kick start.[22]

Sit-back-and-sigh

After you've mapped out visually what happened 'where and when' and have a sense of how the incident came about and came to pass, take a few slow, deep breaths, and think back to that moment when you felt in your body the sense of relief that it was coming to a close or was over.

What did it feel like? Where did you feel it in your body and what do you remember of that moment, what could you see, hear, feel, sense?

Examples that police officers and staff have offered of those moments include:

- watching an offender being removed from a scene;
- that first cup of coffee back at the station;
- getting out of the patrol car and sensing the car door thud shut on the job, now left behind;
- smelling the warmth of their child's head as they tucked them into their bed that night;
- seeing the report or being verbally debriefed about an incident that had been resolved;

- hearing the subtle mutterings and chuckles of relief among peers as they resumed their daily duties.

How does it feel? Are you able to stand down and get back to what you were doing? Is there any sense of warmth and relaxation of muscle tension? Can you feel more open and receptive, friendlier to what is going on around you?

Tip

This can be useful when you can't sleep and can be a useful addition to the sleep debrief. In other contexts, this is sometimes called a 'safety cue'.

Sit-back-and-sigh

Inhale deeply and exhale slowly. Find some space that is free from noise and distraction. Call to mind the incident or experience you want to work with. Ask yourself the question, when did it stop? Let your mind go back to when you felt the most relief. Capture that moment in your mind's eye and sense how it feels in your body to be in that moment of relief. What does that sense of safety feel like? Can you link that sense of safety to your memory of that experience? How good is it to feel safe? Can you learn how this feels and make a note to yourself that you deserve to tap into this relief more often?

REAL-LIFE EXPERIENCES

I live fiercely by 'work hard, play hard' – so when I am not working, my phone and technology is off. It's important to know when to stand down. I even challenge my team who reply to emails immediately when they don't need to. (TIPT trainer for UK police and former inspector)

Ninety-eight per cent of police recruits trained in using 'safety cues' when making sense of traumatic incidents on the job reported that they were immediately able to use the technique and 79 per cent said they went on to share them with family and friends.[23]

Depersonalising experiences

Feeling like you're contracting around an experience and getting way too involved?

Get some separation, find some space, open up your thinking and step back into being yourself.[24] Identifying with the policing role, as being 'a cop' is known to be a strong influence over officers' sense of who they are (as explored in Chapter 2). This may be great when things are going swimmingly, but when things are challenging, over-identifying with 'the job' can feel uncomfortable. If things don't turn out well, if we don't feel supported or respected, or if we're embroiled in an investigation or case which vehemently conflicts with our world views, then this can have a knock-on effect on how we see ourselves.

As we learned in Chapter 3, our brains can default very easily to putting ourselves in the centre of our own drama, to being judgemental about ourselves and comparing ourselves with others. Letting this go on is counterproductive; we seem to do it automatically and yet it feels uneasy. Science demonstrates well how futile and pointless it is to over-identify with a sense of a permanent 'us' in the middle of everything that is going on. As we said in the earlier chapter, there is no location of 'self' to be found anywhere in the human brain, just an array of systems through which we interpret our experiences.[25] Long term, it can take practice[26] to pull ourselves out of thinking about the 'world according to [*insert your name here*]'. Messages about being 'a certain way' or 'kind of person' are likely established early in our childhood development, through our interactions with those who looked after us and those we mixed with. Yet, labelling 'who someone is' takes place in adulthood too. In policing, labels can be inadvertently established by peers, managers, trainers or reinforced by occupational health practices such as personality profiling, psychometric testing and psychological screening (never mind psychological diagnoses). Even if the outcomes of these interventions are intended to be positive (such as enabling us to access support or to understand our motivations for undertaking certain job roles), their effect can limit our beliefs about our capacity as humans to adapt and develop – something we know that the brain is immensely capable of doing. To be resilient in policing, we need to know we can *learn* from experiences and that we can *adapt* how we think and behave in a way that the job demands and our wellbeing deserves. Remove a workforce's right to do this and a force will weaken its resolve (more about this in Chapter 5).

So, what can we do as individuals, regardless of our background or how we may or may not have been screened, tested or profiled by others? There are some very brief techniques that we can practise regularly to help us 'snap out' of contracting around limiting beliefs and to see the world as a bigger place than the one we default to seeing immediately in front of us. This gives us more room to be as much of ourselves as we can be, to change and adapt, learn and move on with resilience for whatever comes next.

'Not me': regain your agency and independence

A very straightforward response to feeling caught up with things that conflict with our views and values, which intrude on our personal space or exceed our boundaries of what we deem acceptable or decent is to say to ourselves, 'This is not me. This is not mine. I am not this'.[27]

This can help us depersonalise (or '*non*-personalise') experiences and stop us from over-identifying with the job at hand.

Not me

Find somewhere where you can speak out loud quietly and not feel self-conscious. Inhale deeply and exhale slowly. Feel a sense of contraction around the incident or experience and the temptation to take it personally or take ownership of it in some way. Sense how that feels in the body. Then say to yourself quietly, 'this is not me, this is not mine, I am not this'. See how it feels when you say that. Keep repeating it, changing the emphasis each time until it starts to have an effect. Sense the distance you start to feel between the experience and you. How does that separation feel in your body? Keep saying the phrases until you feel sufficiently released from the grip of the experience and can open up more to what is going on around you.

REAL-LIFE EXPERIENCES
Cops get involved in so many other people's worst, biggest
and most memorable experiences, and we need to remind
ourselves that we are not the centre of all things. (Response
officer and wellbeing lead)

Body boundaries: stand on your own two feet, separate from but present with what is going on

Sometimes when we are caught up in a very involved situation, it can help to reaffirm boundaries between us and what is going on so that we can maintain objectivity and also look after ourselves. The physical body is an obvious boundary between us and others and between us and our environment. We know from our understanding of body language that it's common to find ourselves mirroring others with whom we empathise or want to understand. We can be skilful with this and actively check in with what our own body is doing before we reflect others'.[28] A good example of where to practise this is in family liaison work.

The technique can be as simple as a light touch 'body sweep' or 'finding your feet' technique where you come into the sense of having a body, limbs and skin, and wearing clothes, and just acknowledge that felt sense of being physically separate from those around you.

You could reinforce this by shifting your posture or deliberately creating a physical sensation, pinching your leg through your trouser pocket, scratching an imaginary itch, briefly rubbing out a tense shoulder muscle or wriggling your feet in your shoes – anything that physically reminds you of your own, separate body.

Body boundaries

When you sense yourself mentally caught up in a very intense, involved situation, remind yourself that you have a body. Inhale deeply and exhale slowly. Find your feet, and if you can, place them on the ground or wiggle your toes. Find some way of physically sensing your body from head to toe, by feeling the clothes on your skin, deliberately moving parts of your body in succession or altering your clothing. Move all the way up your body and then change position if you can. Feel the freshness and agency of having your own physical presence that is separate from those around you before re-engaging.

REAL-LIFE EXPERIENCES

An ideal time to do this is when you've been engaged in a situation for a long time, such as a protracted job where you've felt that you've been going round in circles with a victim, witness or suspect and have almost lost touch with what is going on to some degree. (This can also be good at home when in situations when you sense you've lost the will to live and feel cut off from what is going on around you, such as being with the in-laws and entangled in their latest rant over the kitchen table!) By tuning back into the physicality of your own body, you remind yourself that you are awake, you are yourself and that you can be objective in a situation that has become quite unproductive, draining and over-absorbing.

Sideways shifting: being on an even keel and sensing the broader picture of what is going on around you

We learned in Chapter 3 that when the brain defaults to the midline (when we are busy doing, talking, planning, evaluating) then we can default to 'self-ing'.[29] Activating our lateral networks can reduce this activity. Shifting eye gaze and listening to binaural beats both stimulate the brain laterally and bring their additional benefits.

'Eye gaze': Shifting our eyes from side to side activates large networks responsible for emotional processing[30] and looking toward the horizon or up to the sky produces a non-egocentric focus, 'away from yourself toward the bigger picture',[31] increasing our perspective and objectivity. We can do this in any non-emergency, non-critical situation where we can afford to take a few seconds to divert our eye gaze. It might be particularly useful when being a passenger in a car back from a job or in preparation for an interaction that you know has the propensity to become very involved or claustrophobic.

REAL-LIFE EXPERIENCES

I now know the value of seeing horizons, so when I am particularly stressed I have a local walk I do where there is lots of horizon, sky and nothingness. Being able to see the bigger picture is key to resilience. (Police peer supporter)

'The eye-gaze expansion' worked to take me out of myself and add perspective to whatever I was thinking about. (Response officer)

'Binaural beats' (or soundscape): These are music tracks that play different frequency tones through headphones simultaneously and can generate states of relaxation, concentration and even increase pain tolerance (depending on the frequencies used in the track.)[32] They are good to listen to when we have a chance to take a break from work or after a shift in preparation for relaxing into home life or going to sleep. For many, the beats act as a kind of refreshing 'brain shower'. You can find them on the internet and music download platforms.

Eye gaze

Inhale deeply and exhale slowly. You can practise the eye gaze anywhere. Gently turn your head from side to side to see the full scene of what is going on either side of you. Then just move your eye gaze slowly from one side to the other and see what you can notice. Feel the sense of *seeing* what is on either side of you open up the space around you.

Binaural beats (or soundscape)

If you can find some binaural beat music, start with the volume low and gradually increase it. If you can't access binaural music listen to the sounds on either side of you in the environment. Inhale deeply and exhale slowly. Let the sound fall on each ear rather than wait for it to shift. Feel the sense of *hearing* what is on either side of you open up the space around you.

REAL-LIFE EXPERIENCES

All I can say is that I feel very chilled. I mean, just by plugging into it, it just sets your brain into a different mode. I'm definitely going to use this to zone out when I know that's what I need to do. (Firearms trainer)

Space-making: spaciousness, sensing the bigger picture and open-mindedness

Another way of pulling your brain out of contracting around 'life according to you' is to create some space around you and then step into it. Sensing what is outside of us is sometimes called *proprioception*. Exercises that can help to expand the sense of space around us include horizon jumping, the baked bean tin, atoms in anatomy and 'there are narwhals' (*Ok, stay with us!*).

Horizon jumping

This can work when travelling as a passenger in a vehicle or looking out of an office window, whenever it is safe for you to stand down from the incident which has left you feeling constricted or contracted. Take your eye gaze as far as you can see, preferably outside. Then gradually work your eye gaze from where you are up to the horizon, imagining all the people, buildings, vehicles, trees, foliage, animals and even insects between where you are up to that point on the horizon. Take a moment to acknowledge all that there is other than where you are and where you are looking and also how you are just one component of someone else's horizon.

The baked bean tin

This is an imagination exercise that helps to generate a sense of being just one component of a much bigger interdependent web of activity in the world – beyond the job and all that comes with it. It can be done on a rest break or at the end of a shift, whenever you have a chance to be creative. Take an everyday object (such as a tin of beans, a belt buckle or a pen) and consider all the people who may have been involved in its conception, design, manufacture, sale, transportation, purchase and delivery across the world. Think about all the places where the object has been spoken about or handled. Realising that so much effort is put into so much else around the world can help dilute our sense of responsibility, contracting around the job in hand.

Atoms in anatomy

This is a useful reflection to use in downtime when you have the chance for your mind to wander. We carry a lot of tension in the body; knotted muscles, tight shoulders, inflamed guts and stiff limbs. It can be useful to generate a sense of freedom and spaciousness within the body,[33] especially if we are feeling constricted or weighed down with responsibility. It is rumoured in the world of particle physics that we are 99.9 per cent space – that is, if you removed all the space between the atoms in our bodies (our skin, organs, blood, bone) what is left of your actual body would only be the size of a sugar cube. If we then turn our attention to sensing the space in our breath, between our toes, between our skin and our clothes, our hair and our head, then we can cultivate a sense of lightness and spaciousness to counterbalance the tightness and heaviness of our body. Giving ourselves a few moments to indulge in this can help us release the grip that the job can have on the body.

Space-making

Inhale deeply and exhale slowly. Take your eyes to the horizon and consider all that lies between you and as far as you can see. Think about all the people, buildings, animals, sounds, sights, lives being played out. Then imagine someone looking back at you from the horizon and doing the same. Next, consider any human-made object in front of you. Take a moment to think about all the people involved in getting it to where it is in front of you and all the places it may have been.

Then, think about your body. Think about all the spaces inside your body between your organs, within your lungs, between your pores – all that invisible spaciousness that you are breathing in through the air.

When you have spent enough time in that sense of openness, gradually bring yourself back to where you are.

REAL-LIFE EXPERIENCES

These techniques are probably the most immediately effective that you will come across and have been used in all sorts of settings with all sorts of people, ranging from performance athletes to military and young children.[34] Some of them have been used by over 2,000 UK police officers in 2021 and are being rolled out to a further 10,000 in 2022.[35] They are a great way of simply 'getting some space' – literally and metaphorically.

'There are narwhals': freedom to think about things other than the immediate (OK, bear with us!)

A final offering is a reflection where we imagine the most bizarre, unusual way of living that is so far removed from what we know, habituate and contract around that we can get a sense that there is more to the world than what we are caught up in right here and right now. Again, this is good to do in downtime and is ideal before sleep to relax the brain into a state of ease and creativity.

One way of using this technique is to think about an animal (such as a Narwhal, 'the unicorn of the sea'), a bizarre creature that exists somewhere far away, living its life, doing its thing, with its own worries, desires, plans and habits of thought – just as alive as we are, being in the world just as much as we are. Thinking this way can really depersonalise our immediate situation and allows us to ease back into the sense of being in a much bigger world, whether we can see it or not.

"There are narwhals"

Inhale deeply and exhale slowly. Let your imagination wander far away from your body to the furthest point in the world you can think of and consider the strangeness of all that might go on there in the sea and on the land. Imagine a creature you know exists in a very different environment, which looks very different from you, and maybe even has a bizarre, freaky or magical quality. Remind yourself that other strange and non-conventional lives exist out there. Ones you will likely never know of. They too are going through their daily lives with all its challenges. When you get a sense of acceptance that life can be crazy, check back into yours with a fresh sense that the world is as complex as you are!

REAL-LIFE EXPERIENCES
It's that sense of place and a wider, bigger world where all that bullshit we think is important becomes smaller! There's so much else going on out there! (Response officer)

Using our bodies to tune in to others

Not feeling quite in sync with someone?: how to feel more intuitively informed of others' intentions in order to respond

Our bodies are not just about us. Our brains talk to and listen to other people's body language all the time, much of it without us consciously realising. As spoken about in Chapter 3, the vagus nerve connects mind to body and can tell our minds about other people's minds too. Mirror neurons in our brain also help us to read other peoples' intentions if we mimic their body language and facial expressions. Using these techniques gives us great flexibility in how we tune in to others and how we choose to respond to them. The vagus nerve also releases a chemical called oxytocin which helps us to connect to others, tune into our gut instinct and regulate our threat response.[36] Activating this nerve is a real bonus for policing, offering us the chance to manage our interactions with others skilfully, be it with members of the public, suspects, witnesses, peers, family or friends. The vagus nerve is thought to help us determine the degree of someone's suffering by their facial expression and to increase our odds of connecting with individuals in the most difficult of circumstances on the job. (It is worth noting that practising with it can also help us track voices against background noise and even take a shot with more accuracy.) The vagus nerve (and oxytocin release) is stimulated by making eye contact, friendly gestures (such as smiling and nodding) and sharing or 'disclosing' to demonstrate trust – all of which help to elicit information from those with whom we are engaging.[37] If one considers the interview scenario and the psychological tactic of the 'good cop/bad cop',[38] it becomes clear that it may well be the vagus nerve that the good cop exploits to get results.

'What goes on in vagus, stays in vagus': stimulating the vagus nerve to feel more intuitively informed of others' intentions in order to respond

So, how do we activate and train the vagus nerve to improve our long-term ability to read and get in sync with others? There are several natural ways of stimulating the vagus nerve and releasing oxytocin, which can be used independently or together.[39] These include:

- The long exhale: Take a regular, fairly full inhalation and extend your exhalation as long as possible until your lungs are empty, refill gently and repeat. If you count how long it takes to empty your lungs, use this number as a target each time you practise. If you are in conversation, slow down your speech and breathe out longer on the words you pronounce (this might take a bit of rehearsing!).
- Discrete disclosure: Offering someone a demonstration of trust by disclosing something relatively private or confidential – even if you are only giving the *impression* of its secrecy (it could be an innocuous well-known fact), the effect can be the same.
- Friendly gestures: Making gentle but consistent eye contact, friendly gestures of smiling, nodding and gesticulating affectionately or casually with the arms, an open posture.
- Specific physical activities: Slow breathing exercises, chanting, music therapy, stretching, massage, cold water immersion, fasting and sleeping on the right side of the body are all considered to be conducive to vagal nerve activation.
- Lifestyle choices: Reducing psychological stress, directing positive emotions (such as forgiveness) and laughter are all thought to help regulate the vagus nerve, as does nutrition (such as taking omega 3 and probiotics).

What goes on in vagus *stays in vagus*

Take a deep breath in and count as you exhale as far as you can; repeat six times. In conversation with the other person, offer them a 'share' even if it's mild, to demonstrate trust. Keep eye contact and offer the friendly gesture of smiling. See what effect that has on your rapport and ability to read them. If you sense you need to do more, in your own time look up practices to tune the vagus nerve and incorporate them into your day. Most are very practical and brief and can bring immediate effect.

REAL-LIFE EXPERIENCES

When the body holds stress from challenging incidents, it tends to remove us from others – just a bit, because it wants us to focus on whatever the threat is that we need to gear up for. Unfortunately, for long-term resilience, we need to release body stress and get in synch with each other. A good example of when the vagus nerve can help you out on the job is when we feel we're just not 'getting someone' in an interaction – maybe a witness, a supervisor or even a family member: someone whose point of view or behaviour or reaction seems unfathomable. These techniques can really help you settle into reading what is going on underneath the interaction you are in the midst of and therefore improve your chances of picking up on what's going on. (Even if they don't enable you to find all the answers, they do enable you to accept that you are in an unusual situation and, try as you might, you might have to put this one down to experience.)

'Mirror, mirror': reading facial expressions to feel more intuitively informed of others' intentions in order to respond

As explained earlier in this chapter, faces are not just about recognition and lie detection in policing. In Chapter 3, we learned that mirror neurons are a vital source of information in humans and can be particularly useful in policing in terms of helping individuals to decipher others' emotions and the intentions beneath their behaviour. A good application of mirror neurons in policing is when one is unclear how to interpret someone's facial expression, or be in a live interaction, a recorded interview or a meeting.

A simple approach to exploiting mirror neurons to 'tap in' to what someone is *really thinking* is to mimic their expression and pay attention to any change in your own feeling tone or reaction to the situation. Mirroring body language can be just as useful if the state of mind behind someone's stance is not immediately obvious.

Tip

Subtlety is key here. Many people may be very sensitive to body language and very self-aware and may detect the slightest suggestion of your mirroring them. Others may be much less tuned in and may suddenly notice an out-of-place or new gesture on your part. In both scenarios, your subject may feel unnerved or curious, which may put them off. Make any changes slowly and discretely, easing into the smallest facial expression or shift in posture and make sure you're using this as an opportunity to detect what they might be feeling. (This is different to mirroring body language to make people feel at ease in social situations.)

Mirror, mirror

When you are with someone who you can't seem to understand, take a deep breath in and an extra-long breath out, and gather yourself for a second. Then look at the person's facial expression. Very subtly start to replicate their expression. For more subtlety, turn your head away for a second to do this. As you pull the expression, note intuitively the first emotion you feel. Ask yourself if this emotion fits with the way they are behaving. If it does, go with that new insight into their behaviour. If it doesn't generate any response in you, then accept the fact that you may not fully understand their position in the situation and use *that* as your information on which to base your next decision.

REAL-LIFE EXPERIENCES

This is a technique that can be useful when dealing with someone who is not known to you and their point of view or mood is not immediately clear by their words or body language. However, this is best reserved for when you know you are in a situation where you have the ability to pull a face without being noticed! (That bit is *really important* if you don't want to be suspected of taking the mick!) So, if you are with others who can manage the ongoing exchange while you turn your head or move out of view, or if you can find an opportunity to slip out of view, then go for it.

Smart compassion

It's like suffering with others, only smarter! In Chapter 3 and earlier in this chapter, we learned that fear and compassion (the limbic system in the lizard brain and the prefrontal cortex in the primate brain) can compete for resources, which means if you are activating one, you can't activate the other. One tactic is to play one off against the other, so we can activate compassion to manage a disproportionate fear response. However, there are times when compassion just comes naturally, effortlessly and can even overwhelm us. In Chapter 1 we read that new recruits highly prized empathy as an increasingly valuable skill to master over their first four years in the job,[40] and yet our understanding of burnout in Chapter 2 reminds us that lack of mastery over compassion comes at a cost to our resilience. Recent neuroscience research and the mental discipline of many contemplative traditions offer us a bit of scrutiny on compassion. Compassion can be seen as building on our innate desire to meet the needs of our species: to be free from suffering, to be connected with others (in communities, families), to be free, to be safe (free from harm) and to live peacefully with relative ease (without disorder). However, in day-to-day life, we tend to instinctively think that compassion means 'feeling sorry' for someone or taking on all of their pain as if it were our own. In some disciplines, this is referred to (somewhat brutally) as 'idiot compassion'[41] because it is unsustainable, disempowering and ineffective. Often, we find that out the hard way over time – by 'numbing out' to others' suffering by dissociating (being in denial) or by becoming self-conscious (and beating ourselves up about it). This can be hard if we have some awareness deep down that we joined the service in earnest to help people, to keep them safe, protect their freedom and to keep the peace. The good news is that there is an alternative way to achieve this: *smart* compassion. Smart compassion is when we are able to sense someone else's suffering, to be there next to them for a moment, to do what we can within our capacity to address their suffering and to wish them well as we move on. *Super-smart* compassion is when we then direct proactive compassion back to ourselves, to acknowledge that we've been there for someone else and to then *refuel, resource and reboot* ourselves afterwards, ready for the next challenge. Here are some techniques that can help us master smarter compassion.

When others' distress is just too much to tolerate

'Watching the window:' how to gain control over how much to take on

The phrase 'window of tolerance' can be applied to distress. It is helpful for us to know our limits of tolerating others' distress. It might be useful to use the image of a window in how we manage others' suffering. It's important in our job to be able to see the challenges, problems and issues that people face, mainly because a lot of the time, it is up to us to address and manage some effect or outcome of them. Having visibility of the issues behind and within someone's predicament can be useful. It can help them to feel 'seen' and establish trust if we can acknowledge 'where they are coming from' (even if we don't agree with or understand it fully).

The image of looking through a window is handy if we recognise that visibility is important, but that there is also a clear divide, a separation between our life and theirs (a pane of glass in this analogy). Try to see yourself as an observer who can help through the window but that you can also *shut* the window and even close the curtains and walk away if and when it is right to. When managing others' suffering, there has to come a point where you recognise you have done all that you can do to help.

When you next get embroiled in a scenario where you are feeling too close to someone else's pain, too involved, unable to see a way out, take a step back in your mind and imagine a windowpane between you and them. Notice the glass, the light shining off it, maybe a hint of your reflection looking back at you, recognising you are separate from them, their suffering and their decision-making. When you feel have done all you can do or you realise that the conversation is going nowhere, in your mind's eye mentally reach out and pull the window shut. Find a form of words to summarise your support, what you need them to do next and that you wish them well. Congratulate yourself for being compassionately smart and opening up to what else is going on around you.

Watching the window

When you feel caught up in someone's suffering or predicament, imagine an open window between you and them. Imagine it in detail and feel its presence as a potential barrier but also as a way to see in. Continue your engagement with them with this open window between you. When the interaction needs to end, in your mind's eye, pull the window to. Regardless of their desire to engage you, pull the window closed in your mind and wish them well before turning away. If need be, draw the curtain or pull a blind down as you leave. This is your window of tolerance.

REAL-LIFE EXPERIENCES

The more I read about imagining the window and seeing it, making the barrier between me and the other person, the stronger the image became in my mind. It helped me to focus on the tiny details, the latches, windowsill etc. Picturing my friend on the other side and then picturing the window shutting, creating a barrier was quite effective. It was as if I had given myself permission to put the matter down for a while and know that I didn't have to circle back to it. (Retired officer having worked in roles involving digital trauma exposure)

'The wishing well': trying to fix something that can't be fixed?

An integral component of smart compassion is knowing when you have done your bit. One reason many of us burn out in this line of work is falling prey to the reality that there will always be more people we could help or more time or resources we want to squeeze out of nowhere to give someone one more chance, one more offer of assistance or piece of advice, thinking that it will make all the difference. To offer ourselves some relief from this is to tell ourselves that when we have helped and fulfilled our responsibilities, we can simply (but genuinely and authentically) *wish someone well*. That simple act of wanting things to go well for someone is in itself very powerful for our resilience because it reaffirms our intentions and our values but is realistic in the fact that there is only so much we can do. When the reality is that you can do no more, your intention that someone doesn't suffer anymore and is OK is sometimes just enough for the brain to stand down from that job and redirect its resources to the next, without feeling depleted or in despair. Remembering the phrase 'I wish you well' as you leave a job where you have done your best can offer you that sense of making a difference that you were wanting to achieve all along.

Tip

You can rephrase this to suit your personality or way of relating to people, perhaps saying to them in your mind, 'good luck, buddy' or 'hoping for good things for you'.

The wishing well

When the time has come in an interaction for you to step away, in your mind's eye or even out loud and directly, wish the other party well. If there is a sense in you, them or the process that there is more that you 'could' do but really cannot, this is all the more important. Repeat the phrase with a mental gesture of a salute or a shake of the hand and notice how it is to turn away with a compassionate sense of wanting things to be well for another, regardless of the outcome or your responsibility for it.

REAL-LIFE EXPERIENCES

This technique is the most useful when you just know that your resources for compassion are running at an all-time low. This might be because an immediate situation is becoming unmanageable (either because your compassionate intentions, like advice, are not being received or because there is simply too much suffering in front of you that you can't do anything about). It can also be applied to a longer-term sense of compassion fatigue or burnout where you sense that you just can't take on any more personal cases of disadvantage or distress. Either way, honouring your intention to want others to be well is a way of refuelling your compassion.

You are entitled to care about others *without the expectation that you can magically resolve everything that is wrong with their lives.*

Feeling burned out and invisible?

The flight mask: resource yourself to stand strong

Knowing that we need to look after ourselves to be able to do this job needs to be *tactical and pragmatic*, not just a 'nice idea' that we pay lip service to and then dismiss as we crack on. It's often only self-directed support that leads to sustainable resilience on the job. Unfortunately, waiting for someone to come along and tell you to stand down, take a break, go get yourself a hug or take a day off can be a long, long wait, especially in the current climate. Often the 'fear of missing out' or fear of letting colleagues down can mean we override clear messages from our body and mind that we need to look after ourselves better. Ignoring those messages makes compassion even harder to manage and burnout even more likely. The analogy of the flight mask might be a clichè but it's unavoidable here! Just as the safety instructions on the seat in front on an aircraft advise, we need to *fit our own mask* before helping others, especially those who are very vulnerable.

It might be useful to sometimes wish for yourself what you want for others in your service: that *you* can be free from harm and suffering, that you can be safe, that you too can feel connected to those around you, that you are free to do what you need to do to look after yourself and that you can do your job with ease.

Tip

It's really common to feel real resistance when practising self-compassion and looking after yourself. It takes bravery to do it, but at the end of the day – you are the best person to know what you need and how to get it. Find words that fit the bill for you (excuse the pun). Consider it a tactical move for independent resilience.

The flight mask

The analogy of a parent needing to fix their own oxygen mask in an emergency before attempting to fix their child's is a harsh reminder of the reality that we cannot help others if we are not in a fit state to do so ourselves. Take a few moments after an emotionally draining incident to ask yourself, what is my flight mask right now? What do I need as my resource? Is it a cup of tea? A breath of fresh air, a light-hearted banter with a friend, a good film or a long shower? What is the smallest thing I can do for myself to recharge my inner energy to get out and do this again?

REAL-LIFE EXPERIENCES
You may well have heard of this analogy before and many people say that it is as useful as it is challenging to apply! Especially in roles where we are outward-facing to benefit others, it seems completely unnatural to turn your care and attention inward to yourself first. Yet this is vital. Just like PPE for the body, having what you need for the mind is imperative for resilience.

This requires a shift in mindset to acknowledge that you *matter and you need maintaining*.

It might be helpful to use this technique when you know you are in need of just the smallest of breaks, whether it be a bottle of water, a cup of tea, a day's leave, or to say no to a job that is going to push you beyond what you know your limits are right now.

If it feels uncomfortable to put yourself first on occasion, then maybe you need to get over that discomfort if you are going to be the best you can be for other people.

Getting perspective: putting incidents in their time and place so we can move on

Getting perspective on what happens on the job underpins much operational practice, but it's also important personally. Making sense visually of *what happened when and where* is fundamental to police investigation. Hand-drawn scenes (sometimes called sketch maps for 'mental reinstatement of context') and timelines are already common techniques used in interviewing witnesses.[42] They help witnesses clarify their thoughts about unpleasant experiences and provide a sense of logic and calm to events that may otherwise seem jumbled and stressful to recall. The media are wise to the effect of seeing things laid out in maps and timelines (Figure 4.3), using them as visual aids in news coverage to summarise high-profile critical incidents before going into more nuanced detail. There seems to be a common understanding that humans benefit from organising things visually like this, but how often do we think about doing this for our own life experiences?

We are innately familiar with how useful space and time can be and this is no truer than when we listen to ourselves talking to people going through difficult times. How often do we hear ourselves say things like 'just give it time' or 'I just need some space'? We say these things because we know perspective is important. Sometimes it seems trite to say it as we assume there is nothing tangible, we can *do* to help them get the perspective we know they need.

Yet, recent research has learned from neuroscience, existing investigative processes and therapeutic disciplines[43] about how to clarify and contextualise events in safe and manageable ways, and we can apply this to the front line using specific techniques. The techniques have been rigorously tested in the policing environment and have been used by thousands of officers in

Figure 4.3: An example of a map and timeline used in the press

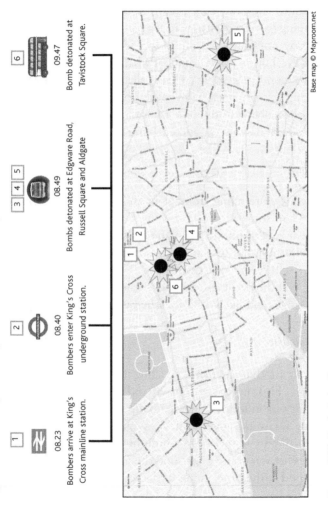

1	2	3 4 5			6
08.23	08.40	08.49			09.47
Bombers arrive at King's Cross mainline station.	Bombers enter King's Cross underground station.	Bombs detonated at Edgware Road, Russell Square and Aldgate			Bomb detonated at Tavistock Square.

Base map © Maproom.net

Source: With thanks to Ian Denness

recent years.[44] They have been designed to target the area of the brain (the *hippocampus*) which is responsible for trauma processing and yet is damaged by trauma (as explained in Chapter 3). Fortunately, the hippocampus is also very trainable and for many, it will grow the more we practise using it.[45]

So, how come maps and timelines help us file traumatic incidents? They do it by giving us a sense of distance from something (we can see it as part of a bigger picture, a bigger map). That way not only does the 'thing' itself appear smaller in the mind's eye, but we can see more of what was happening around it, stuff that *wasn't all about 'us'*. This is called 'allocentric' processing.[46] Applying this approach helps to file things as being in the past, therefore enabling us to come back to the present, reducing the likelihood of flashbacks[47] and enabling us to rest and move on.[48]

Mapping

Find yourself recalling an incident and being right in the thick of it? Gain some visual perspective to give it some space and shrink it in the mind's eye. These three mapping techniques can help the mind to gain perspective so that the event seems smaller with more space around it. They can also help you to realise that the event also involved others who saw it from their perspective (and likely still do, wherever they may be).

The satellite

Bring to mind the incident, recalling it from where you were at the time. Float up above yourself and then look down (if your incident was indoors, imagine taking off the roof and looking down). Draw this overhead view and mark yourself in the picture (Figure 4.4). Zoom a little higher and add more detail about what was going on around the scene. Who else was there or around at the time, either at the scene or in the wider area?

The drone

Fly around the scene as if you were a drone and draw an overhead view from another position in the sky, again, marking where you

Figure 4.4: The satellite mapping technique using an imagined overhead view

Source: With thanks to Police Care UK

Figure 4.5: The drone mapping technique

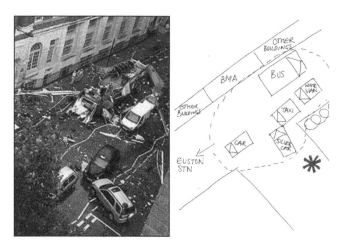

Source: With thanks to Police Care UK, 'Dave', Counter-Terrorism Exhibits Officer, and photographer Nicholas Shanks for the image 'From Behind'. See note 49

were down below (Figure 4.5).[49] (If your incident was indoors you might imagine looking down from different positions in the roof).

The witness

Imagine that there was a witness at the scene (or recall one actually there). Move position to their viewpoint and draw the

Figure 4.6: The witness mapping technique

 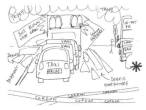

Source: With thanks to Police Care UK and Alex Peart

scene as if looking through their eyes, marking where you were in your original position (Figure 4.6).

Mapping

Find a quiet space where you can concentrate without distractions.

The satellite: Go to the incident in your mind's eye and float up above your head; look down and see yourself. Draw what you see from this overhead view. Mark yourself below you.

The drone: Now imagine you are a drone and move around in this position above the incident. Hover in a new position, looking down from another angle. Draw what you see below you. See if you can mark where you were at the scene. *This sketch should look different from your satellite view.*

The witness: Go to the incident in your mind's eye where you started on the ground. Now try and move around as if you were a different witness there. Imagine if an onlooker took in what was happening. Draw the scene on the ground from this other point of view.

What do you notice that you didn't before? How much more can you see when you zoom out up above? How does it feel to see things from someone else's perspective?

REAL-LIFE EXPERIENCES
Taking myself out of the situation and remembering it from other perspectives has helped me normalise and overcome the feelings I had towards the experience. (New police recruit)

Timelines

Does the worst moment of an incident come to mind as if it's happening right now? Learn to file it as being in the past. Like with the mapping, we can mark events out in a timeline, so we see an episode in a longer context of time – of all that led up to it and all that has happened since. By looking at an incident on a continuum, we have more of an opportunity to consider the cause and effect of other peoples' actions and other external influences (influences that may have had *nothing to do with us*). This can help to release us from trying to understand reasons for why something happened or even from trying to take responsibility for things that were beyond our control – a tendency that can be very natural in policing (as we reflected on in Chapter 2). These three timelines can help file memories in episodic order.

Dawn to dusk

This is a straightforward 'start to finish' way of thinking about an incident that may already be familiar to many of those involved in investigations or anyone who has taken a victimology. The start doesn't have to be in the morning of the day in question, it can be wherever you sensed the incident began.

Begin by recalling the incident from the time point you remember. This is often the most vivid part of the memory and you might remember how it felt in the body at the time. Draw a horizontal line on either side of it and begin to mark the sequence of events before and after. Mark on that timeline the moment when you recall getting a sense that the incident had come to a close when the worst was over and you could begin to stand down and get back to a sense of 'normality'. This

Figure 4.7: The fast forward timeline

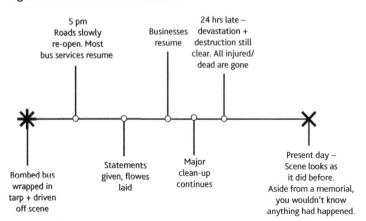

is called a 'safety cue', where we can sit back and sigh, '*it's over*' (further examples are offered in what follows).

Who else might have been involved in the run-up to the event or the fall-out of it?

Buzz back and fly forward

Extend the timeline by rewinding and fast-forwarding. Use your imagination to mark on the extended lines all that might have happened in the lead up to the event that was nothing to do with you, and all that may have happened since. You can add in detail about the location, the lives of the people involved, the investigation or moments in your life that have meant something to you (Figure 4.7).

The time traveller

This technique is a bit more of a stretch and asks us to put what happened in the context of what is important to us in the here and now. Extend your timeline up to the present day and then longer, up to five years from now. Along the line, add in a few things that:

a. have happened (or might have happened) since you or others were involved; and

b. might happen in the next five years, to you or others involved.

Then imagine yourself being able to 'walk back' along the timeline from the future to the here and now. *Ask yourself, given you have all these years ahead, what is most important to you to hold on to, given your experience? What might be good to let go of?*

REAL-LIFE EXPERIENCES

An officer in his 50s spoke of attending a friend's funeral and the widow asking him to imagine himself being at his own funeral in years to come. She asked him what he would want for his family on such a day. The officer replied that he would want his son to look out at a sea of uniforms and to remember his dad was a good cop. The lady replied 'I think that's the saddest thing I've ever heard. ... Would you not like him to remember you as his dad?' This was a real wake-up call for the officer. It reminded him that the job means much to him and yet he means much to others, regardless of it. (Serving superintendent)

Tips

The more you practise the techniques, the easier and more natural they become because the area of the brain responsible can grow the more we use it.[50]

No need to waste time trying to make it into a work of art – you can use symbols, stick people or just blobs of colour, so long as it makes sense to you.

Practise with minor challenges such as arguments or witnessing incidents outside of work. Once you've got the gist of the techniques you can gradually start to apply them to more challenging experiences.

The techniques are harder to use with incidents that involve viewing or listening to digital or audio material. A helpful alternative for this type of exposure is to distract the mind after viewing explicit images undertaking tasks that involve simple spatial processing, such as (non-violent) computer games[51] or even visual puzzles.

Extend the timeline by rewinding and fast-forwarding. Use your imagination to mark on the extended lines all that might have happened in the lead up to the event that was nothing to do with you, and all that may have happened since.

You can add in detail about the location, the lives of the people involved, the investigation or moments in your life that have meant something to you.

Timelines

Dusk to Dawn: Draw a line across a page and mark the start of the incident you are recalling.

Along the line mark the memorable moments for you – this could be things that happened around you, decisions made, what happened at the scene or personal recollections that stand out. Finish with the moment you remember thinking that it was over and that 'normality resumed'.

Buzz back and fly forward: Extend the line in both directions, backwards and forwards. Consider all the things that may have happened in the lead up to the event that were nothing to do with you – beyond your control or your knowledge. Do the same for time going forward, for what may have happened since. You might include social, historical, local and environmental conditions.

The time traveller: Start your timeline from the end of the incident (yup, the end!) and mark 'now' halfway along. Use your memory or imagination to fill in what has happened since the event up until now (in your life, at the scene, in others' lives or in the case). Now extend into the future using your imagination. You might choose to branch out with different future endings or to let your line fade out.

Being objective

Feeling disproportionately negative about an incident? Take the sting out

Laying events out in order also makes space for us to add in other components and realities that we might not automatically recall, such as things that were more positive, neutral or even dull. Science tells us that when we include positive and neutral information in our memory of an unpleasant event like this (especially if we do this within an hour of revisiting the incident in our mind) this brings down the stress response and we can become much more content with letting an experience be what it was and filing it away.[52]

The good, the bad and the boring

Putting events in context and perspective also means adding in all the other information that *wasn't* to do with the threat perception or stress response at the time. This generates an honest, logical and much more realistic appraisal of the entirety of what happened that can be filed to memory safety.

- *What can you remember that was neutral, consistent or unremarkable* (the weather, the vehicles, what someone was wearing)? Mark what you can on each map and timeline.
- *What can you remember that was positive* (a process that worked well, someone showing expertise or professionalism, an act of kindness, something in hindsight that made you smile to yourself)? Mark what you can on each map and timeline.

Tip

When we have 'carte blanche', an open opportunity to add in *any detail we want* about an incident that we have up until now always labelled in our memory as 'difficult', it can be hard to know where to start. It's as if we almost need permission that 'anything goes'. What can be helpful when we are hesitant or self-conscious about detailing our experiences (even if it's privately to ourselves) is to remind ourselves of the phrase 'There is nothing human that is new under the sun' – that there is likely nothing so different in our own minds and experiences that others haven't thought or felt before. So, we are free to accept all of the experiences as they were in their entirety, the good, the bad and the ugly.

REAL-LIFE EXPERIENCES

These techniques have been practised by thousands of officers over time, either in the context of interviewing witnesses, talking therapies or trauma impact interventions. The reason they are so effective is that they offer a structured way of reflecting on cause and effect but in a more open-minded way than simply reporting 'this happened, then that happened'. By allocating yourself time and space to get down on paper in front of you how things unfolded from our perspective and possibly from the perspective of others, we give ourselves a chance to appreciate all the different influences on why things happen as they do and how some things can lead to another.

Next time you have an incident or experience where what happened when doesn't seem to make sense, try grabbing a pen and paper and giving your brain a few minutes to work out what you *do know* and to accept what perhaps you'll *simply never know*. The difference between the two can be the difference between a sleepless night and a decent nocturnal recharge!

Bossing the mind

To get the most out of any new way of thinking, it helps to get into the habit of being able to prepare and steer the brain. Some of these techniques come from neuroscience, some from those already on the job.

> Between stimulus and response, there is a space. In that space is our power to choose our response. In our response lies our growth and our freedom. (A quote about the work of Victor Frankl, Auschwitz survivor, psychiatrist and neurologist)[53]

There are times in any job when all the planning, analysing and organising our responses to all that is going on around us can mean that our headspace is a very busy, fragmented place. It can also feel somewhat lonely as we contract around everything through our own eyes. In policing, having a clear mind is vital to decision-making, tactical manoeuvres and accountability. Knowing where our mind is at, what it is capable of (and what it is not) is important – not just to protect the integrity of our actions but also to keep us in tune with others. It's only when we learn to keep track of our thinking that we have a chance at genuine resilience. As we appreciated in Chapter 3, mind-wandering sounds pleasant (if we think of lazy, fanciful daydreaming), but the reality of a wandering mind under daily pressure is very different.[54] When a mind is left to its own devices it can wander into ruts, get caught in cyclical thinking and come up against many dead-ends. This doesn't make for good threat perception or decision-making on the job. Stressful tasks and high-pressured incidents require our minds to be at their sharpest, and for this reason, we need to take more control of our thinking to direct our actions. There are techniques we can use that, with practice, can become part of the way we approach our work and, over time, enable us to develop a more proactive, constructive and friendly rapport with our minds.

For when mind wandering and getting lost in thought kinda hurts: get in command and control of your thoughts

Spotting the default

The wandering mind is an unhappy mind.[55]

In Chapter 3 we learned that the mind can easily default to thinking in certain ways which are not always conducive to being effective on the job – or happy in it. These states of mind emerge from the human brain's natural default[56] to areas of activity (often along the midline of the brain[57]) which involve:

- incessant planning and ruminating;
- self-ing;
- comparing ourselves to others;
- going over old ground; or
- thinking about what we want or crave.

In doing so, our inner voice is quietly reaffirming to ourselves what we *don't* have, who we are *not like* and what we *haven't* done. We can appreciate that all brains do this – sometimes for good reason (sometimes we need to make plans or go over old ground), but often the mind defaults to these habits of thought not because they are required, but simply because there is nothing else to occupy its attention at the time. Our challenge is to learn to spot when we have slipped into these habits unnecessarily and the thoughts are going nowhere (compared to consciously thinking along these lines because we have a task in hand which requires it). As individuals, we might be more prone to some defaults than others and it's good to know which defaults we are likely to slip into and when.

If you are feeling industrious, do some homework for yourself – find out what your style of default is. Get to know it. Then own it.

It might be useful to revisit Chapter 2 and create your checklist of modes of thinking that you tend to find yourself in and when and where they tend to be most common. Once you are familiar with your defaults, you can start to find ways of redirecting your thoughts more constructively with new 'go-to' mindsets that give you what you need or want. Repeatedly pulling your mind toward what you need can build strong neural pathways for long-term resilience – and *this* is the *self-directed neuroplasticity* that we mentioned in Chapter 3 getting in action, in your mind (Table 4.1).[58]

REAL-LIFE EXPERIENCES
Here are some examples of mind-wandering that we might observe on the job. With them, some alternative directions to where we might guide our thoughts, and examples of how we can learn to spot when we are wandering off somewhere unhelpful.

Spot your defaults

Keep a piece of paper on you for a few days to scribble down where your mind goes when it wanders. Then come up with a plan for how to help yourself spot your mind wandering and what you can do to gently bring it back to think more tactically about what you need to. You might think of labelling where your mind defaults to, without giving yourself a hard time about it. You could just note 'Ah, comparing' or 'Oh, planning again' or 'Hmmm, wanting'. This noting gives you the chance to decide if thinking like this is really what you want to be doing, or if another way of thinking might be more constructive.

Table 4.1: Quick reference guide for resilience techniques in policing

Daily techniques

Stimulus	Technique	Felt benefit
Morning (or pre-shift) Starting your day	Morning mindset: beginning again, being resourced, part of a team which means something	Fully resourced, prepared, supported, open to and inspired for the day ahead
Noon (or mid-shift) During your day	Checking-in: the 'body sweep', breathing space, eye-gaze expansion	Steady in the present, with clarity and perspective on how the day is progressing
Night (or post-shift) At the end of your day	Sleep debrief: standing down with gratitude, little wins and giggles	Satisfied with the day, connected, in tune with what's important to you and relaxed, ready for sleep

Mastering threat perception

Stimulus	Technique	Felt benefit
For when you're sensing a threat but you need to get the measure of it	What's for lunch? F.E.A.R. vs T.H.R.E.A.T Fear face-off	More in command and control of the threat response
Feeling disproportionately anxious about a harmless interaction	From F-word to C-bomb	Imagining life from someone else's disadvantage (Smart compassion)
When the day's events are a heavy weight to carry home	Boots-at-the-door	A clear boundary between job and home, coming back to life outside work
Constructing a personal story in your mind about an incident?	Labelling 'There is...' Getting creative (bit weird)	Acknowledging the discomfort and neutralising the narrative in your head
For when your body is holding tension and it's starting to be uncomfortable	Shake it out Feeling your feet	Reset your body, feel accomplished, at ease and present in the here and now

Table 4.1: Quick reference guide for resilience techniques in policing (continued)

Knowing when to stand down

Stimulus	Technique	Felt benefit
For when your stress response is lingering and not subsiding after an incident	Sit-back-and-sigh	Being able to stand down mentally and relax back into the body and open up to what is going on around you

Depersonalising experiences

Stimulus	Stimulus	Technique
For when you find yourself contracting around an experience and getting way too involved	Not me	Regaining agency and independence
	Body boundaries	Standing on your own two feet, separate from but present with what's going on
	Sideways shifting: eye gaze and binaural beats (or soundscape)	Being more on an even keel and sensing the broader picture of what is going on around you
	Space-making: horizon jumping, baked beans, atoms and narwhals	Spaciousness, sensing the bigger picture and open-mindedness
	'There are narwhals'	Freedom to think about things other than the immediate

Using our bodies to tune in to others

Stimulus	Technique	Felt benefit
Not feeling quite in sync with someone?	In vagus Mirror, mirror	How to feel more intuitively informed of others' intentions in order to respond

Smart compassion

Stimulus	Technique	Felt benefit
When others' distress is just too much to tolerate	Watching the window	In control of how much to take on
For when you're trying to fix something that can't be fixed	Wishing well	Be satisfied you've done your best
Feeling burned out and invisible?	Flight mask	Resource yourself to stand strong

Table 4.1: Quick reference guide for resilience techniques in policing
(continued)

Getting perspective

Stimulus	Technique	Felt benefit
For when you keep recalling an incident as if you're right in the thick of it	Mapping: the satellite, the drone and the witness	The event seems smaller with more space around it, not all about you and that you are back right here
When the worst moment of an incident keeps reappearing in your mind's eye as if it's now	Timelines: dawn to dusk, buzz back and fly forward, and the time traveller	The event seems more distant, further away in the past – they weren't all about your part in them. You are back in the now

Being objective

Stimulus	Technique	Felt benefit
Feeling disproportionately negative about an incident?	The good, the bad and the boring	The sting of the event is neutralised as you recognise more about the whole memory

Bossing the mind

Stimulus	Technique	Felt benefit
For when mind-wandering and being lost in thought kinda hurts	Spotting the default	Getting in command and control of thoughts, knowing your mental 'kit'
Feeling unprepared and vulnerable, sense of foreboding, over-stressing	Priming the brain: eyes in, tactical filtering, body prep, you got this	Prepared, focussed, resilient, tactical
Obsessing, ruminating, trying to figure out something you can't – feeling uncomfortable	Befriending *don't know*	A sense of detached ease with what is, strong in yourself to reaffirm what is important *to you* in the here and now, what you *can* act on

Permission to lighten up

Stimulus	Technique	Felt benefit
When you can feel negativity creeping up on you	RAIN: Recognise, Accept, Investigate, Non-Identify	Get savvy, intervene and activate your resilience
For when healthy stress morphs into a very slight whiff of panic	STOP: Stop, Take a breath, Observe, Proceed	Regroup, refocus and resume

Table 4.1: Quick reference guide for resilience techniques in policing (continued)

For those times where we make a bad thing worse in our minds	The second punch	Acknowledging something for what it is without additional suffering
For when there is a flicker of something positive!	HEAL: Have, Enrich, Absorb and Link	Feel resourced, inspired, confident, grateful (without losing your edge)
Feeling like it's Ground Hog Day or that life is a bit tired and stale	The hand swap	Refreshed, skilful, amused, open-minded and lightly accomplished
For when things are a bit 'meh'	S' funny...	Brightness and connection with others

Priming the brain

Feeling unprepared, stressed or with a sense of foreboding about a job? This is a way to feel more together, focussed, resilient and tactical. We have talked much about how threat perception is integral to working in emergency response, perhaps particularly so in policing. It is natural for stress to build prior to an event that we anticipate being either physically or psychologically threatening, and which will require from us a steady, tactical and strong response. In our observational research with those in high-risk roles,[59] resilience came thick and fast for those who had developed the habit of *priming* (preparing) their brain before dealing with such a job. In other neuropsychological studies with Special Forces, physiological (body-based) approaches proved effective for immediate resilience in stressful critical incidents.[60] Here are some techniques which can help to prime the brain in anticipation of managing threatening scenarios.

Getting your eyes in

This is a technique described by someone we worked with in public protection which epitomises the idea of priming the brain. When preparing to shift into a mode of working where you are going to be exposed to potentially traumatic material such as digital images (from CCTV, body-worn video, counter-terrorism propaganda or child sexual exploitation cases) or audio input (such as taking 999 calls or reviewing distressing recordings), it is useful to mark that transition.

You can take a moment to note that you are moving from the everyday world of working with what you can see, hear and understand in front of you, to the (limited) digital realm of sounds and images which may be disjointed, fragmented and without context. Give yourself permission to adjust to this new form of input and remind yourself of the specific task you have to complete and what completing that task will look, sound and feel like. Tactically preparing the brain can help you get in, and out, of the zone of that particular threat more smoothly and with agency.

Tactical filtering

It is also important to prepare the brain before entering a scene or a scenario that you anticipate will be physically 'full-on' in terms of live trauma exposure. In these incidents, we can help the brain to mark the transition from ongoing, habitual 'everyday life' thinking to a more time-critical, focussed, task-oriented mentality required for the extraordinary conditions ahead. The stress response in the body does this for us naturally, but we can help the mind even further by turning its attention to the task at hand to improve performance and to help avoid over-exposure to traumatic stimulus from an extreme situation.

Setting clear tactical objectives of what we need to assess, find out and execute at the scene, primes the brain to filter out any superfluous information that it doesn't need for you to carry out your task. Thankfully, this is likely to include filtering out superfluous evocative, sensory material which is more likely to make trauma impact harder to process.

In preparation for such an incident, take a few deliberate moments *en route* or before entering the scene to set yourself between one and three clear objectives, establish an early line of sight as to where you need to look to perform your duties and, if you can, where your exit point will be. On completion, be sure to acknowledge what has been accomplished before refocussing your objectives on moving to the next stage of the incident management process. This can help transition out of the incident maintaining a sense of agency and purpose until you are ready to stand down.

Tip

You might want to consider marking the transitioning out of this type of incident with the 'sit-back-and-sigh' safety cue technique.

Body prep

There are more physiological means of preparing the mind and body for situations in which you anticipate a heightened stress response and more intensive threat management. Also known in US SWAT teams as 'combat breathing', some resilience programmes train participants in controlling their breathing (while engaging in positive affirmations) to manage adrenalin spikes and reactivity prior to exposure.[61] This stimulates the 'anti-stress' mechanisms in our body (also called the *parasympathetic nervous system*). A simple approach is to inhale and exhale deeply five times, each time elongating the exhalation. Take a moment to acknowledge the breath as a resource in itself, carrying oxygen to your cells throughout your body to give you all the physical and mental strength you need. Acknowledge to yourself that these resources enable you to realise your good intentions for a positive outcome ahead.

'You got this'

A simple way of preparing the brain before exposure to threatening scenarios is to remind it that it has (*you have*) resources to carry out the task at hand. Even if your resources are not the best or in the greatest supply, it is important to let your brain recognise those resources it very much has, so it is more likely to make use of them when they are needed most. Examples of resources include the physical kit you have (protection, equipment), the team you are with (and the wider team elsewhere or back up available to you) and the knowledge and skills you carry (from your training and experience). It can be really helpful to add to this the faith and trust that your team and force have *in you* (otherwise you wouldn't be on the job). The support of all those who care about you and wish you well and are proud of you is good to recognise every so often (even the people out there you have never met, and possibly never will, but who support the service).

Bossing your mind

Getting your eyes in: When you are preparing to view challenging material or a disturbing scene, make a mental note that you are transitioning out of the everyday sights and sounds of where you are to a temporary state to fulfil a specific task. If the task is digital, note that the images and audio will likely have a disjointed or unreal quality as they are mediated through technology. Focus on only what you need to for completing the task. When you are done, notice the transition to the reality of the daily sights and sounds around you – as neutral or unremarkable as they may be, this is where you are.

Tactical filtering: As you join an incident, set yourself three clear objectives of what you need to achieve. Establish an early line of sight of where you need to be and where to exit. Make a deliberate note to yourself when all objectives are fulfilled and when you are transitioning or 'demobilising'.

Body prep: Inhale deeply and exhale slowly and repeat three or four times. As you do so, think about the oxygen being taken to all the cells in your body and brain, making you steady and ready.

You got this: Take a few seconds to think about the resources you have available to you at any one time, right now: your physical kit, your team, your training and skills, the support of your loved ones.

Remember that it is because of the faith in you that others have that you are doing the job you do.

REAL-LIFE EXPERIENCES
These techniques have all been taken from face-to-face research with officers in high-risk roles which involve

exposure to atypical trauma (ranging from digital imagery work to evidence recovery in counter-terrorism). Reaffirming our commitment to focus *only on what we need to* in order to get through an adverse experience is hugely protective for our brain and also very empowering. We are perhaps at our most resilient when we know that we can *trust ourselves to use our minds* in the ways we know work well (especially when they are under the most pressure).

If you have a way of prepping your mind that helps you steady your focus and attention and which pays respect to the personal challenge ahead, use it. If it works well, consider it part of your arsenal and consider sharing it with others in similar roles.

Obsessing, ruminating or fixating on trying to figure something out? Find a sense of ease with what is, reaffirming what you can do and what you do know

Befriending 'don't know'

Another default position in the human brain (that may be particularly familiar to those in policing) is grappling with trying to work something out – ruminating on an issue, planning a way of finding something out or trying to make sense of the unfathomable. Policing is a role where questions need answers, the experiences are extraordinary and we feel an inherent responsibility to fix and make right as much as we can.

Sometimes, it's important to fully accept that there will be things that cannot be fully understood or filed in a nice, neat category, clearly labelled and fully defined.[62] Sometimes we can feel quite empowered by being honest enough to recognise that for some issues and problems we simply D.O.N.'T. K.N.O.W.

By acknowledging this fact of life (and, more importantly, to each other) we galvanise greater respect and trust in what we categorically *do know*. This trust in ourselves (with a healthy dollop of humility) can build a resilient core to our personality, our reputation and our approach to whatever is to come our way.

'Don't know'

When you sense your thoughts contracting around something problematic, increasing in intensity and speed as you frantically try to figure something out, take a deep breath and exhale slowly. Think about what is the *nub* of what you are grappling with not knowing? Then simply and calmly say to yourself very slowly 'Don't know'. Spell it out: D.O.N.'T. K.N.O.W. Breathe out again. Let yourself be for a second, release the tension in your body and look upward.

How does it feel to accept it? Do you feel relieved? A little rebellious even? However you feel is fine. The fact is you are accepting a limitation of being a human being. This makes more room and releases more energy for you to then think about what you *do* know and therefore what you *can* do and motivates pragmatic action. Be confident. (It's OK not to know it all, 24/7 about everything ever).

REAL-LIFE EXPERIENCES

This is the simplest and bravest of practices when you are telling yourself that you absolutely *have to* resolve or answer something you realise deep down is pretty impossible. It can be used as a private practice to acknowledge that it's OK not to have all the answers – or, if appropriate, you can even share it with others. In the right circumstances, it may be good for others to hear that you are comfortable (enough) with *not knowing* all the answers to an issue. It can be especially settling to let go of the battle against 'not knowing' if there is a consensus that the battle is unlikely to be won. This might resonate in times officers and staff are concerned about outcomes of cases which are now out of their hands, such as in call handling or counter-terrorism.

Permission to lighten up

Feeling it's all getting a bit much? It's OK to let go just a little. It's OK to look out for your happiness. You have permission.

145

We finish this section with a final tool kit of ways in which we can bring a little more lightness and an element of ease to our thinking on the job.

(If you are interested in developing these practical suggestions further, many are covered in much more detail in their original texts, in particular, those by psychologists Rick Hanson[63] and Tara Brach[64].)

Is feeling negativity creeping up on you? Be savvy, intervene and activate your resilience

RAIN: Recognise, Accept, Investigate and Non-identification

The RAIN technique is a very effective way of dealing responsibly with negative experiences. Practising RAIN can limit the tendency to dissociate from (or numb out to) that which we find difficult or unpleasant. As discussed throughout the book so far, if we don't make time to acknowledge the impact that experiences have on us at the time, we allow stress and the 'drip-drip-drip' effect of trauma exposure to accumulate. To avoid burnout, it is extremely important in policing that we practise being proactive in the immediacy of a negative experience and put the event into as much perspective as possible.

When you **R**ecognise that an incident or situation has been challenging or upsetting, take a moment to inhale deeply to the count of four and exhale to the count of six. See the incident for what it is – what has happened and why it's negative. After realising the negativity (and this is the difficult bit) we need to **A**ccept that this is the reality; it's just the way things are right now. This doesn't mean we have to be passive or agree with what happened or condone it; we are simply acknowledging the uncomfortable truth that this thing has happened.

This releases more of our mental energy to **I**nvestigate it responsibly. We can do this *mentally*, by considering why something has occurred, the conditions in which it did, cause and effect, influences (seen and unseen) that may have been at play. We can also do this *physically* by investigating in our body where we are holding a stress response to it – is it a tightening in the chest, a grip in our muscles, a contraction of the throat or a shadow in our stomach? Investigating gives us a sense of agency, an ability to understand an issue (as best we can) and to connect with our physical response to it.

Once we have done this, we can relax our reaction to it by **N**ot identifying with it, making the effort to step back from it being 'about us' or 'signifying something' and resist the temptation to start building a 'case' and a narrative around it. We can see it objectively for what it is, acknowledge it had an effect on us, and then step aside from it and let it be what it was. A good sign that this has been effective is slightly less bracing in the body when we think about it.

Tip

If you prefer, you can replace 'non-identification' with 'nurture' for times when you need a bit of a boost and some 'super smart compassion'. Ask yourself 'What do I really want or need right now?'

It could be as simple as a hot drink, a change of clothes, texting a friend or taking a breath of fresh air. Or it could be more substantial, like contacting a TRiM[65] practitioner for a debrief or organising a leisure activity for your next day off.

Is a moment of healthy stress taking on a very slight whiff of panic? Learn how to regroup, refocus and resume

STOP: Stop, Take a breath, Observe, Proceed

Being able to immediately diffuse stress is something we would all love to naturally have as a personal trait, but in occupations such as policing, our brains and bodies simply spend so much time in that reactive mode that this expectation is a little unrealistic – you'd think. Yet, as we practise being able to spot when that reactivity is getting a grip and then just pausing for one breath, we soon realise that we can feel a lot more in control and a lot more ready to deal with what we know life is about to hurl at us. The memory aid for this is the word STOP, which stands for:

- **STOP** interrupting your racing thoughts or reactive actions.
- **TAKE A BREATH,** inhale deeply through the nose and exhale as long as you can through pursed lips.
- **OBSERVE,** take a step back from yourself and the situation and become a witness of your thoughts, your body and your emotional tone – tune in to and be with what's arising, however it is.
- **PROCEED** after being objective like this; think clearly about how you might respond. The advice is to choose *one* thing that you can focus on right now, and go with that focus.[66]

Making a bad thing worse in your mind? Just let something be a bit 'yuk'

The second punch

Accepting that something negative has happened is critical for resilience. Science has shown that we feel significantly less pain when we accept it than if we try to distract ourselves from it.[67] Physical and psychological pain or discomfort happens – it's a fact of life – especially in a job that deals daily with people's worst experiences (as we spoke about in Chapters 1 and 2). Neuroscience has also shown that there are benefits to ways of thinking about pain that have been practised for many years in contemplative traditions, but which we can easily replicate ourselves.[68]

Specifically, the advice is to differentiate between pain and suffering. Pain is what happens. If someone punches you in the face, it's going to hurt. Suffering is our reaction to that. If we react in a way that resists what has happened, arguing that it was unfair, riling with the fact that it shouldn't have happened or could have gone differently or punishing ourselves for letting it happen, then we introduce suffering. We might as well punch ourselves in the face a second time.

If we learn to pause after feeling the effect of pain before we start launching into a whole internal dialogue of mind-wandering, comparing and judging then we have more of a chance of feeling less pain for less time.

For when there is a flicker of something positive: feel resourced, inspired, confident and grateful, without losing your edge

HEAL: Have, Enrich, Absorb and Link

Positive experiences are really rich resources for resilience. As we learned in Chapter 3, they often go unnoticed, perhaps particularly so in occupations that are geared toward the negativity bias of threat. Trusting our positive thoughts is not something that always comes naturally to anyone, let alone those in challenging roles.[69] Yet, spending time recognising those better moments (even if they are very brief and *especially* if they are rare) can help us meet the core needs of our brains, which we learned in Chapter 3 are safety, satisfaction and connection.

When you notice that you have had a positive moment or experience, take a moment to inhale deeply to the count of four and exhale to the count of six. See what happened for what it is – an incident that was well managed, a successful outcome of an investigation, a compliment from a supervisor, a team showing trust, a family member recognising what you do, a pleasurable day off, a tasty meal, an unexpected smile from someone or a funny observation.

Then (and this can feel indulgent but is very effective) quietly Enrich the experience by noticing its qualities. Use your senses – what does it look, sound or feel like? Check in with your body – do you feel warm, energised, tingly, at ease, relaxed, excited? Giving the experience a physical presence inside yourself can help make it stick so you can bank it for use later when you need a pick-me-up.

Next, take some time to let the experience 'soak in', really Absorb it into how your day is going, what it means to you in general, how it perks you up or entertains you. Really let it land and be part of you.

The final stage is optional and is to Link the positive experience with a situation in the past where you have felt the opposite, perhaps a time when you have *not* felt friendship or support or have been in physical discomfort.[70]

Tip

It is best to use the Link phase carefully and only apply to mild negative experiences if you have had a lot of trauma exposure on the job. Many people don't feel the need to link positive experiences and just enjoy them for what they are in the present.

Permission to lighten up

RAIN: Recognise an uncomfortable or painful thought, Accept that it's there, Investigate where it might come from and if you can sense its tension or feeling tone in your body, then try Not to identify with it too much. It's a temporary state that's there for many reasons, manifesting in many ways, but it's not something you need to bind yourself to or take on. You can nurture yourself while it's here.

STOP: When you sense fear or agitation building, Stop. Take a deep breath in and exhale slowly. Observe what it is that is happening and how you are responding to it. Proceed in a more together, aware way as a response to what is happening rather than a knee-jerk reaction.

The second punch: When you experience something uncomfortable or annoying, painful or even distressing, see it for what it is. Accept that it's here but try not to add to it. Try not to rally against it, contest it, add in judgements as to whether it's fair or not or debate its legitimacy. All these reactions are second punches that you give yourself, which you can probably do without.

HEAL: When you Have a sense of a positive moment, a vibe, a gesture, memory and observation or a rapport with someone, really notice it. Then Enrich it by thinking about all the sensations you feel in your body in response to it, making a mental note of the senses, sights, sounds, smells, what it feels like in the body. Then take a moment to Absorb it into your experience, one to remember as you go to sleep, to match or Link to other experiences which could have done with a bit of what this positive experience has offered you.

Feeling a bit like you're stuck in Ground Hog Day? Life a bit same-y?

The hand swap

Learn how to rejuvenate your brain and kick start it with a sense of energetic accomplishment. A very refreshing way of getting the brain into a receptive state for feeling resilient is to move its energy about a little, in particular, moving it from the midbrain towards the front, where we know from Chapter 3 is where we are often at our best for decision-making, compassion management and seeing things with clarity.[71]

A somewhat entertaining way of redirecting this energy is to simply swap hands. Regularly using your non-dominant hand for everyday activities[72] can also increase a sense of self-control and is also thought to help regulate aggressive emotion.[73]

This is good to use for everyday non-demanding tasks such as stirring a cup of tea, brushing teeth or opening a laptop. It's also a little amusing and the novelty can be very satisfying.

Feeling a bit 'meh'? A bit distant from others? Generate some light relief and a sense of connection with those who 'get you'

'S' funny...'

Our final technique is perhaps one of the most essential, accessible and familiar – lightening up with humour. It's not surprising that police humour has been shown to help 'anchor' crime scene investigators into a sense of 'normalcy' for their emotional survival,[74] to create bonds with those in other emergency response roles (such as ambulance crew) on the front line,[75] reinforce group values and exchange social support among new recruits.[76]

Taking time to exchange a humorous reflection can release reward chemicals (such as dopamine) in our fear response circuitry (the amygdala), which can bring much-needed relief after challenging experiences.[77]

As with all humour, timing is everything and choosing the right time and place to avoid offence when emotions are running high is a vital skill to master.

REAL-LIFE EXPERIENCES

Giving yourself permission not to over-identify with negativity and to see a lighter way through difficult situations is a good thing. This is very different to 'toxic positivity' (a tendency to suspend and dissociate from the darker reality of a situation by trying to celebrate small wins in a veil of disproportionate and disingenuous optimism). When others advise '*just think positively*', it can be hard not to react in exactly the opposite way! These techniques offer a more down-to-earth way of tackling the negativity bias without denying that sometimes life is the way it is.

It might be useful to keep the RAIN, HEAL and STOP acronyms to hand on a piece of paper. The hand swap is good for early morning teeth-brushing to open the mind for the day ahead. Humorous reflections can be useful at the end of a challenging job or day to settle the brain's stress response.

How to get the most out of the techniques

The untrained mind is stupid. (Ajachn Cha)[78]

So, we have a pretty full tactical toolkit at our disposal, evidenced by a lot of science, research and lived experience of those who understand the brain, resilience and what it's like to work in

Table 4.2: Bossing your brain – an example of notes to observe your defaults and get more tactical

Mind wander	Circumstances	Thoughts	Effect	Alternative	Prompt
Comparing myself to a crew member	Dealing with a domestic	'I haven't got the patience, I'm no good at the job'	Low self-esteem, disproportionate	Talk to the team, realise my strengths	Call out to Domestic Violence job
Planning detail of the evening	Bored in morning meeting	'Too much to do, it won't turn out the way I want it to'	Building panic and distraction about what to say and do, what might go wrong	Set aside planning to later in the day and go with the flow	Being bored or wanting something to control

policing and emergency response. The challenge now is what we as individuals do with it.

Research suggests that we have around 6,000 thoughts per day to grapple with, but that (much to do with the technological impact of our devices) a study by Microsoft has revealed that our 'attention capital' is reducing through our use of social media. Other research has shown more specifically that our attention span has dropped in recent years from 12 seconds to 8 seconds.[79] So, we have less of an attention span to deal with this huge volume of thought traffic. What we need to do is upgrade our attention so we can practise the techniques we need to, to establish smarter traits of thinking and build resilience. Thankfully, training the mind in attention has been going on for thousands of years and now modern neuroscience is taking to a whole different level, opening up new opportunities for everyday people living everyday lives to change their minds for good. Police included.

The solution for dealing with this daily barrage of thoughts seems to be *to get in between them* and then take control. The techniques provide us with the instructions for the control. But we have to establish a strong command first if we want to see real improvement.

In policing, it could be helpful to think about this in terms of operational tactics for crowd management.[80] We're talking about being able to see the crowd of thoughts not as one big mass but as a gathering made up of individual components that can come and go. Sometimes we can disperse them, sometimes we can cordon some off and intercept them, sometimes we need forward intelligence to see where the thoughts are going, sometimes we may even need to negotiate with them, and sometimes we can just let them burn themselves out. Whichever tactic we choose and whichever tool we select from our toolkit to implement it with, we need to know when to move in. That kind of command takes experience and practice. Table 4.2 is an example of what that might look like in action.

Practising with the brain isn't new to the front line. In 2017, one Miami university was training combat troops, firefighters and New York City front-line trauma response workers during the Ebola epidemic, as well as 80 prisons, in cognitive practice.[81]

And as former US CNN newscaster Dan Harris points out, when delivering to law enforcement in Arizona, this isn't a 'crunchy granola thing'.[82] The chief involved in delivering the training was well aware of cultural barriers in policing, acknowledging 'a lot of risk of not looking hard core' but that this type of training 'makes us more *tactically* sound', and another sergeant (a former marine) explained that it 'sharpens [our] edge on the street'.[83] In another US study, even those experiencing high levels of stress, with histories of trauma exposure, reaped lasting benefits from an eight-week course of mindfulness training.[84]

More recently, the UK has been catching up with the notion that policing minds deserve a bit of time, care and attention for them to perform at their best. During an intense period of heightened stress and demands on police officers around the world, His Holiness the 14th Dalai Lama participated in his first-ever dialogue with Western police officers from his residence in the foothills of the Indian Himalayas. In the early hours of Tuesday, 8 July 2020, nearly 1,000 London Metropolitan Police officers gathered via the internet to participate in a live video dialogue with Nobel Peace Prize winner and exiled Tibetan leader to discuss 'Developing Compassion During Uncertain Times'.[85] Since the event, an eight-week course has been taught to over 200 officers, with impressive results that make practical sense in a very testing operational environment, against all odds. One officer shared, 'I must admit I was a sceptic of mindfulness prior to undertaking this programme. This was due to the way it has been portrayed. I will continue to practice often and add it to my toolbox'. Rising above the initial scepticism came with reward, with evaluation data demonstrating significant and positive differences in mood, stress, calmness, self-compassion, perspective and resilience – states and traits we now know to be integral to policing in the current climate.

The work in the US also recognised that one of the biggest challenges of police work is not to take the anxiety and anger from your previous call into the next one and, equally important, was 'not to carry the disquiet of the day back into your personal life'.[86] In Chapter 1 we saw in the UK that over half of police officers rarely (or never) have time to make sense of one job before moving on to the next.[87] We know that with trauma exposure being part of policing, this can make us especially prone to having our brains propelled into the next emergent issue without having a chance to prepare. The risks of this are clearly acknowledged in neuroscience: 'Overwhelming trauma resets to a hair trigger the amygdala's threshold of hijacking the rest of the brain to what it perceives as an emergency'.[88]

So, our starting point in policing (and perhaps in other areas of emergency response) is a little on the back foot, perhaps – but *we are where we are* and it's what we choose to do with our predicament that counts. The smart move is to be as present as possible for each experience *and its impact* as it is before the next experience. As Jeff Warren states, 'Instead of white-knuckling it through your experience, you're opening to the experience, and that's what allows you to reset'.[89]

How do we do that? We need to take the same approach to our experiences on the job as we do to our thoughts: we need to get in between them. We need command and control. We can achieve this with five simple steps:

1. Stop overdoing
2. Start surveillance
3. Get your body on board
4. Make time
5. Train up

Stop overdoing

To be able to magic up resources so that officers and staff across the UK can pause and take a second in between tasks, jobs, incidents and cases would be a wonderful thing, but it's not going to happen. If we can't generate time out of nowhere, then we need to be more efficient with the time we have. The first thing we need to do is identify when those times, those opportunities to gain command and control are.

In a post-COVID world at work, we are likely to be engaging more and more frequently with the technologies and communications that enabled us to work remotely and maintain performance through a time when face-to-face interaction was limited. This is also likely to be the case outside of work in terms of our social connectivity. But, as the research by Microsoft revealed even back in 2019,[90] our attention span, our ability to engage our brains constructively, is diminishing. Especially when we are under time pressure at work, we become more and more fragmented, trying to do 500 things at once while being continually distracted by radios, mobiles, fit bits, smart watches, social media pinging, news alerts, email notifications and calendar reminders. This is on top of those roles in policing that may (operationally) necessitate multi-tasking (such as working in some control rooms, processing 999 and 101 calls, dealing with social media and incoming email, which all has to happen at the same time).

Some of us would love to boast that this means we are becoming *multi-taskers* like that's a good thing. Neuroscience, unfortunately, puts us right on that one: 'multi-taskers are suckers for irrelevancy'.[91] The reality is that when we do lots of things at once, there is a chance we will be doing lots of things not very well *and* (more importantly) our minds become fragmented, disjointed and scattered, making work and life more difficult and un-fun than it needs to be.

The good news is that we don't have to fall into that default mode of multi-modal reactivity, of *over-doing-ness*. A neuroscience study from 2012 proves that just three ten-minute sessions of counting the breath were enough to appreciably increase the attention skills of heavy media multi-taskers. What is more, those who were worse on the tests made the greatest gains (a shot in the foot for those who label themselves or others as 'just not having the kind of brain' that can pay attention to one thing at a time[92]). Once we learn to pay attention more, we are more likely to spot those times in between tasks where we can (literally) catch our breath before moving on to the next task. These micro-moments of sanity might be all we need to steady our reactivity and stress response, and gradually build a stable core of resilience over time.

Everyday practice

When you feel the 'buzz' of moving at speed within and between tasks, just take a second to ask yourself if what you are doing needs to be done; a) right now, b) all at the same time or even, c) at all. Once you answer those questions, you are likely to be much better placed to triage and prioritise what is most useful to turn your attention to right at that moment, and what will bring the best outcome and most pleasing reward.

Start surveillance

Of the simplest tasks in the world, watching your breath, surely, is one of them. Yet, it still takes skill and practice, especially if you are easily distracted. The rewards, however, are great. The techniques are core to attention training and are recommended for anyone wanting to improve their resilience.

That said, studies have shown that they are also specifically pertinent to work involving disturbing images. In a 2017 study using images of burns victims, attention training reduced amygdala activity (the alarm bell in our brains) in participants who repeatedly viewed the images.[93]

These positive results are likely very transferable to processing digital material in child sexual exploitation and counter-terrorism work.

Everyday practice

Allocate a few minutes of the day. You can do this in the car before a shift or coming back from a job, after a shower before getting dressed, on a break or before you go to sleep.

Practise watching your breathing, then watching your thoughts come in and out while you keep focussing on the breath, and then watching yourself watch both your breath and your thoughts.

Start small: try watching just three breaths and gradually increase to ten. As you get good at that, take it up a level and see if you can watch your breaths without intervening with them in any way – so not regulating them yourself, just watch them happen as if you weren't looking at all. This can take a while. (Like, a year).

For some of us, watching the breath has connotations and can make us feel uncomfortable. So, an alternative is to listen. Tune in to the sounds around you and again, *try not to intervene* by labelling the sounds or trying to find out from where they are coming. Try to observe the sounds as one big 'soundscape' that you can listen to, happening as if you weren't there at all.

At some point, you will know you are ready to move on to the 'super practice': watching your thoughts. Just as you did with breathing and or sounds, apply the same approach to your thinking. Watch your thoughts come and go, *without intervening in them*, without following them or being hijacked by them, watch them come into your mind and wander off, as they do. Remember, there are 6,000 of them coming and going every day, and you don't have to invest in or finish any one of them.

Use breathing or sounds as your anchor – keep watching your breath or sounds and wait.

Soon enough, a thought will pop up (that's what the brain does!). See if you can notice when you start following it. When you do notice, come back to breathing or sounds and start again. You'll be surprised how many times you get pulled away by the thought, but each time you come back from it, it's a win.

Treat it like training a puppy, each time your mind comes back from being distracted, give yourself a biscuit (a 'well done me') and acknowledge the discipline you're cultivating. With solid training, you can start to reap the rewards of resilience.

Super practice

Find a quiet space free from interruption or distraction. If you can, set a timer for one minute, then increase the time of each practice by another minute. Take a few minutes being with your breath, counting in and out until you feel relatively steady and calm. When you are aware of your first thought, note it with a very short label, even just 'thinking'. Then don't follow it. Just go back to breathing. Counting in and out.

When the next thought comes up, again, label it 'thinking'.

Keep going until your timer sounds the end of your practice. Then say 'well done me' and get back to your day.

Tip

At first, you will be inundated with lots of labels of 'thinking' and very few breaths to notice. That's because we have busy minds and it takes a lot of practice to slow them down. When you slow them down, that's where the sense of command and control comes in. Soon enough, you will free up more mental space and time to make smarter decisions and will have the confidence to trust them more.

Get your body on board

It's important to know what the brain's mental and physical requirements are to rewire it for resilience. Your mind and brain are stimulated by your attitude and fuelled by what you put in your body. Neuroscience shows us that there are certain conditions in which new neural pathways thrive: repetition (repeating the exercises), emotional arousal and reward (really congratulating yourself on getting proactive on this), novelty (trying new things and sometimes improvising a bit) and careful attention to how it all feels.[94]

Physically, aerobic exercise and a ketogenic diet (high fat, zero sugar, very low carbohydrate and moderate protein) is known to help neuroplasticity and to protect key areas of the brain such as the hippocampus, helping it release vital proteins (which is harder to do for some genotypes than others).[95]

Together, these mental and physical components produce protective sheaths around neurons which enable them to increase their conduction of electricity by 100 times.[96] This means we can develop new thought processes with greater ease and efficiency, super-charged, physically *feeling* this upgrade of cognitive function.

Lifestyle improvements[97] are greatly enhanced by your mental attitude. Both your body and brain benefit from an approach to resilience that taps into a sense of purpose both on the job and in life more generally. We know from earlier chapters that policing seem to lose its meaning over time for some, and can also take its toll on the human body. Neuroscience has shown that reinforcing a sense of purpose in cognitive practice can help rectify damage to our immune systems, increasing the activity of an enzyme (called telomerase) in our immune cells which helps them live longer – even five months later.

> It's as if the body's cells were saying, stick around, you've got important work to do.[98]

Tip

In your daily techniques (be it the morning mindset, check-in or sleep debrief), try to include an affirmation of why you were motivated to sign up to the police in the first place, what you get most out of a working day and how it feels to finish the day with a sense of a 'job well done'.

Make time

The most important component of rewiring your brain for resilience is the same in policing as it is in any profession, discipline, country or lifestyle the world over: *making time to do it*. As we have appreciated, time is not in abundance in this line of work and finding those moments for practice is critical – but it's at our discretion.

Many forces set aside an hour every month or so for time to support personal development, exchange news or debrief – sometimes called 'power hour'. The suggestion here is to encourage you to make your own 'discretionary power hour' once a week or fortnight to take stock. You can use this allocated time to gently assess how your command and control on your brain is doing, and how you might tweak your practice or approach to your advantage going forward.

Finding the right times to practise that work for you is critical, and finding time can be a practice in its own right, so don't be hard on yourself if you struggle at first. Take a moment to look at the rhythm of your workflow, your work-life balance and your personal time, and see what practices might slip into that rhythm with the least disruption and greatest gains, even if the windows of time are few and far between (they can always increase in number and regularity).

Everyday practice

You might consider how to create small, accessible windows of practice – to and from work, scheduled during holidays, integrated into leisure time, coming back into force after an external job, within family time, before or after meetings or within shift breaks. The trick is to start with a brief, easily achievable, unobtrusive time slot that you can make your best effort to invest in.

Tip

When you have established some regular time for personal practice, it can be good to embed the results by carving out some time with others on the job. Research has shown that in emotionally trying occupations, checking in with others over a cup of coffee can make the world of difference to resilience.[99]

Train up

Armed with a toolkit and with all the intention in the world to create time to practice is a great start. Yet, many of us benefit from the occasional nudge or from a more structured approach to practising something new. If this applies to you, then you're in good company. Neuroscience has been tracking the benefits of structured cognitive practice for many years now and has very good news for those working day-to-day in professions like policing:[100]

- After just 30 hours on one attention for stress reduction course, participants grew new neural pathways to regulate their threat perception and emotional regulation and on another.
- Those who practised for more hours over another five-month attention for stress course recovered more quickly from blood pressure spikes in stressful scenarios.
- Even just seven minutes of a wishing well attention practice boosted participants' good feelings and sense of connection and peer support.
- Three days of a basic attention course (for complete novices) showed they had more ability to snap out of the 'personal melodrama' of the default mode of thinking and improved their control circuitry in the brain.[101]

With the evidence already established that these kinds of meditative attention practices work and are highly relevant to policing, nothing is stopping you from finding out for yourself and exploring the many applications and courses available online (and even through the NHS in some areas). Meditation[102] is a practical, effective (and let's face it, quite entertaining) way of building resilience for life that works. It just does.

Karma police

What we have learned is that we can hardwire the policing brain by regularly practising resilient thinking techniques that can be applied on the job.[103] This has the potential for a profound impact on policing beyond the mind of any one individual. Laying down new neural pathways has long been used at the micro-level in the health sector (to support stroke rehabilitation for example) and in elite sport – but it has also been taught at a more macro level to teams and whole organisations in competitive arenas of business and technology (ranging from Google to NASA[104]).

The reason for this broader application of neuroplasticity techniques is that once an individual uses the new pathways that they lay down, once they practise these resilient habits of thought, they are more receptive to resilient behaviour around them. (As we know from our understanding of mirror neurons, our brains will activate in areas we use for certain activities simply by watching others performing that activity.[105]) This is how collective resilience builds for an organisation.

One could argue that the mythical notion of 'karma' isn't about the 'universe paying us back' for our actions, it's actually about the brain: practise thinking in a certain way and you will become more receptive to it in the world around you. Practise thinking resiliently and resilience will come your way, as an individual officer, as a unit, a team or a whole force.

Chapter 4 snapshot

- 'If you keep doing what you've always done, you'll keep getting what you always got.' (*Unknown*)
  The practices offered in this chapter offer readers the chance to experiment with different ways of thinking in bite-sized chunks of practice, five or ten minutes at a time. Some techniques will resonate with you more than others, and some might grow on you either time. The point is to have them available to you, to try them out, practice the ones that work for you, and every so often try something new.
- The four key areas of the brain which can be trained to help the *policing mind* become as resilient as can be are:
  - the prefrontal cortex (the newest part of the brain, right at the front behind the forehead);
  - the language centres (these go off-line when we feel under threat, but are needed to make sense of experiences once the threat has passed);
  - our sensory systems (that can help enrich our experiences and help us remember the ones that really mean something to us);
  - our midbrain or mammalian brain (also called our limbic system, which specifically helps us make sense of our traumatic memories and is also responsible for our situational awareness – our understanding of where we are); and
  - the nerve connecting our mind and body (the vagus nerve, which refines our ability to resonate with and read others).

- Together, these areas of the brain help us with the essential demands of policing: focus, understanding others' motivations and anticipating their behaviour, making sense of the unusual and traumatic, filing incidents away logically, making good use of the resources available to us, snapping ourselves out of unhelpful or unpleasant mind-wandering and working smartly with our bodies to manage the stress response.
- We can rewire the brain by becoming more aware that we have one at all and watching what it does. This often just comes down to the simple act of *noticing what we are thinking* and how we are responding to what is going on around us – rather than needing to do anything terribly clever or remarkable with it. Yet this noticing takes practice itself. It's simple. But it's not always that easy! Especially if we have a lot going on. This is why committing to having a go regularly is so important.

Checklist

☐ Now you have an idea that the human brain adapts to the job and that a 'policing mind' has common habits, adaptations and traits, how do you feel about engaging with it more pragmatically? Can you feel any resistance to trying out techniques to develop your thinking? Can you feel a sense of urgency to have a go or to rise to the challenge? Do you sense a bit of both? *However you feel before trying, can you just notice that, choose one and have a go anyway?*

☐ Which demands on the policing mind do you most resonate with? Focus? Predicting others' behaviour? Managing difficult incidents? Allocating resources? Managing stress? *Which demand calls to you the most? Are there any other demands of your job which one of the techniques might be useful for?*

☐ Which of the techniques did you immediately resonate with? *Can you work out why?*

☐ How do you feel about setting a few minutes aside each day to practise working with your thinking? What are the challenges of finding that time? *Where might you find the space to practise where you won't be disturbed? Would it be helpful to let anyone know you are taking a few minutes for yourself when you do, to protect that time? How might you establish a routine so that a short amount of practice is just part of your day, like brushing your teeth or eating? Can you place reminders in your day – either visibly or using alerts on your phone?*

☐ If you find something that works well – how would you feel about sharing it with your peers? What if someone were to ask you how you manage your thinking on the job? *Would you feel prepared to share the possibilities of practising to rewire the mind for resilience? How would you describe it?*

5

What now? The big step change

In our concluding chapter, we consolidate our shared understanding of the 'policing brain' and begin to form an action plan – taking a realistic, honest approach to what this means in operational terms on the ground, for individuals and organisations. Our exploration ends with a question put to you, the reader.

What we know about the 'policing brain'

What we know is that the concept of *the policing brain* has earned its place on the front line and supports very much needed resilience out there in the everyday reality of life on the job. Contemporary policing now has a chance to catch up with the latest neuroscience that helps explain why working in policing looks and feels the way it does.

Key learning points include the following:

- Science shows that training the brain can improve key areas of function to support policing, such as increasing connectivity between and redirecting energy towards specific regions, as well as breaking unhelpful or unproductive habits of thought.
- Areas of the brain that can become compromised (by unprocessed trauma exposure, habits of thought or under-use/ neglect) can be effectively reactivated with simple, short techniques which can cultivate lasting resilience when applied regularly.

Figure 5.1: The policing brain – a summary of key features

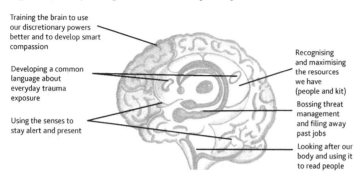

Training the brain to use our discretionary powers better and to develop smart compassion

Developing a common language about everyday trauma exposure

Using the senses to stay alert and present

Recognising and maximising the resources we have (people and kit)

Bossing threat management and filing away past jobs

Looking after our body and using it to read people

- Our perceptions of our policing role and identity, how we relate to others and where we see ourselves in the broader context of our lives and the world around us can all come down to practising what we choose to pay attention to (how we steer our thinking).
- Figure 5.1 summarises components of the policing brain that can be exploited (in a good way!) to develop resilient traits. These include: developing our decision-making skills and smartening up our compassion management, expanding and enriching a rational, common language about the uncomfortable truths on the job, reconnecting with our senses and communicating better with our bodies to manage stress and refine our intuition about other people, priming our brain for task-specific focus, resourcing ourselves more consciously with what we have in place to do the job, and professionalising our mastery over threat perception and our expertise in processing the experiences which make us who we are.

'The only thing to fear is fear itself': getting real with threat perception

If we put it like that, everything seems so hopeful and straightforward.[1] But, realistically, we all know that if it was so easy to master threat, we wouldn't be in the predicament we are, looking for new resilience in an undeniably difficult era for emergency response. If we are to make any genuine steps towards a new approach to police wellbeing, we have to be brutally honest about the fact that the dynamics that threat management requires set policing aside from other 'front line' roles. In Chapter 1 we recognised that threats come from the nature of crime and public opinion on law enforcement, as well as the immediacy of dangerous physical environments of emergency response.

We observed in Chapter 2 that threat management is one of the predominant skills required on the job and because of this we might be tempted to assume that managing threats becomes second nature. However, a more honest appraisal of the situation for many might be more than day-to-day, we are *trying as best we can to keep on top of threats, from wherever they are coming*. Essential to that is keeping in sync with the alarm signal alerting us to threats: fear. The starting point for resilience is acknowledging that the F-word (fear) is a biological response to the nature of the work, the single most important component of our human survival kit, a response that deserves respect, not a blind eye. A culture that cannot accept that, cannot effectively support its workforce in managing it.

It's important to appreciate that here in the UK we are fortunate to have trauma exposure being more publicly accepted as part of policing. But how far does this acceptance go? Do forces genuinely, daily, look at trauma exposure head-on, talk about it openly, quantify it responsibly, process it effectively and accept it *without rejecting or inadvertently shaming those who show its impact on them*?

It's been too easy to:

- label and medicalise trauma impact *out* of the way (through transfers away from the front line or early retirements);
- hide trauma impact within sickness absence data (describing generic 'stress' or filing it under physical symptoms of its manifestation); and
- disguise trauma impact with presenteeism (blaming other policing challenges for its effect on our professionalism or demeanour when we turn up at work, affected by it).

The fact is, trauma exposure and its impact are already part of policing life, and many are finding ways through and out the other side.[2] However, are we giving ourselves the chance to learn anything from these people? Do we even know who they are?

Neuroscience suggests we really should. Research has shown that trauma exposure can refine certain areas of cognitive function that are essential in front line response (one such function being situational awareness). Data collected as part of a study into individual variation in trauma impact in police, military and civilian populations suggests that those who have been exposed to trauma (without current disorder) are more accurate in their ability to judge their own navigation competency, compared to those who were trauma naïve.[3] This is just one example of how science demonstrates that a trauma-experienced brain can also be a resilient and more skilful one, compared to its less experienced counterparts.

Looking forward to the future, we are much more likely to be able to make the most of the lessons learned from trauma experience if we accept that trauma impact (and the transient experience of fear that accompanies it) happens in the first place. That is where we have to start to catch up with what the human brain may be capable of in emergency response occupations. A simple way to start is by recognising trauma exposure, using tools such as the Police Traumatic Events Checklist,[4] which categorises incidents and jobs in policing which are most frequently reported as officers and staff's worst on the job (Table 5.1).

By encouraging officers and staff to self-monitor trauma impact, recognise its accumulation and see their own experiences being recognised on paper (or digitally) is a big step change, for the policing brain and the culture. If forces can then take on that recognition into its processes, support and common language, threat management will become something that is respected and not feared.

Responsibility in forces

What forces do collectively matters. Individuals may make strong, autonomous decisions to establish a new approach to their thinking lives, taking resilience into their own hands – but if they are met with push-back from the organisation, they

Table 5.1: The Police Traumatic Events Checklist

Police Traumatic Events Checklist — This matrix shows the most common 'worst' experiences described in UK policing. It describes common worst events and situational factors at the time. *How do your experiences compare?*	A — Exposure to gruesome events or scenes (eg disrupted bodies or gory injuries)	B — Organisation pressure (eg lack of resources or support)	C — Cumulative exposure (eg a build up of small traumas over time or within a job)	D — Being the first person on scene	E — Personal resonance (eg the victim was known or resembled someone, it was a birthday, etc)	COVID-19 — Victim vulnerability (eg elderly, signs of deprivation or animal cruelty)	Another situational factor that worsened impact (please describe)	NONE
1 — Incidents involving children (eg fatalities, abuse or exploitation)								
2 — Sudden or unnatural death (eg murder, suicide or hanging)								
3 — Road traffic collision and/or rail incident								
4 — Seeing or working with a dead body								
5 — Serious injury or physical assault to yourself								
6 — Major incident (eg terrorism, national or transport disasters)								
7 — Supporting families (eg delivering death messages, family liaison)								
8 — Incidents involving weapons (especially knives and including firearms, taser)								
9 — Vicarious or secondary trauma (eg distressing calls, case notes, images)								
10 — Incidents involving fire (including explosions)								
COVID-19 — Being exposed to toxic or infectious exposures or hazards								
Another type of incident (please describe in a few words)								

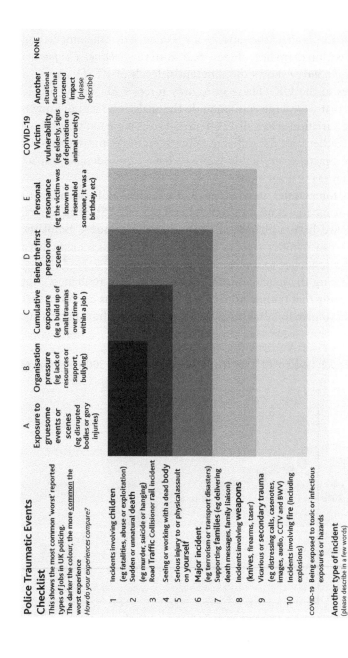

Police Traumatic Events Checklist

This shows the most common 'worst' reported types of jobs in UK policing.
The darker the colour, the more common the worst experience
How do your experiences compare?

	A Exposure to gruesome events or scenes (eg disrupted bodies or gory injuries)	B Organisation pressure (eg lack of resources or support, bullying)	C Cumulative exposure (eg a build up of small traumas over time or within a job)	D Being the first person on scene	E Personal resonance (eg the victim was known or resembled someone, it was a birthday, etc)	COVID-19 Victim vulnerability (eg elderly, signs of deprivation or animal cruelty)	Another situational factor that worsened impact (please describe)	NONE
1 Incidents involving children (eg fatalities, abuse or exploitation)								
2 Sudden or unnatural death (eg murder, suicide or hanging)								
3 Road Traffic Collision or rail incident								
4 Seeing or working with a dead body								
5 Serious injury to or physical assault on yourself								
6 Major incident (eg terrorism or transport disasters)								
7 Supporting families (eg delivering death messages, family liaison)								
8 Incidents involving weapons (knives, firearms, taser)								
9 Vicarious or secondary trauma (eg distressing calls, casenotes, images, audio, CCTV and BWV)								
10 Incidents involving fire (including explosions)								
COVID-19 Being exposed to toxic or infectious exposures or hazards								

Another type of incident
(please describe in a few words)

Source: With thanks to Police Care UK and the Police Federation of England and Wales

will be doing so with one hand tied behind their back. With or without mandates from the Home Office or assertions from police and crime commissioners, local decisions made within single forces affect the capacity for resilience that the officers and staff within them have. Figure 5.2[5] from the *Policing: The Job and the Life Survey* shows the differential levels of PTSD across 18 forces in the UK. These were only forces with survey sample sizes that were large enough to do the analysis, so it's not known if the variation across all 42 territorial areas is greater than this or not. Either way, the differences between forces mean that local force practices are highly likely to have a considerable impact on trauma management.[6]

So, forces differ, so what? Well, if we can identify reasons as to why some forces might have higher levels of PTSD than others, then we have a chance of addressing those causes. Similarly, if we can identify reasons as to why some forces might have higher resilience to trauma impact, then we have a good chance of sharing the practices that help facilitate that resilience. Not accepting that trauma impact comes with trauma exposure isn't going to give forces what they need. Just as the human nervous

Figure 5.2: Levels of PTSD by territorial police force (n > 300 in each force)

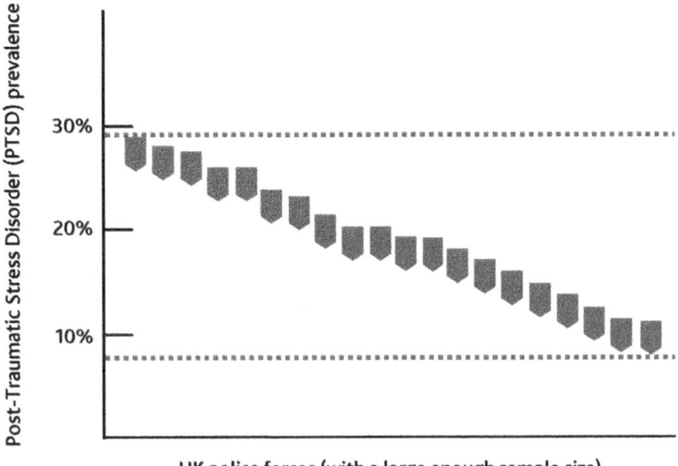

Source: Image reproduced by author, with thanks to Police Care UK. See note 6

system doesn't have a 'delete' button for traumatic impact, nor does an organisation. Denying trauma impact and hoping for the best isn't playing out the way that many might have hoped for – the effects are everywhere. What is more, the effects more likely originate from the process of denial than the trauma exposure itself. Trauma exposure, like pain, is inevitable on the job – but the suffering that comes with it is more optional.[7] Whether the suffering originates from the individual's relationship to trauma exposure or the organisation's is a controversial question worth asking in any force. It may well transpire that it is not about an individual being 'weak' in the face of trauma but the organisation.

Here is an example. Figure 5.3 is an analysis of (as yet unpublished[8]) data extracted from the same survey which shows a direct correlation between PTSD and time pressure within forces. This illustration alone shows that there is something very real about how deadlines and pace of workflow may jeopardise officers' and staff's ability to make sense of one incident before moving on to the next – a complaint from over 55 per cent of respondents, which was highly correlated with perceptions of trauma management in-force. So, denying the impact of a job by denying time to acknowledge that impact is directly correlated with the level of the disorder within the organisation.

Further analysis of this data suggests that other working conditions in forces are closely and strongly related to PTSD prevalence.[9] These include:

- lack of peer support;
- having little time to process an incident before the next;
- solving unforeseen problems on your own;[10]
- experiencing humiliating behaviours;
- experiencing sexual harassment in-force (by employees as well as the public);
- lack of support from line manager.

Addressing force working conditions such as these may have an indirect *but significant* impact on PTSD prevalence. What is more, addressing these factors may ignite subtle changes in organisational culture, of tone. It's not always (or indeed ever) going to be possible to compel people to become friends at

Figure 5.3: Correlation between PTSD prevalence and working time pressure in 18 UK territorial police forces

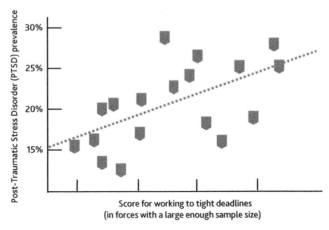

Note: n > 300 in each force
Source: Unpublished data from *Policing: The Job and The Life* survey, University of Cambridge and Police Care UK (2019) with permission from Police Care UK

work, to magic up time off between incidents, to prevent single crewing or officers turning up alone first on the scene, to stop public humiliation or to end sexual harassment – but so much can be done in the right direction. Honestly recognising that the less palatable conditions of the workplace often come down to how we treat each other (as well as the demands of the job) is important. If there aren't the resources to make the changes we need, there can be the right attitude. If there can't be time off, there can be time together. If there can't be time together, there can be a shared language. If there can't be unilateral respect for each other, there can be a culture that does not tolerate *dis*respect. The conditions of the workplace are as much the result of how we as individuals conduct ourselves and relate to each other as they are of labour market dynamics.

Behavioural change in forces

Taking responsibility within forces can be hard to get to grips with. It's no mean feat for leaders, managers or peers to bring into action changes that are guaranteed to make these 'softer' kinds of impacts, regardless of how vital those changes clearly are. Instructions on how to change behaviour around trauma in forces are yet to be found in any operational handbook, training manual or national guidance. Yet, there may be other areas of modern life from which we can borrow.

'Behavioural science' is used in wider industry all the time, encouraging us to buy things, to engage in healthy (or unhealthy!) lifestyles, to donate to good causes, to develop new management styles and, more recently, to interact with our devices. Combining simple lessons from behavioural science with the insights we have gained about the policing brain may be all we need to get started. The Cabinet Office and Institute for Government offer a tool called MINDSPACE, a checklist of influences on human behaviour used for policy-making.[11]

Table 5.2[12] illustrates how the tool can be applied to working on trauma resilience, be it in the context of personal development, daily management, tasking wellbeing working groups or at a strategic, leadership level.

Being a human leader

Leadership is often cited as being pivotal to an organisation's capacity for cultural change, especially for contemporary trauma resilience. In recent times, it features strongly in guidance for emergency responders in the post-COVID environment – and not in the conventional 'strategic' and 'organisational development' sense that one might expect from talk about 'all things governance'. Advising the National Health Service, front line trauma expert Professor Neil Greenberg[13] urges leaders to task themselves in very human ways to achieve real results: improved performance, reduction of sick leave and increase in returns to duty. This 'nip-it-in-the-bud' approach includes reinforcing social bonds between supervisors and colleagues, structuring peer support (such as 'buddying up' shift staff to ensure end-of-shift reviews are conducted) and helping supervisors feel confident to speak to team members about their mental health. What is more, Greenberg reinforces the need to embrace the potential for officers and staff to develop resilience in the post by avoiding harmful processes (such as

Table 5.2: MINDSPACE checklist of influences on our behaviour for use when making policy

MINDSPACE	Influences on our behaviour	Notes on police trauma resilience
Messenger	We are heavily influenced by who communicates information	Share experiences – genuine stories of getting through difficult jobs or times in policing
Incentives	Our responses to incentives are shaped by predictable mental shortcuts such as strongly avoiding losses	Incentivise teams to realise trauma impact isn't a 'loss' to avoid at all costs, but an opportunity for collective learning and resilience
Norms	We are strongly influenced by what others do	'Start by joining': lead by example of acknowledging that trauma impact happens
Defaults	We 'go with the flow' of pre-set options	Insert trauma impact monitoring as a pre-set option in sickness, risk and occupational health data
Salience	Our attention is drawn to what is novel and seems relevant to us	New recruits, new post-COVID working practices offer forces a fresh chance to put faces and voices to new trauma resilience work
Priming	Our acts are often influenced by subconscious cues	Formalise basic awareness training and key mental resilience techniques into initial training and CPD
Affect	Our emotional associations can powerfully shape our actions	Include emotional tone in communications about trauma exposure and performance and use science
Commitments	We seek to be consistent with our public promises and reciprocate acts	Communicate more openly and respectfully about the meaningfulness of the job that remains
Ego	We act in ways that make us feel better about ourselves	Promote self-care as a selfless way of ensuring we are fit and ready to be there for others on the job

Source: Dolan et al, 2020, adapted with considerations for the policing brain. See note 12

psychological screening) that can medicalise trauma impact and deter individuals from positively engaging with their shared experience of it on the job.

As we alluded to before, how an organisation builds a service's trauma resilience may well be determined by the extent to which the impact of trauma is acknowledged in the first place. This is where the voice of leadership can really resonate. Using words like 'resilience' when talking about trauma, has connotations of proactivity, dynamism and strength and can sound inspiring (in a detached kind of way), but does it show understanding of the whole, up-close everyday experience on the job? To reach resilience, we have learned that the brain needs to accept and deliberately work with our sense of vulnerability. We know from Chapter 3 that the 'F-word'[14] really needs to become part of our vocabulary for our brain to be able to regulate our responses. By avoiding fear, we inadvertently *get in our own way* of moving past it. We know from recent survey data that (even pre-COVID) 90 per cent of UK police were already trauma-exposed and had faced those moments of vulnerability (with over one in five of them currently living with its harmful impact[15]). The uncomfortable truth is that none of us are invincible, none of us are immune to indiscriminate incidents of shock, terror or suffering, and the human brain *has* to respond to such experiences with alarm (and fear) for us to be able to take action and survive. These vulnerable experiences are rich sources of learning how we make sense of our lives on the job, and leaders are missing a treat if they only engage with the stories of the seemingly unscathed. To borrow from a football analogy, in his book *Fever Pitch,* Nick Hornby talks about the Gus Caesar story to demonstrate the reality that we can get so far in life thinking we are invincible and yet, at the last hurdle, we can find ourselves tripped up by our own very human vulnerability: 'I think there is a real resonance in the Gus Caesar story: it contains a terrifying lesson for any aspirants who think that their own unshakable sense of destiny is significant'.[16]

Even if we retire relatively unscathed, it is very common for police to feel the impact of their experiences in their career when life becomes a little quieter (without the distractions that our avoidant tendencies relished on the job). Without preparation, the sudden shift to retirement can be little short of painful.[17] By embracing these techniques to master trauma resilience daily as best we can, we are avoiding the impact of avoidance in later life. But we need the opportunities to do this, and leadership has a responsibility to honour that.

Being human is about being authentic, honouring the reality of our experience. Authenticity in leadership has been valued across many disciplines in recent years, but there is little literature which talks about it specifically in the policing realm.[18] Authentic leadership is said to be about self-awareness, relational transparency (revealing information, thoughts and emotions to others), unbiased openness (being open to differing perspectives on oneself) and authentic behaviour (self-regulation guided by personal values and standards[19]). The way that these attributes are described echoes many of the benefits of the simple, everyday techniques described in Chapter 4, such as developing better self-awareness by training attention, using our biofeedback to understand others' motivations, using the chemical messengers of 'feelings' to guide our response to the demands around us, being open to fresh perspectives and reminding ourselves at the beginning of the day what our intentions are. All these attributes of leadership can be enhanced by working more smartly with the brain we already have, using the techniques that have already been shown to work – and practical application of these skills is worth considering for personal and professional development in leadership programmes.

Finally, taking pride at the top has the potential to do wonders for any workforce. Shame, humiliation and a lack of sense of doing meaningful work are now known to be a toxic mix for trauma impact in contemporary policing.[20] A great gift for any officer, team or police family would be hearing that the commitment and sacrifices that they make because of their service are being respected – and for that respect to be heard in everyday language in the workplace (rather than reserved for formal commendations, impact reports or bravery award ceremonies). Furthermore, to hear that leading a police force is something that brings someone else pride could make the world of difference to those in need of feeling that what they are going through as an officer or a family member is truly worth it.

Being a whole human

Recognising that police leaders can be human is something from which leaders, their officers and staff can benefit, and that benefit can resonate across an institution over time.[21] What is more, having permission to be a 'whole' human is integral for trauma resilience. Extraordinary things may happen in service, but that doesn't require us to be super-human in our experience of them.

In Chapter 2, we talked about how being in the police service can feel divided and fragmented as we compartmentalise our identity as being in work mode or non-work mode (such as being a family member, a friend or a citizen). For some, the split is too much and overwhelmingly identifying with policing can be appealingly straightforward. For example, we might often hear in work circles, officers proudly proclaiming 'Oh, I'm a 24/7 cop, I am – cop by day, cop by night; always a cop' (possibly in response to the legal requirement to deal with offences off duty, unless under the influence of alcohol). As inspiring as this 24/7 duty seems – we all know deep down that all of us were something or someone *before* we joined the service, and all of us have ideas, thoughts, senses, perceptions, roles, likes and dislikes every day that sometimes aren't anything to do with the fact we work with the police. And yet, the urge to be 'completely something' is clearly there. We want to feel wholly recognised, fully here. This was reflected in a very powerful media campaign by the Police Federation of Northern Ireland in 2016 called 'We Are Fathers/Mothers/Granddaughters' and for good reason.[22] Integrating who we are in our different roles makes a brain happy (as we learned in Chapter 3). By maintaining a false divide between life (or a self) in policing and life (or a self) outside of it, we prevent ourselves from seeing the whole picture of our experience and we avoid using our whole minds understand it – and because of this, genuine resilience is all the more likely to evade *us* over time.

This translates at an organisational level too. It may be tempting to encourage officers and staff to prioritise their job above other aspects of their lives, but this temptation seems to come from a place of uneasiness – almost as if the culture needs us to negate everything else that we think or feel, in case policing loses its edge or forces lose the commitment of their workforce. The irony is, by ignoring the whole person, institutions lose their edge by not tapping into sources of resilience that may come from individuals' whole life experience, and they also risk losing the respect, trust (and therefore commitment) of those they employ. If we as individuals hand over our mental health to an organisation[23] that cannot see a whole human, then we have little hope of feeling a genuine part of it.

Policing processes can mitigate against this by making practical moves toward treating officers and staff as whole humans, as people with lives and experiences and resources that extend beyond the immediacy of the job or task they are currently undertaking. Some simple recommendations are:

- Recognise that many police are part of wider families: include information for families of officers and staff about what it's like to support a loved one in their service on the job. Generate and sustain peer support networks for families and friends with opportunities for meaningful contact either online or face-to-face.
- Strategically reconsider policies that only provide support for officers on issues or for conditions that are directly, exclusively and demonstrably related to their employment. A core example is access to mental health treatment. Attempting to avoid having to deal with a person's non-work issues at work is a false economy, delaying access to swift treatment, disempowering individuals and compromising their relationship with their employer.
- Developing a language to describe the humanity of a police officer is worth working towards in internal and external force communications. By representing basic needs in communications (need for water, rest, time with family) grants those in service permission to self-care, strengthening their resilience and reminding the wider public that *to police is also to be human.*

It's happening

What makes all of this a lot more encouraging is that change is already happening. In Chapter 1, we were introduced to the idea of a #newbreed of police and Sarah Charman's hope for 'cultural plasticity'[24] through the new generations of recruits joining the service. It is reasonable to expect that millennial cohorts may have more awareness of how different brains work differently (or 'neurodiversity'), of how brain chemicals guide us in our behaviour ('emotional intelligence') and of how personal characteristics are more fully expressed in the community, than generations before them. With this awareness comes a need for a steady and firm grasp on what this means for the workplace and how those new in service can work with their own minds to steady their steer through the practical reality of contemporary law enforcement and public service. Here, we have a chance. Policing traits most prized by new recruits (in Chapter 1) comprised communication, empathy and gut instinct. What we have learned about the human brain (in Chapter 3) is that it has the *capacity for plasticity*, in specific areas, including communication, empathy and gut instinct. By introducing neuroplasticity to policing in ways such as these (and more), we have a chance of true, savvy cultural change – a new advantage for 2020s policing.

Post-COVID-19, the labour market and social world is proving to be different to life before the virus. We see changes in our relationships to the NHS, to public protection, changes in our working styles, our interconnectivity, our relationships to technology and our social integration. The relationship between the police and the public has to navigate these new landscapes. But before that, relationships *within* policing will also have to adapt to what this new world means for different policing roles, units, ranks, localities and even generations.

Just as fragmentation can be challenging for the human brain on an individual level (in terms of identity and sense of self), so too can it present challenges at the more macro level. Bonds within the 'policing family' need attention for them to be able to offer connection and stability in an increasingly divided and changing wider world. Social isolation (be it a sense of loneliness or a more tangible lack of social networks) is a formidable factor in physical disease, known to be directly responsible for the exacerbation of poor cardiovascular health, stroke, physical mobility, cognitive decline and dementia, Parkinson's, depression and severe mental illness in older adults and adolescents.[25] There is an irony here: eventually, one of the most significant risks to human health from COVID-19 may not be what the virus was (or is) itself, rather it will be the effect it had on isolating us as people, people who need(ed) each other in times of crisis. We can learn from this at a local level. Now more than ever, there is a need for police forces across the UK to take responsibility for the impact of reducing time for peers to spend making sense of their difficult experiences and of their policing lives in general. Again, the false economy of removing places for meaningful contact on (and after) shift may prove costly to a police service already struggling to deal with the fall-out from lack of investment in mental health – a cost largely unquantified, yet acutely felt by those on the front line. Losing connection between each other means losing hope for resilience. Increasing connection means increasing resilience. Biologically, neurologically, socially, psychologically, personally and professionally, quality time with each other prevents disease, dis-ease and promotes survival. Fact.

Quick practical wins

So, we have new generations, cultural changes, new techniques to help wire-in resilient policing traits. Before we go, where do we *start*? Research into trauma resilience in UK policing has been an adventure in itself -and along the way, we have met many individuals, teams and leaders who have made undeniably smart decisions and astute observations that bring home (to force) what resilience has the potential to *really mean*. These people have started from where they are, and not from a place which they think it might be nice to be seen to be starting from. Some of these decisions and observations speak for themselves and are shared here to give you a sense of the opportunities out there to explore in your own way.

Refresh induction

- Be up-front in job descriptions: highlight high-risk areas of work,[26] be explicit about the need for self-awareness and that certain cognitive traits can be usefully developed to do the job well.

- Ensure scrutiny over any psychological screening already in place to prevent unnecessary tick-box pre-recruitment exclusion of individuals to roles in which they may well come to thrive.
- Provide information and support for families and friends of new recruits in induction packs and encourage in-force engagement with families and activities with police family children and teens.

Introduce trauma impact monitoring

- Introduce practical trauma exposure and trauma impact monitoring. There are validated checklists and screens online that are ready (and easy) to use by individuals in non-clinical environments such as policing.[27] Effective signposting to sufficient and appropriate support to address the needs captured through monitoring is also highly recommended.
- Integrate traumatic event exposure monitoring as part of regular force workflow, such as task allocation (in-force control rooms, for example), in supervisions and continued professional development.
- Offer officers the option of flexible psychological assessments or supervisions which can be diarised on a needs basis (rather than allocating scheduled yearly appointments).
- Task the human resources team to include a new 'post-incident trauma impact' item on sickness absence recording. Being able to self-report trauma impact and then a healthy return to work afterwards is empowering for individuals' resilience and this is likely to be reflected at force level over time. It is highly recommended that finance teams work with human resources teams to assess the impact of new trauma monitoring on other sickness data and ill-health retirement (and their associated costs) regularly, such as annually.

Enhance communications

- Create new communications activities to develop a bespoke local common language and vocabulary on trauma exposure and trauma impact, which can be integrated into everyday internal communications and promoted through trauma impact-specific campaigns.

- Task communications and training teams to develop light-touch guidance for managers and supervisors to help them initiate trauma-confident conversations with teams. Include input from individuals who are known to be good communicators on awkward issues to help humanise and naturalise the supervision process.
- Establish a programme of trauma resilience-themed activities to encourage peer learning and personal practice, such as a force *think-off* challenge day, inviting officers to share their experiences and exchange tips, anecdotes and intentions for the year ahead. Encourage leaders to participate – either to share their experiences of trauma resilience or at least their interest in it.
- Communicate regularly and engagingly on all trauma resilience initiatives to normalise them as everyday practice in-force. Consider external local media communications on the impact of trauma on local officers, perhaps related to a local news item or wider current affairs.

Widen wellbeing workflow

- Avoid compartmentalising wellbeing as the responsibilities of certain areas or silos of force business. By assigning wellbeing to specific territories, it reduces collective responsibility, stunts cultural change and separates individuals from their sense of a shared experience on the job. Assigning wellbeing to specific business areas also increases the risks of forces being exploited by expensive contracts with external providers and limits engagement with the wider remit of trauma support in the public sector and other areas of emergency response.
- Join up areas of force business providing trauma impact interventions to work with communications and leaders to improve fluidity between initiatives and to offer peer support for those managing and delivering them.
- Be aware of equality of access to trauma management. There are many 'gaps' through which officers and staff may slip due to different infrastructures around their roles. Examples

include those working in family liaison and counter-terrorism networks, civilian vs staff roles, those working undercover or with other partners, such as the NCA and even those placed temporarily on scene guard on traumatic incidents.[28]

- Ensure clinical governance is in place to maximise the efficacy of trauma management interventions and to limit risks to reputation and harm from un-tested offers of support which have not been ethically cleared for safety and GDPR.[29] Work with other forces or bodies with research capacity or clinical leads (such as chief medical officers) if need be. Ensure that health and retirement decision-making boards are aligned with clinical governance and legal teams to protect individuals and forces from litigation or exploitation based on poor trauma management.

- Support officers and staff accessing therapies and interventions which come with an inherent understanding and experience of working with those on the front line. So many who are in police service report being put off by talking treatments because they feel they waste so much time educating their therapist or counsellor on the subtle and sometimes extreme working conditions and cultural differences (to other areas of the labour market), that they run out of energy and confidence to get to the heart of the matter on which they need clarity.[30]

- Reach out to other areas of emergency response to understand pressures on trauma resilience that front line work presents to individuals, in areas such as fire and rescue, the NHS, the RNLI,[31] Search and Rescue and the military. Policing may be unique in many ways but there is a lot to be said for sharing common ground with other key workers, especially in times of crisis.[32]

Conclusion

This book has intended to open up a new way of perceiving police resilience – from the inside out. By using the lens of science, we have looked at functions, structures and chemicals in the human brain that can explain much about how the human mind adjusts to policing as an everyday job. More than anything, we hope that you have also come to the conclusion that, albeit interesting, knowing about the biology of our brain isn't as important as establishing some clearer awareness of what is already – and has perhaps always been – going on underneath, in our thoughts, sensations, behaviour and (inter)actions on the job.

As we continue through the 2020s, ahead of us are many unknowns: the long-term impact of COVID-19, the practical and economic impact of Brexit, the future of ever unstable relationships between the public and police.[33] Yet, there is a certain resilience growing within the service, through engagement with new initiatives based on compassion and being trauma informed. What is more, officers are increasingly reporting that they are being treated with empathy when they disclose help-seeking and feel more confident in forces that are more open about mental health and all that comes with it. The last 15 or so years of neuroscience has brought insight into how the brain can change for good to a service that is already showing signs of change.

The question is, can individuals and forces work together to bring into action what is so pressingly needed *right now*: the chance for meaningful contact with someone who 'gets it' after a difficult incident, a common way of phrasing experiences that helps us communicate what we know we need to be able to say, deep down (without raising eyebrows or stiffening upper lips), ways of keeping connections between work and family intact so we don't feel so divided, the daily practice of being able to accept and go with the job, just as it is, without having to cut off, dissociate or pretend that things aren't as they are?

We hope that this exploration of the human brain (as applied to policing) has shown how we can go 'below the line' of our everyday understanding of how things are going, to honestly and robustly enquire to see clearly, and then to emerge again, intact and engaged, ready to reach out to others on and off the job and participate in a full and rewarding life.

If only in the simplest of ways, we have the chance to befriend the brain, befriend the lizard, mouse and monkey of our inner life and step back from their chatter for long enough to choose how *we* want to respond to the demands of the environment we find ourselves in. By regularly taking the briefest of time out, we have the chance to use our cognitive skills, to build on our innate intentions to help others, to maximise our inherent skills of getting to the facts, of reading people, of making sense of the problematic or difficult, of supporting people and by standing by what is right – to be police officers and staff, and to be human.

We have a kit we can pick up and put aside, we have some instructions we can follow and tweak, and we have a team of those who work with us, for us, who lead us and who stand beside us.

In each moment we can ask ourselves, how can I use *my mind's full capability* to take this task (this day, this job, this life) in the way I want it to go?

At that moment we have a choice.

But before we make the most of that choice, we have to ask ourselves a question, *do we want to change our minds*? What if when we changed our minds, we weren't racked with thinking we must have been 'wrong' before, but rather we became enthused, excited and proud that now we can change it, just to *get more right*.

To change our minds also takes bravery – bravery to take off the labels we have given ourselves, to step out of the boxes we operate from within, to turn away from the biases we have absorbed and propagated over time, to open up to trusting ourselves and our gut instincts, and to reconnect with what it *really is* that we want out of our lives – to be happy.

Chapter 5 snapshot

- The big step change we have in UK policing is to realise that how we go about our job is about how much we check in with how we think- and this works at an individual level and an institutional level.
- We know from neuroscience that the brain adapts to life on the job, it's just no one until now has explained how and why and what we can do about it.
- It's understandable that, particularly because of how the early 2020s are unfolding, forces can too easily step back from facing the impact of trauma on the front line because it can, quite frankly, seem overwhelming and untameable.
- On the flip-side, the UK police service is actually in a very strong position to progress like it never has before. With

the evidence base to prove that *accepting* trauma exposure as part of the job is the *ultimate key to resilience*, we can let the unhelpful coping mechanisms of denial and dissociation from the issue (on a personal and cultural level) take a back seat, and confident pragmatism steer us into a new era.

- Forces can make changes locally that count: they can improve open communication on normalising trauma exposure without making it 'a thing', they can monitor trauma impact in sickness data to demonstrate that it happens and the force accepts that people get over it, they can lead by being human and not reverting to archaic notions of machismo and denial, passed down from long-gone generations, and they can welcome all sides to being a person into policing, bringing in opportunities to support employees by factoring in families and life outside the job, relieving officers and staff of feeling split between their job and their life.
- There are quick wins: refreshing induction packages, introducing trauma impact monitoring, enhancing communications in forces and with the media and public and widening out where resilience can feature as an integral part of work across many areas of the organisation, ranging from policy to tactical command, workplace design to social media.
- Policing is not on its own. There is so much to share with other areas of emergency response, from all the life lessons and organisational traits of those in the ambulance service, fire and rescue, search and rescue, home and abroad.

Checklist

☐ What does the phrase 'policing mind' mean to you? How does realising that the human brain adapts to life on the job in good ways and bad change how you see yourself and others you work with or know in the service? How can you get to know your own unique policing mind better? *Does it start with five minutes a day? Does it start with protected time with a professional? Does it start with a humorous reflection on the craziness of the job (and your thinking) with a friend?*

☐ What do you think the future might look like with more of an understanding of how police think and are affected by life on the front line? Who needs to know about it and why? *What can you do in your 'bit' of the bigger picture to improve that understanding? Can you bring in some insights into police thinking on the job? Can you see what your wellbeing team is up to? Can you write an email to your local police commissioner, join an online group or speak to your federation?*

☐ How do you think you might be able to talk about the job now? *Has anything changed in the words you might choose to use or the things you might want to express to those around you or those who want to know what it's like to work for the police? Can you change your voice, raise it or both?*

☐ To what extent do you think you might have gone 'below the line' of everyday life into the adventure of the brain, and what might you tell others about that as you resurface and put the book down? *Is there a you-shaped tool kit you can show other people who might need to borrow from you? Or is it more about how you quietly go about the life you live? What is the smallest change you see in front of you now?*

☐ What does being happy on the job already mean to you? What means more to you now? *How can you go about looking after that and being proud to be doing what you do? Do you know what pride feels like? Can you let yourself feel it just a little bit more? Do you realise you deserve it?*

(*We do.* Good luck!)

Epilogue: 'Veil'

By Mark Chambers

Rolling from the yard to start
another job: professional mode engaged.
Seen as a uniform rescuer,
viewed as a sharp investigator,
heard as authority on difficult calls.
Never even skin-deep recognition:
just a role or a function.
Not bad enough to keep them off sick,
this day's peaks and troughs of home;
the officer on the cordon grieves for their nan,
the interviewing officer's last IVF try failed today,
the negotiator fears another death in contact.
You wore no seatbelt and had no clue
the ticket was written by a heartbroken hand.

From *Blue Verse* (2020)

Notes

Chapter 1

[1]   McDonald, H. (2020) 'Domestic abuse surged in lockdown, Panorama investigation finds', *The Guardian*, [online] 17 August, Available from: https://www.theguardian.com/society/2020/aug/17/domestic-abuse-surged-in-lockdown-panorama-investigation-finds-coronavirus [Last accessed 16/11/20].

[2]   Kilo, O. (2020) 'Dealing with Deaths and Bereavements', [online] 6 April, Available from: https://oscarkilo.org.uk/dealing-with-covid-19-deaths-and-bereavements/ [Last accessed 16/11/20].

[3]   Frith, B. (2020) 'Supporting police mental wellbeing through COVID-19 and BLM', *Mental Health at Work*, MIND, [online] Available from: https://www.mentalhealthatwork.org.uk/blog/supporting-police-mental-wellbeing-through-covid-and-blm/ [Last accessed 02/12/20].

Police Federation of England and Wales HQ (2020) 'Police Wellbeing and Coronavirus Anxiety', [video] 17 April, Available from: https://www.youtube.com/watch?v=JcLo2qKcNxA&feature=youtu.be [Last accessed 02/12/20].

University of Cambridge (2020) Police Resilience and Covid 19: An interview with Rick Hanson', [online] Available from: https://www.policingtrauma.sociology.cam.ac.uk/RickHansonandJess [Last accessed 02/12/20].

Waseem, Z. and Laufs, J. (2020) 'Policing a Pandemic: Impact of the COVID-19 Pandemic on Law Enforcement Agencies', Jill Dando Institute, University College London, [online] Available from: https://www.ucl.ac.uk/jill-dando-institute/sites/jill-dando-institute/files/impact_on_law_enforcement_final_no_11_.pdf [Last accessed 22/11/20].

[4]   Douaud, G., Lee, S., Alfaro-Almagro, F., Arthofer, C., Wang, C., Lange, F. et al, 'Brain imaging before and after COVID-19 in UK Biobank', *medRxiv* [preprint] Available from: https://www.medrxiv.org/content/10.1101/2021.06.11.21258690v1. doi: 10.1101/2021.06.11.21258690 [Last accessed 27/10/21].

[5]   Rowe, M. (2014) *Introduction to Policing* (5th edn), London: SAGE.

[6]   *BBC News* (2020) 'Man jailed for urinating at PC Keith Palmer memorial during protest', [online] 26 March, Available from: https://www.bbc.co.uk/news/uk-england-london-53051096 [Last accessed 02/12/20].

7   Gregory, A. and Deardon, L. (2021) 'Bristol protest: Seven arrested after 20 police officers injured in "Kill the Bill" demo "hijacked by extremists"', *The Independent*, [online] 26 March, Available from: https://www.inde pendent.co.uk/news/uk/crime/bristol-protest-police-arrest-riot-b1820 467.htmlt [Last accessed 24/03/21].

8   Author replaced Independent Police Complaints Commission with IOPC. Italics author's own.

    Sutherland, J. (2017) *Bue: Keeping the Peace and Falling to Pieces*, London: Widenfield and Nicholson, Orion Publishing, p 215.

9   Waddington, P.A.J. (1999) 'Police (canteen) sub-culture – an appreciation', *British Journal of Criminology*, 39(2): 287–309.

    Hesketh, I. and Williams, E. (2017) 'A new canteen culture: The potential to use social media as evidence in policing', *Policing* 11(3): 346–355.

10 Houdmont, J., Elliott-Davies, M. and Donnelly, J. (2019) 'Single crewing in English and Welsh policing: frequency and associations with violence towards and injuries in officers', *Policing and Society*, 29(7): 820–833.

11 Elliott-Davies, M. and Houdmont, J. (2018) *Officer Demand, Capacity, and Welfare Survey Initial Report – Descriptive Results*, Leatherhead: Police Federation of England and Wales R101/2018.

12 Rowe, M. (2020) *Policing the Police: Challenges of Democracy and Accountability* (1st edn), Bristol: Policy Press.

13 Police Federation 'Protect the Protectors', [online] Available from: https://www.polfed.org/campaigns/protect-the-protectors/ [Last accessed 15/11/20].

14 Hesketh, I. and Cooper, C. (2017) *Managing Health and Wellbeing in the Public Sector: A Guide to Best Practice.* London: Routledge Psychology Press.

15 Oscar Kilo (2020) [online] Available from: https://www.oscarkilo.org/ [Last accessed 17/11/20].

16 Direct quote from author S.-J. Lennie, see Lennie, S.-J., Crozier Sarah, E. and Sutton, A. (2019) 'Robocop – The depersonalisation of police officers and their emotions: A diary study of emotional labor and burnout in front line British police officers', *International Journal of Law, Crime and Justice*, [online] June, Available from: https://www.sciencedirect.com/scie nce/article/abs/pii/S1756061619302836 [Last accessed 27/10/21].

17 Meechan, F. (2017) 'The compassion at work toolkit', *Compassion at Work Sub-Group of the National Forum for Health and Wellbeing at Work*, [online] Available from: https://oscarkilo.org.uk/app/uploads/2017/12/Compass ion-at-Work-Toolkit-FINAL-5-December-2017.pdf [Last accessed 22/11/20].

18 Grove, R. and O'Connor, M. (2020) 'We asked for workers, they sent us humans: Examining trauma informed supervision for police officers', *Achieving for Children with Camden and Islington NHS Trust*, [online] Available from: https://www.achievingforchildren.org.uk/news-trauma-informed-police-supervision/ [Last accessed 27/10/21].

[19] Brewin, C. and Burgess, N. (2014) 'Contextualisation in the revised dual representation theory of PTSD: A response to Pearson and colleagues', *Journal of Behavior Therapy and Experimental Psychiatry*, 45(1): v217–219.

[20] Porges, S.W. and Carter, C.S. (2017) 'Polyvagal theory and the social engagement system', *Complementary and Integrative Treatments in Psychiatric Practice*, 221.

[21] Office for National Statistics, Elkin, M. (2020) 'Child sexual abuse in England and Wales', Office for National Statistics, [online] 5 March, Available from: https://www.ons.gov.uk/peoplepopulationandcommun ity/crimeandjustice/bulletins/childabuseinenglandandwales/march2020 [Last accessed 24/11/20].

[22] Park, C.L., Mills, M.A. and Edmondson, D. (2012) 'PTSD as meaning violation: testing a cognitive worldview perspective', *Psychological Trauma*, 4(1): 66–73.

Williamson, V., Murphy, D., Phelps, A., Forbes, D. and Greenberg, N. (2021) 'Moral injury: the effect on mental health and implications for treatment', *The Lancet* 8(6): 453–455.

[23] Commission for Countering Extremism (2020) 'COVID-19 How Hateful Extremists Are Exploiting the Pandemic', [online] July, Available from: https://assets.publishing.service.gov.uk/government/uploads/sys tem/uploads/attachment_data/file/906724/CCE_Briefing_Note_001. pdf [Last accessed 24/11/20].

[24] Richards, A. (2015) *Conceptualizing Terrorism*, Oxford: Oxford University Press.

Lowe, D. (2017) 'Prevent strategies: the problems associated in defining extremism: the case of the United Kingdom', *Studies in Conflict & Terrorism*, 40(11): 917–933.

[25] Canetti-Nisim, D., Halperin, E., Sharvit, E. and Hobfoll, S.E. (2009) 'A new stress-based model of political extremism: personal exposure to terrorism, psychological distress, and exclusionist political attitudes', *Journal of Conflict Resolution* 53(3): 363–389.

[26] The NPCC reports in their 2019 National Strategy on Policing and Mental Health that 'Her Majesty's Chief Inspector of Constabulary warned (2018) that over-reliance upon the police had become a "national crisis" because of a "broken mental health system"'. National Police Chiefs' Council (2019) 'National Strategy on Policing and Mental Health', [online] Available from: https://www.npcc.police.uk/Mental%20Health/Nat%20Strat%20Fi nal%20v2%2026%20Feb%202020.pdf [Last accessed 26/11/20].

[27] Campbell, D. (2020) 'Police 999 callouts to people suffering with mental health crises soars', *The Guardian*, 18 October, [online] Available from: https://www.theguardian.com/society/2020/oct/18/police-999- callouts-to-people-suffering-mental-health-crises-soars [Last accessed 26/ 11/20].

28 National Police Chiefs' Council (2019) 'National Strategy on Policing and Mental Health', [online] Available from: https://www.npcc.police.uk/Mental%20Health/Nat%20Strat%20Final%20v2%2026%20Feb%202020.pdf [Last accessed 26/11/20].
    Police Service of Northern Ireland, 'Multi Agency Triage Team Pilot', [online] Available from: https://www.psni.police.uk/advice_information/policing-and-mental-health/ [Last accessed 26/11/20].

29 National Police Chief's Council (2019) 'National Strategy on Policing and Mental Health', [online] Available from: https://www.npcc.police.uk/Mental%20Health/Nat%20Strat%20Final%20v2%2026%20Feb%202020.pdf [Last accessed 26/11/20].

30 Bayley, D. (1994) *Police for the Future*, New York: Oxford University Press, in Rowe, M. (2014) *Introduction to Policing* (5th edn), London: SAGE.

31 HMICFRS (2019) 'State of Policing: The Annual Assessment of Policing in England and Wales', London: Her Majesty's Chief Inspector of Constabulary, p 9, [online] Available from: https://www.justiceinspectorates.gov.uk/hmicfrs/wp-content/uploads/state-of-policing-2019.pdf [Last accessed 26/11/20].

32 National Police Wellbeing Service https://www.college.police.uk/News/College-news/Pages/National_well_service_launch_April_2019.aspx [Last accessed 29/11/20].

33 Policing Research Unit, University of Durham (2020) 'National Policing Wellbeing Survey 2019: Summary of Evidence and Insights', [online] Available from: https://oscarkilo.org.uk/app/uploads/2020/06/ISSUED-2019-National-Police-Wellbeing-Survey-1.pdf [Last accessed 29/11/20].

34 The report offers the reader an average score of anxiety in the past three months and on a scale of 0 to 10, using an unknown scale, at 6.37.

35 Miller, J.K., McDougall, S., Thomas, S., Wiener, J.M. (2017) 'Impairment in active navigation from trauma and post-traumatic stress disorder', *Neurobiology of Learning and Memory*, 140: 114–123.

36 Police Care UK is a registered charity in England and Wales (1151322) and Scotland (SC0047767). Company limited by guarantee registered in England and Wales (08426630). Previously the Police Dependants' Trust, Registered Charity Number: 251021.

37 Brewin, C.R., Miller, J.K., Soffia, M., Peart, A. and Burchell, B. (2020) 'Posttraumatic stress disorder and complex posttraumatic stress disorder in UK police officers', *Psychological Medicine*: 1–9.

38 Hansard (2020) 'Mental health and policing', *House of Commons Chamber*, Vol. 684, [online] Available from: https://hansard.parliament.uk/commons/2020-11-25/debates/09498FC1-A8DE-4A80-AA61-0BEC55FF251E/MentalHealthSupportPolicing [Last accessed 01/12/20].

39 Syed, S., Ashwick, R., Schlosser, M., et al (2020) 'Global prevalence and risk factors for mental health problems in police personnel: a systematic review and meta-analysis', *Occupational and Environmental Medicine*, 77: 737–747.

40 Stevelink, S., Opie, E., Pernet, D., Gao, H., Elliott, P., Wessely, S., Fear, N.T., Hotopf, M. and Greenberg, N. (2020) 'Probable PTSD, depression and anxiety in 40,299 UK police officers and staff: Prevalence, risk factors and associations with blood pressure', *PloS One*, 15(11).

41 Brewin, C.R., Andrews, B. and Valentine, J.D. (2000) 'Meta-analysis of risk factors for posttraumatic stress disorder in trauma-exposed adults', *Journal of Consulting and Clinical Psychology*, 68(5): 748–766.

42 Brewin, C.R., Miller, J.K., Soffia, M., Peart, A. and Burchell, B. (2020) 'Posttraumatic stress disorder and complex posttraumatic stress disorder in UK police officers', *Psychological Medicine*: 1–9.

43 Miller, J.K., Brewin, C.R., Burchell, B.J. Soffia, M., Elliot-Davies and Peart, A. (2021) 'The development of a UK Police Traumatic Events Checklist', *The Police Journal*, Available from: https://journals.sagepub.com/doi/full/10.1177/0032258X211002597 [Last accessed 27/10/21].

44 Miller, J.K., Soffia, M., Brewin, C.B. and Burchell, B. (2020) 'Policing: The Job and the Life Survey 2018 Summary Report', *Police Care UK*, [online] Available from: https://www.policecare.org.uk/wp-content/uploads/PoliceCareUK_TJTL-Report-.pdf [Last accessed 01/12/20].

45 Miller, J.K., Brewin, C.R., Burchell, B.J., Soffia, Elliot-Davies, M. and Peart, A. (2021) 'The development of a UK Police Traumatic Events Checklist', *The Police Journal*, Available from: https://journals.sagepub.com/doi/full/10.1177/0032258X211002597 [Last accessed 27/10/21].

46 Foley, J., Hassett, A., Williams, E. (2021) 'Getting on with the job: A systematised literature review of secondary trauma and post-traumatic stress disorder (PTSD) in policing within the United Kingdom (UK)', *The Police Journal*, [online] Available from: https://journals.sagepub.com/doi/full/10.1177/0032258X21990412 [Last accessed 27/10/21].

Bride, B.E., Robinson, M.M., Yegidis, B. and Figley, C.R. (2004) 'Development and validation of the secondary traumatic stress scale', *Research on Social Work Practice*, 14(1): 27–35.

Hurrell, A.-K., Draycott, S. and Andrews, L. (2018) 'Secondary traumatic stress in police officers investigating childhood sexual abuse', *Policing: An International Journal*, 41(5): 636–650.

Tehrani, N. (2018) 'Psychological well-being and workability in child abuse investigators', *Occupational Medicine*, 68(3): 165–170.

Gray, C. and Rydon-Grange, M. (2020) 'Individual characteristics, secondary trauma and burnout in police sexual and violent offending teams', *The Police Journal*, 93(2): 146–161.

47 Perez, L.M., Jones, J., Englert, D.R. and Sachau, D. (2010) 'Secondary traumatic stress and burnout among law enforcement investigators exposed to disturbing media images', *Journal of Police and Criminal Psychology* 25(2): 113–124.

Burruss, G.W., Holt, T.J., and Wall-Parker, A. (2017) 'The hazards of investigating internet crimes against children: digital evidence handlers' experiences with vicarious trauma and coping behaviors', *American Journal of Criminal Justice* 43(3): 433–447.

48 Golding, S.E., Horsfield, C., Davies, A., Egan, B., Jones, M., Raleigh, M., Schofield, P., Squires, A., Start, K., Quinn, T. and Cropley, M. (2017) 'Exploring the psychological health of emergency dispatch centre operatives: a systematic review and narrative synthesis', *PeerJ*, 5: e3735.

49 Robinson, H.M., Sigman, M.R. and Wilson, J.P. (1997) 'Duty-related stressors and PTSD symptoms in suburban police officers', *Psychological Reports*, 81(3): 835–845.

Wilson, F.C. (1997) 'Psychological distress in police officers following critical incident's', *The Irish Journal of Psychology*, 18(3): 321.

Wilson, L.C. (2015) 'A systematic review of probable posttraumatic stress disorder in first responders following man-made mass violence', *Psychiatry Research*, 229(1): 21–26.

Green, C. (2001) 'Human remains and the psychological impact on police officers: excerpts from psychiatric observations', *Australasian Journal of Disaster and Trauma Studies*, 5(2).

Gersons, B. (1989) 'Patterns of PTSD among police officers following shooting incidents: a two-dimensional model and treatment implications', *Journal of Traumatic Stress*, 2(3): 247–257.

Lonsway, K.A. and Welch, S. (2004) 'Witnessing an accidental shooting at the police training academy: Professional and psychological outcomes', *Women & Criminal Justice*, 15(3–4): 59–79.

Colin, L., Nieuwenhuys, A., Visser, A. and Oudejans, R.R.D. (2014) 'Positive effects of imagery on police officers' shooting performance under threat', *Applied Cognitive Psychology*, 28(1): 115–121.

Novy, M. (2012) 'Cognitive distortions during law enforcement shooting', *Activitas Nervosa Superior* (54): 60–66.

50 Charman, S. (2017) *Police Socialisation, Identity and Culture: Becoming Blue*, London: Palgrave Macmillan.

51 Kaku, M. (2014) 'The golden age of neuroscience has arrived', *Wall Street Journal*, [online] August 20, Available from: https://www.wsj.com/artic les/michio-kaku-the-golden-age-of-neuroscience-has-arrived-1408577 023 [Last accessed 27/10/21].

52 Schwartz, J.M. and Begley, S. (2002). *The Mind and the Brain: Neuroplasticity and the Power of the Mental Force*, New York: HarperCollins Publishers.

53 Functional Magnetic Resonance Imaging (fMRI)

54 Covey, T.J., Shucard, J.L., Violanti, J.M., Lee, J. and Shucard, D.W. (2013) 'The effects of exposure to traumatic stressors on inhibitory control in police officers: A dense electrode array study using a Go/NoGo continuous performance task', *International Journal of Psychophysiology*, 87(3): 363–375.

55 Green, B. (2004) 'Post-traumatic stress disorder in UK police officers', *Current Medical Research and Opinion*, 20 (1): 101–105.

Novy, M. (2012) 'Cognitive distortions during law enforcement shooting', *Activitas Nervosa Superior* (54): 60–66.

Kavanagh, E.L. (2006) 'A cognitive model of firearms policing', *Journal of Police and Criminal Psychology*, 21: 25–36.

Williot, A. and Blanchette, I. (2020) 'The influence of an emotional processing strategy on visual threat detection by police trainees and officers', *Applied Cognitive Psychology*, 34: 295–307.

Mercadillo, R.E., Alcauter, S., Fernândez-Ruiz, J. and Barrios, F.A. (2015) 'Police culture influences the brain function underlying compassion: A gender study', *Social Neuroscience*, 10(2): 135–152.

McPherson-Sexton, S.A. (2006) 'Normal memory versus traumatic memory formation', *Journal of Police Crisis Negotiations*, 6(2): 65–78.

Tegeler, C.L., Shaltout, H.A., Lee, S.W., Simpson, S.L., Gerdes, L. (2020) 'Pilot trial of a noninvasive closed-loop neurotechnology for stress-related symptoms in law enforcement: improvements in self-reported symptoms and autonomic function', *Global Advances in Health and Medicine*, 9.

Henig-Fast, K., Werner, N.S., Lermer, R., Latscha, K., Meister, F., Reiser, M., Engel R.R. and Meindl, T. (2009) 'After facing traumatic stress: Brain activation, cognition and stress coping in policemen', *Journal of Psychiatric Research,* 43(14): 1146–1155.

Lindauer, R.J.L, Booij, J., Habraken, J.B.A, Uylings, H.B.M, Olff, M., Carlier, I.V.E. et al (2004) 'Cerebral blood flow changes during script-driven imagery in police officers with posttraumatic stress disorder', *Biological Psychiatry*, 56(11): 853–861.

Van Zuiden, M., Savas, M., Koch, S.B.J., Nawijn, L., Staufenbiel, S.M., Frijling, J.L., Veltman, D.J., Van Rossum, E.F.C. and Olff, M. (2019) 'Associations among hair cortisol concentrations, posttraumatic stress disorder status, and amygdala reactivity to negative affective stimuli in female police officers', *Journal of Traumatic Stress*, 32(2): 238–248.

Galatzer-Levy, I.R., Steenkamp, M.M., Brown, A.D., Qian, M., Inslicht, S., Henn-Haase, C., Otte, C., Yehuda, R., Neylan, T.C. and Marmar, C.R. (2014) 'Cortisol response to an experimental stress paradigm prospectively predicts long-term distress and resilience trajectories in response to active police service', *Journal of Psychiatric Research*, 56(1): 36–42.

Yao, Z., Yuan, Y., Buchanan, T.W., Zhang, K., Zhang, L. and Wu, J. (2016) 'Greater heart rate responses to acute stress are associated with better post-error adjustment in special police cadets', *PloS One*, 11.7.

Shucard, J.L., Cox, J., Shucard, D.W., Fetter, H., Chung, C., Ramasamy, D. and Violanti, J. (2012) 'Symptoms of posttraumatic stress disorder and exposure to traumatic stressors are related to brain structural volumes and behavioral measures of affective stimulus processing in police officers', *Psychiatry Research Neuroimaging*, 204(1): 25–31.

Lindauer, R.J.L, Vlieger, E-J., Jalink, M., Olff, M., Carlier, I.V.E, Majoie, C.B.L.M. et al (2004) 'Smaller hippocampal volume in Dutch police officers with posttraumatic stress disorder', *Biological Psychiatry*, 56(5): 356–363.

Miller, J.K., McDougall, S., Thomas, S. and Wiener, J. (2017) 'The impact of the brain-derived neurotrophic factor gene on trauma and spatial processing', *Journal of Clinical Medicine*, 6(12): 108.

Baldacara, L., Araujo, C., Assuncao, I., Da Silva, I., Jackowski, A.P. (2016) 'Reduction of prefrontal thickness in military police officers with post-traumatic stress disorder', *Archives of Clinical Psychiatry*, 44(4): 94–98.

Van Der Werff, S.J.A, Elzinga, B.M, Smit, A.S and Van Der Wee, N.J.A. (2017) 'Structural Brain Correlates of Resilience to Traumatic Stress in Dutch Police Officers', *Psychoneuroendocrinology*, 85: 172–178.

Smith, N.I.J., Gilmour, S., Prescott-Mayling, L., Hogarth, L., Corrigan, J.D. and Williams, W.H. (2020) 'A pilot study of brain injury in police officers: a source of mental health problems?' *Journal of psychiatric and mental health nursing*, 7(30).

Subramaney, U., Vorster, M. and Pitts, N. (2011) 'HPA axis and immune responses in a Metro police cohort susceptible to PTSD', *Brain, Behaviour, and Immunity*, 25(2): 239.

Kaldewaij, R., Koch, S.B.J., Zhang, W., Hashemi, M.M., Klumpers, F. and Roelofs, K. (2019) 'High endogenous testosterone levels are associated with diminished neural emotional control in aggressive police recruits', *Psychological Science*, 30(8): 1161–1173.

Peres, J.F.P., Foerster, B., Santana, L.G., Fereira, M.D., Nasello, A.G., Savoia, M., Moreira-Almeida, A., and Lederman, H. (2011) 'Police officers under attack: resilience implications of an FMRI study', *Journal of Psychiatric Research*, 45(6): 727–734.

Setroikromo, S.N.W., Bauduin, S.E.E.C, Reesen, J.E, Der Werff, S.J.A, Smit, A.S, Vermetten, E. and Der Wee, N.J.A. (2020) 'Cortical thickness in Dutch police officers: an examination of factors associated with resilience', *Journal of Traumatic Stress*, 33(2): 181–189.

Lansing, K. (2005) 'High-resolution brain SPECT imaging and eye movement desensitization and reprocessing in police officers with PTSD', *The Journal of Neuropsychiatry and Clinical Neurosciences* 17(4): 526–532.

Vythilingam, M., Nelson, E.E., Scaramozza, M., Waldeck, T., Hazlett, G., Southwick, S.M, ... Ernst, M. (2009) 'Reward circuitry in resilience to severe trauma: an fMRI investigation of resilient special forces soldiers', *Psychiatry Research. Neuroimaging*, 172(1): 75–77.

Groer, M., Murphy, R., Salomon, K., Diamond, D., Van Eepoel, J., Bykowski, C. and White, K. (2009) 'Salivary biomarkers in law enforcement officers engaged in stressful virtual simulated training scenarios', *Brain, Behavior, and Immunity*, 23(S39).

Colin, L., Nieuwenhuys, A., Visser, A. and Oudejans, R.R.D. (2014) 'Positive effects of imagery on police officers' shooting performance under threat', *Applied Cognitive Psychology*, 28(1): 115–121.

Wei, Y. (2017) 'Assessment study on brain wave predictive ability to policemen's safety law enforcement', *Journal of Discrete Mathematical Sciences & Cryptography*, 20(1): 193–204.

Covey, T.J., Shucard, J.L, Violanti, J.M., Lee, J. and Shucard, D.W. (2013) 'The effects of exposure to traumatic stressors on inhibitory control in police officers: a dense electrode array study using a go/nogo continuous performance task', *International Journal of Psychophysiology* 87(3): 363–375.

Skurko, E.V. (2011) 'Models of artificial neuron networks and latent semantic analysis during monitoring of legislation and in the law-enforcement practice of Russia', *Scientific and Technical Information Processing* 38(3): 207–211.

[56] UNSUNG is another initiative established in 2020 which is committed to supporting Armed Forces, doctors, nurses and paramedics, firefighters, law enforcement and rescue services by raising money to develop a platform to support, honour and heal the individuals and families across the globe facing the long-term impact of serving in the provision of critical services to humankind. Available from: https://www.unsungfoundation.org/ [Last accessed 11/02/21].

[57] Sharp, M.L., Harrison, V., Solomon, N., Fear, N., King, H. and Pike, G. (2020) 'Assessing the mental health and wellbeing of the Emergency Responder community in the UK', *Open Research Online* Open University, The Royal Foundation and King's College London (King's Centre for Military Health Research, KCMHR), [online] Available from: https://kcmhr.org/erreport2020-mentalhealth-wellbeing/ [Last accessed 27/10/21].

Chapter 2

[1] University of Cambridge and Police Care UK (2019) *Policing: The Job and the Life* (unpublished data, with permission from Police Care UK). Comments from police and staff were offered freely in response to the open question, 'Is there anything else you'd like to say?'

[2] © 2020 Home Box Office, Inc. All Rights Reserved.

[3] Oskar Kilo (2017) 'From Surviving to Thriving', [video] Available from: https://oscarkilo.org.uk/command-resilience-wellbeing-surviving-thriving/ [Last accessed 04/01/21].

[4] The phrase is associated with Darwin but actually derives from a contemporary, Herbert Spencer. Spencer, H. (1864) *Principles of Biology*, London: Williams and Norgate.

[5] Ekman, P. (1999) in *Handbook of Cognition and Emotion*, T. Dalgleish and M. Power (eds), London: Wiley and Sons, p 138.

[6] Ekman, P. (1992) 'An argument for basic emotions', *Cognition and Emotion*, 6(3–4): 69–200.

[7] Cowen, A.S., Manokara, K., Fang, X., Sauter, D., Brooks, J.A., and Keltner, D. (2021, June 9) 'Facial movements have over twenty dimensions of perceived meaning that are only partially captured with traditional methods'. https://doi.org/10.31234/osf.io/hc93t.

[8] Manning, P.K. (2014) 'Policing: privatizing and changes in the policing web', in J. Brown (ed) *The Future of Policing*, Abingdon: Routledge, pp 23–39.

Niederhoffer, A. and Niederhoffer, E. (1978) *The Police Family: From Station House to Ranch House*, Lexington, MA: Aero Publishers.

Ryan, A.M., Kriska, S. David, K.S., West, B.J., and Sacco, J.M. (2001) 'Anticipated work family conflict and family member views: role in police recruiting', *Policing: An International Journal of Police Strategies and Management*, 24(2): 228–239.

Carpenter, D. (2001) 'Police with families: states with obligations', *Law and Order*, 49(5): 119.

9 Wolter, C., Santa Maria, A., Gusy, B., Lesener, T., Kleiber, D. and Renneberg, B. (2019) 'Social support and work engagement in police work. The mediating role of work-privacy conflict and self-efficacy', *Policing: An International Journal of Police Strategies and Management,* 42(6): 1022–1037.

10 University of Cambridge and Police Care UK (2019) *Policing: The Job and the Life.* Available from: https://www.cam.ac.uk/sites/www.cam.ac.uk/files/inner-images/thejobthelife_findings.pdfs.pdf (cam.ac.uk) [Last accessed 24/03/21].

11 Miller, J.K., Brewin, C.R., Soffia, M., Elliott-Davies, M., Burchell, B. and Peart, A. (2021) 'The Development of a UK Police Traumatic Events Check list', *The Police Journal*, [online] Available from: https://doi.org/10.1177/0032258X211002597 [Last accessed 27/10/21].

12 University of Cambridge and Police Care UK (2019) *Policing: The Job and the Life* (unpublished data, with permission from Police Care UK).

We use the term 'flashbacks' to summarise 'powerful images or memories that sometimes come into their mind in which they felt the experience was happening again in the here and now' and the term 'nightmares' to summarise 'upsetting dreams that replayed part of that experience or were clearly related to the experience'.

13 University of Cambridge and Police Care UK (2019) *Policing: The Job and the Life.* Available from: https://www.cam.ac.uk/sites/www.cam.ac.uk/files/inner-images/thejobthelife_findings.pdfs.pdf (cam.ac.uk) [Last accessed 24/03/21].

14 Miller, J.K. (2016) 'Navigating trauma: how PTSD affects spatial processing', *Police Professional* (532).

Miller, J.K., McDougall S., Thomas, S. and Wiener, J.M. (2017) 'Impairment in active navigation from trauma and post-traumatic stress disorder', *Neurobiology of Learning and Memory* 140: 114–123.

Smith, K., Burgess, N., Brewin, C.R. and King, J.A. (2015) 'Impaired allocentric spatial processing in posttraumatic stress disorder', *Neurobiology of Learning and Memory*, 119: 69–76.

15 Brewin, C.R. (2018) 'Memory and forgetting', *Current Psychiatry Reports*, 28(10): 87.

16 Van der Kolk, B.A. (2014) *The Body Keeps the Score: Brain, Mind, and Body in the Healing of Trauma*, New York: Viking.

[17] With permission from Nick Cave. See also: https://www.independent. co.uk/arts-entertainment/films/nick-cave-financed-documentary-one-more-time-feeling-so-he-would-not-have-speak-journalists-about-death-his-son-bad-seens-album-skeleton-seeds-a7228331.html [Last accessed 24/ 03/21].

[18] Charman, S. (2017) *Police Socialisation, Identity and Culture: Becoming Blue*, London: Palgrave Macmillan.

[19] Police Care UK (2020) *Policing: The Job and the Life Survey 2018 Summary Report*, [online] Available from: https://www.policec are.org.uk/wp-content/ uplo ads/Police Care UK_TJTL-Rep ort-.pdf [Last accessed: 20/03/21].

[20] Caplan, J. (2003) 'Police cynicism: police survival tool?', *Police Journal (Chichester)*, 76(4): 304–313.

Skolnick, J. (2008) 'Enduring issues of police culture and demographics', *Policing and Society*, 18(1): 35–45.

[21] United States Study: Enciso, G., Maskaly, J., and Donner, C.M. (2017) 'Organizational cynicism in policing: examining the development and growth of cynicism among new police recruits', *Policing: An International Journal of Police Strategies and Management,* 40(1): 86–98.

Richardsen, A.M., Burke, R.J. and Martinussen, M. (2006) 'Work and health outcomes among police officers', *International journal of stress management,* 13(4): 555–574. The study addressed Type A personality with characteristics of competitiveness, ambitiousness, time urgency, impatience and hostility.

[22] Caplan, J. (2003) 'Police cynicism: police survival tool?', *Police Journal (Chichester)*, 76(4): 304–313.

[23] Caplan, J. (2003) 'Police cynicism: police survival tool?', *Police Journal (Chichester)*, 76(4): 311.

[24] Finnish Study: Papazoglou, K., Koskelainen, M. and Stuewe, N. (2019) 'Examining the relationship between personality traits, compassion satisfaction, and compassion fatigue among police officers'. *SAGE Open*, 9(1).

UK study: Burnett, M.E., Sheard, I. and St Clair-Thompson, H. (2020) 'The prevalence of compassion fatigue, compassion satisfaction and perceived stress, and their relationships with mental toughness, individual differences and number of self-care actions in a UK police force', *Police Practice and Research,* 21(4): 383–400.

[25] Burnett, M.E., Sheard, I. and St Clair-Thompson, H. (2020) 'The prevalence of compassion fatigue, compassion satisfaction and perceived stress, and their relationships with mental toughness, individual differences and number of self-care actions in a UK police force', *Police Practice and Research,* 21(4): 383–400.

[26] Sansô, N., Galiana, L., Oliver, A., Cuesta, P., Sânchez, C. and Benito, E. (2018) 'Evaluation of a mindfulness intervention in palliative care teams', *Psychosocial Intervention*, 27(2): 88–91.

[27] Stamm, B.H. (2002) 'Measuring compassion satisfaction as well as fatigue: developmental history of the compassion satisfaction and fatigue

test', in C.R. Figley (ed.) *Treating Compassion Fatigue*, New York: Brunner-Routledge, pp 107–119.

28 Papazoglou, K., Koskelainen, M. and Stuewe, N. (2019) 'Examining the relationship between personality traits, compassion satisfaction, and compassion fatigue among police officers', *SAGE Open*, 9(1).

29 Greenberg, N. and Wignall, M. (2012) 'An organizational approach to the management of potential traumatic events: trauma risk management (TRiM) – the development of a peer support process from the Royal Navy to the Police and emergency services', in R. Hughes, A. Kinder and C. Cooper (eds) *International Handbook of Workplace Trauma Support*, Oxford: Wiley-Blackwell, pp 181–198.

30 Boag-Munroe, F. (2019) *Pay and Morale Survey R048/2019*, Leatherhead: Police Federation of England and Wales.

31 Jackman, P.C., Henderson, H., Clay, G. and Coussens, A.H. (2020) 'The relationship between psychological wellbeing, social support, and personality in an English police force', *International Journal of Police Science and Management*, 22(2): 183–193.

32 University of Cambridge and Police Care UK (2019) *Policing: The Job and the Life*, [online] Available from: https://www.cam.ac.uk/sites/www.cam.ac.uk/files/inner-images/thejobthelife_findings.pdfs.pdf (cam.ac.uk) [last accessed 27/10/21].

33 Violanti, J.M., Ma, C.C., Gu, J.K., Fekedulegn, D., Mnatsakanova, A. and Andrew, M.E. (2018) 'Social avoidance in policing: associations with cardiovascular disease and the role of social support', *Policing: An International Journal of Police Strategies and Management*, 41(5): 539–549.

34 Taylor, S.E., Stanton, A.L. (2007) 'Coping resources, coping processes, and mental health', *Annual Review of Clinical Psychology*, 3(1): 377–401.

Jackman, P.C., Henderson, H., Clay, G., and Coussens, A.H. (2020) 'The relationship between psychological wellbeing, social support, and personality in an English police force', *International Journal of Police Science & Management*, 22(2): 183–193.

35 Sutherland, J. (2017) *Blue: A Memoir*, London: Orion.

36 Van der Kolk, B.A. (2014) *The Body Keeps the Score: Brain, Mind and Body in the Healing of Trauma*, New York: Viking.

37 Guha, A., Spielberg, J.M., Lake, J., Popov, T., Heller, W., Yee, C.M. and Miller, G.A. (2020) 'Effective connectivity between Broca's area and amygdala as a mechanism of top-down control in worry', *Clinical Psychological Science*, 8(1): 84–98.

38 Police Care UK (2020) *Policing: The Job and the Life Survey 2018 Summary Report*, [online] Available from: https://www.policecare.org.uk/wp-content/uploads/PoliceCareUK_TJTL-Report-.pdf [Last accessed: 20/03/21].

39 Van der Kolk, B.A. (2014) *The Body Keeps the Score: Brain, Mind and Body in the Healing of Trauma*, New York: Viking.

40 Van der Kolk, B. (2015) *The Body Keeps the Score: Brain, Mind, and Body in the Healing of Trauma*, New York: Viking.

41 Fredrickson, B.L. (2014) *Love 2.0: Creating Happiness and Health in Moments of Connection*, New York: Penguin Group.

42 With Devon and Cornwall Police and University of Exeter.

Tourky, M., Harvey, W. and Badger, L. (2021) *Quick Wins to Long-Term Outcomes: An Evaluation of Surfwell for Promoting the Health and Wellbeing of Police Officers*. Exeter University Business School, [online] Available from: https://ore.exeter.ac.uk/repository/bitstream/handle/10871/125 398/Surfwell%20Report%20%28March%2c%202021%29.pdf?sequence= 1&isAllowed=y [Last accessed 28/06/21].

Also see: https://whatworks.college.police.uk/Research/Research-Map/Pages/ResearchProject.aspx?projectid=815 [Last accessed 27/12/20].

Top findings included immediate personal gains through positive changes in mood, a sense of achievement, improved confidence, acceptance of mental health difficulties and renewed motivation. Sustained benefits included greater resilience to cope with future stressors, increased hope of coping with difficulties more effectively, optimism represented in an ability to see the world in a more positive light, a stronger belief in their own ability to improve their wellbeing and improved self-efficacy. Some officers also developed lasting self-care tools to help them to manage their wellbeing, such as setting boundaries, social reconnection and mindfulness. Benefits for the police force included the development of a positive view of the force because of the implementation of the Surfwell project, less sick leave and decisions by some officers to stay in their jobs because of their heightened sense of resilience.

43 Chandler, N. (2020) *Pay and Morale Survey 2020: Covid 19*, [online] Available from: https://www.polfed.org/media/16411/pay-and-morale-covid-report-v03.pdf [Last accessed 27/12/20].

44 University of Cambridge and Police Care UK (2019) *Policing: The Job and the Life* (unpublished data, with permission from Police Care UK).

45 Burke, R.J. and Mikkelsen, A. (2006) 'Burnout among Norwegian police officers: potential antecedents and consequences', *International Journal of Stress Management*, 13(1): 64–83.

Bakker, A.B. and Demerouti, E. (2014) 'Job demands-resources theory', in C. Cooper and P. Chen (eds), *Wellbeing: A Complete Reference Guide*, Chichester: Wiley-Blackwell, pp 37–64.

Wolter, C., Santa Maria, A., Gusy, B., Lesener, T., Kleiber, D. and Renneberg, B. (2019) 'Social support and work engagement in police work The mediating role of work-privacy conflict and self-efficacy', *Policing: An International Journal of Police Strategies & Management*, 42(6): 1022–1037.

46 Keltner, D. (2017) *The Power Paradox: How We Gain and Lose Influence*, New York: Penguin Books.

47 Wang, M. and Shi, J. (2014) 'Psychological research on retirement', *Annual Review of Psychology*, 65: 209–233.

48 Bullock, K., Garland, J. and Coupar, F. (2019) 'Police officer transitions to retirement in the United Kingdom: Social identity, social support, and (in)justice', *Policing & Society*: 1–15.

49 Marshall, R.E., Milligan-Saville, J.S., Steel, Z., Bryant, R.A., Mitchell, P.B., Harvey, S.B. (2020) 'A prospective study of pre-employment psychological testing amongst police recruits', *Occupational Medicine*, 70: 162–168.

Rona, R.J., Burdett, H., Khondoker, M., Chesnokov, M., Green, K., Pernet, D., Jones, N., Greenberg, N., Wessely, S. and Fear, N. (2017) 'Post-deployment screening for mental disorders and tailored advice about help-seeking in the UK military: a cluster randomised controlled trial', *Lancet*, 389: 1410–1423.

See: Greenberg, N. (2020) 'Mental Health Screening within Organisations: What's the Evidence?' Kings Centre for Mental Health Research, [webinar] Available from: https://www.youtube.com/watch?v=eNSOB1vh05s&feature=youtu.be [Last accessed 04/01/21].

50 This model proposes that personality consists of five dimensions which comprise: (1) agreeableness (ie likeability and cooperativeness with others); (2) conscientiousness (ie degree of organisation, persistence and motivation to achieve a goal); (3) neuroticism (ie opposite of emotional stability); (4) extraversion (ie level of assertiveness and contrasts with introversion); and (5) openness to experience (ie desire to seek out new experiences).

51 Costa, P.T. and McCrae, R.R. (1980) 'Influence of extraversion and neuroticism on subjective well-being: happy and unhappy people', *Journal of Personality and Social Psychology*, 38(4): 668–678.

52 Campbell, J. (1968) *The Hero with a Thousand Faces*. Princeton, NJ: Princeton University Press.

53 Baůarici, S.M. and Kilièaslan, Y. (2017) 'Hero's Journey as a Lattice Structure: A Case Study of Star Wars', *Journal of Balkan Libraries Union*, 5(2): 17–23.

54 Brach, T. (2021) *Remembering Our Belonging*, [Blog] Available from: https://www.tarabrach.com/remembering-belonging-1/ [Last accessed 24/03/21].

Chapter 3

1 Harari, Y.N. (2014) *Sapiens: A Brief History of Humankind*, Toronto: Signal.

2 Huff, T. (2010) *Intellectual Curiosity and the Scientific Revolution: A Global Perspective*, Cambridge: Cambridge University Press.

3 Harari, Y.N. (2014) *Sapiens: A Brief History of Humankind*. Toronto: Signal.

4 Schwartz, J.M. and Begley, S. (2002) *The Mind and the Brain: Neuroplasticity and the Power of the Mental Force*, New York: HarperCollins Publishers.

Hanson, R. (2020) *Neurodharma: New Science, Ancient Wisdom and Seven Practices of the Highest Happiness*, New York: Harmony.

Davidson, R.J. and McEwen, B. (2012) 'Social influences on neuroplasticity: stress and interventions to promote well-being', *Nature Neuroscience*, 15: 689–695. doi: 10.1038/nn.3093

5 Raichle, M.E. and Gusnard, D.A. (2002) 'Appraising the brain's energy budget', *Proceedings of the National Academy of Sciences*, 99(16): 10237–10239.

6 James, W. (1914) *The Energies of Men*, New York: Moffat, Yard and Company.

7 Siegel, D.J. (2010) *Mindsight*, Melbourne: Scribe.

8   Adapted from Siegel, D.J. (2010) *Mindsight*, Melbourne: Scribe.

9   Hanson, R. (2020) *Neurodharma: New Science, Ancient Wisdom and Seven Practices of the Highest Happiness*, New York: Harmony, p 107.

10   Hanson R. (2011) 'Hug the monkey', *Psychology Today*, 20 December, [online] Available from: https://www.psychologytoday.com/us/blog/your-wise-brain/201112/hug-the-monkey [Last accessed 130121].

11   Hanson, R. (2020) *Neurodharma: New Science, Ancient Wisdom and Seven Practices of the Highest Happiness*, New York: Harmony, p. 113.

12   Van der Kolk B.A. (1994) 'The body keeps the score: memory and the evolving psychobiology of posttraumatic stress', *Harvard Review of Psychiatry*, 1(5): 253–265.

13   Miller, J.K. (2016) 'Navigating trauma: how PTSD affects spatial processing', *Police Professional*: 532.

     Miller, J.K., McDougall S., Thomas, S. and Wiener, J.M. (2017) 'Impairment in active navigation from trauma and post-traumatic stress disorder', *Neurobiology of Learning and Memory*, 140: 114–123.

     Smith, K., Burgess, N., Brewin, C.R. and King, J.A. (2015) 'Impaired allocentric spatial processing in posttraumatic stress disorder', *Neurobiology of Learning and Memory*, 119: 69–76.

     Hanson, R. (2020) *Neurodharma: New Science, Ancient Wisdom and Seven Practices of the Highest Happiness*, New York: Harmony.

     Covey, T.J., Shucard, J.L., Violanti, J.M., Lee, J. and Shucard, D.W. (2013) 'The effects of exposure to traumatic stressors on inhibitory control in police officers: a dense electrode array study using a go/nogo continuous performance task', *International Journal of Psychophysiology*, 87(3): 363–375.

     Meyer, T., Smeets, T., Giesbrecht, T., Quaedflieg, C.W.E.M., Girardellie, M.M., Mackay, G.R.N. and Merckelbach, H. (2013) 'Individual differences in spatial configuration learning predict the occurrence of intrusive memories', *Cognitive, Affective and Behavioural Neuroscience*, 13: 186–196.

14   Miller, J.K., Peart, A. and Soffia, M. (2020) 'Can police be trained in trauma processing to minimise PTSD symptoms? Feasibility and proof of concept with a newly recruited UK police population', *The Police Journal*, 93(4): 310–331.

15   Kessler, H., Holmes, E.A., Blackwell, S.E., Schmidt, A.-C., Schweer, J.M., Býcker, A., Herpertz, S., Axmacher, N. and Kehyayan, A. (2018) 'Reducing intrusive memories of trauma using a visuospatial interference intervention with inpatients with posttraumatic stress disorder (PTSD)', *Journal of Consulting and Clinical Psychology*, 86(12): 1076–1090.

16   Neves, G., Cooke, S.F. and Bliss, T.V.P. (2008) 'Synaptic plasticity, memory and the hippocampus: a neural network approach to causality', *Nature Reviews Neuroscience*, 9: 65–75.

     Miller, J.K. and Peart, A., Soffia, M. (2020) Can police be trained in trauma processing to minimise PTSD symptoms? Feasibility and proof of concept with a newly recruited UK police population. *The Police Journal*, 93(4): 310–331.

17 Rozin, P. and Royzman, E.B. (2001) 'Negativity bias, negativity dominance, and contagion', *Personality and Social Psychology Review* 5(4): 296–320.

18 Hanson, R. (2020) *Neurodharma: New Science, Ancient Wisdom and Seven Practices of the Highest Happiness*, New York: Harmony.

19 Fredickson, B.L. (2013) Love 2.0: *Creating Happiness and Health in Moments of Connection*, New York: Plume, p 13.

20 Thanks to Forest Hanson on Patreon: https://www.rickhanson.net/being-well-podcast-the-optimism-bias-and-influencing-other-people-with-dr-tali-sharot/

   Sharot, T., Riccardi, A., Raio, C. Phelps, E.A. (2007) 'Neural mechanisms mediating optimism bias', *Nature*, 450: 102–105.

   Garrett, N., González-Garzón, A.M. Foulkes, L., Levita, L. and Sharot, T. (2018) 'Updating beliefs under perceived threat', *Journal of Neuroscience*, 38(36): 7901–7911.

21 Hanson, R. (2020) *Neurodharma: New Science, Ancient Wisdom and Seven Practices of the Highest Happiness*, New York: Harmony.

22 University of Cambridge and Police Care UK (2019) *Policing: The Job and the Life* (unpublished data, with permission from Police Care UK).

23 Siegel, D.J. (2010) *Mindsight*, Melbourne: Scribe.

24 Brewin, C.R., Miller, J.K., Soffia, M., Peart, A. and Burchell, B. (2020) 'Posttraumatic stress disorder and complex posttraumatic stress disorder in UK police officers, *Psychological Medicine*: 1–9.

25 Fredickson, B.L. (2013) *Love 2.0: Creating Happiness and Health in Moments of Connection*, New York: Plume.

26 Hull, A.M. (2002) 'Neuroimaging findings in post-traumatic stress disorder: Systematic review', *British Journal of Psychiatry*, 181(2): 102–110. Cambridge University Press.

   Rauch, S.L., van Der Kolk, B.A., Fisher, R.E., Alpert, N.M., Orr, S.P., Savage, C.R., Fischman, A.J., Jenike, M.A. and Pitman, R.K., et al (1996) 'A symptom provocation study of post-traumatic stress disorder using positron emission tomography and script driven imagery', *Archives of General Psychiatry*, 53: 380–387.

27 Stephens, R. and Robertson, O. (2020) 'Swearing as a response to pain: assessing hypoalgesic effects of novel "swear" words', *Frontiers in Psychology*, 11: 723.

28 Stephens, R. and Robertson, O. (2020) 'Swearing as a response to pain: assessing hypoalgesic effects of novel "swear" words', *Frontiers in Psychology*, 11: 723.

29 Siegel, D.J. (2010) *Mindsight*, Melbourne: Scribe.

30 Killingsworth, M.A. and Gilbert, D.T. (2010) 'A wandering mind is an unhappy mind', *Science*, 330: 932.

31 Raichle, M.E., MacLeod, A.M., Snyder, A.Z., Powers, W.J., Gusnard, D.A., Shulman, G.L. (2001) 'Inaugural article: a default mode of brain function', *Proceedings of the National Academy of Sciences*, 98(2): 676–682.

[32] Raichle, M.E., MacLeod, A.M., Snyder, A.Z., Powers, W.J., Gusnard, D.A., Shulman, G.L. (2001) 'Inaugural article: a default mode of brain function', *Proceedings of the National Academy of Sciences*, 98(2): 676–682.

[33] Hanson, R. (2020) *Neurodharma: New Science, Ancient Wisdom and Seven Practices of the Highest Happiness*, New York: Harmony.

[34] Andrews-Hanna, J.R. (2012) 'The brain's default network and its adaptive role in internal mentation', *The Neuroscientist: A Review Journal Bringing Neurobiology, Neurology and Psychiatry*, 18(3): 251–270.

[35] Hanson, R. (2020). *Neurodharma: New Science, Ancient Wisdom and Seven Practices of the Highest Happiness*, New York: Harmony.

[36] Courtesy of Tara Brach, Brach, T. (2013) 'Practicing Meditation: "Getting Out of Your Own Way"', [podcast] 13 May, Available from: https://www. tarabrach.com/practicing-meditation-getting-out-of-your-own-way-audio/ [Last accessed 17012021].

[37] Dispenza, J. (2010) *Evolve Your Brain: The Science of Changing Your Mind*, Florida: Health Communications.

[38] Hanson, R. (2020) *Neurodharma: New Science, Ancient Wisdom and Seven Practices of the Highest Happiness*, New York: Harmony.

[39] Hanson, R. (2020) *Neurodharma: New Science, Ancient Wisdom and Seven Practices of the Highest Happiness*, New York: Harmony.

[40] BBC News (2006) 'Spike "wrote world's best joke"', *BBC News*, 9 June, [online] Available from: http://news.bbc.co.uk/1/hi/5064020.stm#quote Last accessed 30/01/2020

[41] Hanson, R. (2020) *Neurodharma: New Science, Ancient Wisdom and Seven Practices of the Highest Happiness*, New York: Harmony.

[42] Calancie, O.G., Khalid-Khan, S., Booij, L., Munoz, D.P., Kingstone, A. and Miller, M.B. (n.d.) 'Eye movement desensitization and reprocessing as a treatment for PTSD: Current neurobiological theories and a new hypothesis', *Annals of the New York Academy of Sciences*, 1426(1): 127–145.

[43] Siegel, D.J. (2010) *Mindsight*, Melbourne: Scribe, p 62.

[44] Fitzgibbon, B.M., Kirkovski, M., Fornito, A., Paton, B., Fitzgerald, P.B. and Enticott, P.G. (2016) 'Emotion processing fails to modulate putative mirror neuron response to trained visuomotor associations', *Neuropsychologia*, 84: 7e13.

[45] Dan Siegel on his book, *Mindsight* (2010), What is mindsight? An interview with Dr. Dan Siegel, [Online] Available from: www.psychalive.org [Last accessed 11/21].

[46] P.G. Enticott, P.J. Johnston, S.E. Herring, K.E. Hoy and P.B. Fitzgerald (2008) 'Mirror neuron activation is associated with facial emotion processing', *Neuropsychologia*, 46(11): 2851–2854.

[47] Ekman, P. (1992) *Telling Lies Clues to Deceit in the Marketplace, Politics, and Marriage*, New York: W.W. Norton.

[48] Porges, S. (2011). *The Polyvagal Theory: Neurophysiological Foundations of Emotions, Attachment, Communication, and Self-Regulation*, New York: W.W. Norton.

Featured in: Being Well Podcast, Series 3, Episode 107 (2020). Available from: https://www.rickhanson.net/being-well-podcast-polyvagal-theory-with-stephen-porges/ [Last accessed 30/01/2021].

49 Alshami, A.M. (2019) 'Pain: is it all in the brain or the heart?' *Current Pain and Headache Reports*, 14; 23(12): 88.

50 Kulkarni, S., Ganz, J., Brayer, J., Becker, J., Becker, L., Bogunovic, M. and Rao, M. (2018) 'Advances in enteric neurobiology: the "brain" in the gut in health and disease', *Journal of Neuroscience*, 38(44): 9346–9354.

51 Hashemi, M.M., Gladwin, T.E., de Valk, N.M., Zhang, W., Kaldewaij, R., van Ast, V., Koch, S., Klumpers, F. and Roelofs, K. (2019) 'Neural dynamics of shooting decisions and the switch from freeze to fight', *Scientific Reports*, 9(1): 4240.

52 Fredickson, B.L. (2013) *Love 2.0: Creating Happiness and Health in Moments of Connection*, New York: Plume, p 118.

53 De Couck, M., Nijs, J. and Gidron, Y. (2014) You may need a nerve to treat pain: the neurobiological rationale for vagal nerve activation in pain management. *Clinical Journal of Pain*, 30(12): 1099–1105.

54 Immordino-Yang, McColl, A., Damasio, H. and Damasio, A. (2009) 'Neural correlates of admiration and compassion', *Proceedings of the National Academy of Sciences*, PNAS 0810363106 in Fredickson, B.L. (2013) *Love 2.0: Creating Happiness and Health in Moments of Connection*, New York: Plume.

55 Andrew, M.E., Violanti, J.M., Gu, J.K., Fekedulegn, D., Li, S., Hartley, T.A., Charles, L.E., Mnatsakanova, A., Miller and D.B., Burchfiel, C.M. (2017) 'Police work stressors and cardiac vagal control', *American Journal of Human Biology*, 29: e22996.

56 Cicchetti, D. and Rogosch, F. (2012) 'Gene × Environment interaction and resilience: Effects of child maltreatment and serotonin, corticotropin releasing hormone, dopamine, and oxytocin genes', *Development and Psychopathology*, 24(2): 411–427.

Hanson, R. (2020) *Neurodharma: New Science, Ancient Wisdom and Seven Practices of the Highest Happiness*, New York: Harmony.

57 Campbell A. (2010) 'Oxytocin and human social behavior', *Personality and Social Psychology Review*, 14(3): 281–295.

Fredickson, B.L. (2013) *Love 2.0: Creating Happiness and Health in Moments of Connection*, New York: Plume, p 51.

58 Merzenich, M., Nahum, M. and Van Vleet, T. (2013) 'Changing Brains', *Progress in Brain Research* (Volume 2, 1st ed), Oxford: Elsevier.

See also: https://www.rickhanson.net/get-started/ [Last accessed 31/ 01/21].

59 Hebb, D.O. (1949) *The Organization of Behavior*. New York: Wiley & Sons.

60 Miller, J.K., McDougall, S. and Thomas, S., Wiener, J. (2017) The impact of the brain-derived neurotrophic factor gene on trauma and spatial processing. *Journal of Clinical Medicine*, 6(108).

We will be sure to take genetic differences into consideration in Chapter 4 by offering alternative practices to ensure everyone has an equal chance of benefitting from the exercises.

61 Molteni, R., Barnard, R.J., Ying, Z., Roberts, C.K. and Gômez-Pinilla, F. (2002) 'A high-fat, refined sugar diet reduces hippocampal brain-derived neurotrophic factor, neuronal plasticity, and learning', *Neuroscience,* 112(4): 803–814.

Ji, D. and Wilson, M.A. (2007) 'Coordinated memory replay in the visual cortex and hippocampus during sleep', *Nature Neuroscience* (10): 100–107.

Ma, C.L., Ma, X.T., Wang, J.J., Liu, H., Chen, Y.F. and Yang, Y. (2017) 'Physical exercise induces hippocampal neurogenesis and prevents cognitive decline', *Behavioural Brain Research*, 317: 332–339.

Siegel, D.J. (2010) *Mindsight: The New Science of Personal Transformation,* New York: Bantam Books.

62 Hanson, R. (2020) *Neurodharma: New Science, Ancient Wisdom and Seven Practices of the Highest Happiness*, New York: Harmony.

63 In particular, compassion management: Mercadillo, R.E., Alcauter, S., Fernãndez-Ruiz, J. and Barrios, F.A. (2015) 'Police culture influences the brain function underlying compassion: A gender study', *Social Neuroscience*, 10(2): 135–152.

64 With reference to psychologist Bruce Perry, quoted by Forrest Hanson. Available from: https://www.rickhanson.net/being-well-podcast-polyva gal-theory-with-stephen-porges/ [Last accessed 20/02/2021].

Chapter 4

1 Jessie Potter speaking at the 7th Annual Woman to Woman conference, covered by T. Ahern in his article in *The Milwaukee Sentinel* (p 5, column 5), 24 October 1981.

2 Our use of the word 'unhelpful' is deliberate here: too often we use the word phrase 'bad habit' and this brings an unnecessarily 'judge-y' attitude to understanding how the brain works. Brains develop habits because they are trying to respond efficiently – that's all. Sometimes this works out well for us, sometimes it doesn't.

3 PPE = personal protective equipment.

4 Schuler, A.-L., Tik, M., Sladky, R., Luft, C.D.B., Hoffmann, A., Woletz, M., Zioga, I., Bhattacharya, J. et al (2019) 'Modulations in resting state networks of subcortical structures linked to creativity', *Neuroimage*, 195: 311–319.

Hagger, M.S., Wood, C., Stiff, C., Chatzisarantis, N.L. (2010) 'Ego depletion and the strength model of self-control: a meta-analysis', *Psychological Bulletin*, 136(4): 495–525.

5 Raichle, M.E.; MacLeod, A.M.; Snyder, A.Z.; Powers, W.J.; Gusnard, D.A. and Shulman, G.L. (2001) 'Inaugural Article: A default mode of brain function', *Proceedings of the National Academy of Sciences*, 98(2): 676–682.

6   Van der Kolk, B.A. (1994) 'The body keeps the score: memory and the evolving psychobiology of posttraumatic stress', *Harvard Review of Psychiatry*, 1(5): 253–265.

7   Police Care UK (2020) *Policing: The Job and the Life Survey 2018 Summary Report*. Available from: https://www.policecare.org.uk/wp-content/uplo ads/PoliceCareUK_TJTL-Report-.pdf [Last accessed: 200321].

8   53 per cent of over 16,000 respondents reported persistent difficulty getting to sleep in 2018. See: Miller, J.K., Soffia, M., Brewin, C.B. and Burchell, B. (2020) *Policing: The Job and the Life Survey 2018 Summary Report*, Police Care UK. Available from: https://www.policecare.org.uk/wp-content/ uploads/PoliceCareUK_TJTL-Report-.pdf [Last accessed 20/03/20].

9   Trauma Risk Management, [online] Available from: https://www.marcho nstress.com/page/p/trim [Last accessed 11/08/21].

10   Acheson, D.T., Gresack, J.E. and Risbrough, V.B. (2012) 'Hippocampal dysfunction effects on context memory: possible aetiology for post-traumatic stress disorder', *Neuropharmacology*, 62: 674–685.

11   Bate, S., Frowd, C., Bennetts, R., Hasshim, N., Portch, E., Murray, E. and Dudfield, G. (2019) 'The consistency of superior face recognition skills in police officers', *Applied Cognitive Psychology*, 33(5): 828–842.

     Rutkin, A. (2015) 'Lie-detecting algorithm can spot a guilty face', *New Scientist*, 228(3046): 22.

12   Shumen, J.R., Lang, P.J. and Keil, A. (2018) 'Face perception in social anxiety: visuocortical dynamics reveal propensities for hypervigilance or avoidance', *Biological Psychiatry*, 83(7): 618–628.

13   Threat perception becomes 'maladaptive' in police where there is over-exposure to trauma, leading to hypervigilance and inaccurate perceptions of what is a threat and what is not, and what is safe and what is not. Sixty-seven per cent of officers showed high levels of hypervigilance either by way of their having clinical levels of post-traumatic stress disorder (of which is a key symptom, a maladaption) or as being otherwise healthy officers (adapting to the demands of the job).

     Miller, J.K., Soffia, M., Brewin, C.B. and Burchell, B. (2020) *Policing: The Job and the Life Survey 2018 Summary Report*, Police Care UK. Available from: https://www.policecare.org.uk/wp-content/uploads/PoliceCare UK_TJTL-Report-.pdf [Last accessed 20/03/20].

14   Polite reminder: this is a reflective practice for working with anxiety in interpersonal relationships and is in no way a tactical practice for dealing with threatening behaviour in an operational context.

15   With great thanks to Lee and Steph for sharing their experiences of the police family for the benefit of others.

16   Hanson, R. (2020) *Neurodharma: New Science, Ancient Wisdom and Seven Practices of the Highest Happiness*, New York: Harmony, p 113.

17   Siegel, D.J. (2010) *Mindsight*, Melbourne: Scribe, p 187.

18   Ridley, J. (1935) 'Studies of interference in serial verbal reactions', *Journal of Experimental Psychology*, 18(6): 643–662.

19 Trauma Impact Prevention Techniques (TIPT), [online] Available from: https://policecare.org.uk/get-informed/trauma-impact-prevention-techniques-tipt/ [Last accessed 11/08/21].

20 Wimberger, L. (2017) 'Using Neuroscience to Find Healing and Happiness' Neuroscience Training Summit, published by Sounds True, Inc., [online] Available from: https://neuroscience-training-summit-2017-sfn.soundstrue.com/?sq=1 [Last accessed 28/10/21].

21 De Zavala, A.G., Lantos, D. and Bowden, D. (2018) 'Corrigendum: yoga poses increase subjective energy and state self-esteem in comparison to "power poses"', *Frontiers in Psychology*, 9 February.

22 Morgan, C.A., Grillon, C., Southwick, S.M., Davis, M. and Charney, D.S. (1995) 'Fear-potentiated startle in posttraumatic stress disorder', *Biological Psychiatry*, 38(6): 378–385.

  Andersen, P., Morris, R., Amaral, D., Bliss, T. and O'Keefe, J. (eds) (2007) *The Hippocampus Book*, Oxford University Press: London.

  Andero, R. and Ressler, K.J. (2012) 'Fear extinction and BDNF: translating animal models of PTSD to the clinic', *Genes, Brain and Behavior*, 11 (5): 503–512.

  Heldt, S.A., Stanek, L., Chhatwal, J.P. and Ressler, K.J. (2007) 'Hippocampus-specific deletion of BDNF in adult mice impairs spatial memory and extinction of aversive memories', *Molecular Psychiatry*, 12(7): 656–670.

  Maren, S. (2011) 'Seeking a spotless mind: extinction, deconsolidation, and erasure of fear memory', *Neuron* 70(9): 830–845.

  Peters, J., Dieppa-Perea, L.M., Melendez, L.M. and Quirk, G.J. (2010) 'Induction of fear extinction with hippocampal-infralimbic BDNF', *Science* (328): 1288–1290. Rosas-Vidal, L.E., Do-Monte, F.H., Sotres-Bayon, F. and Quirk, G.J. (2014) 'Hippocampal–prefrontal BDNF and memory for fear extinction', *Neuropsychopharmacology*, 39: 2161–2216.

23 Miller, J.K., Peart, A. and Soffia, M. (2020) Can police be trained in trauma processing to minimise PTSD symptoms? Feasibility and proof of concept with a newly recruited UK police population. *The Police Journal*, 93(4): 310–331.

24 It is important to distinguish here between passive, unintentional depersonalisation that can kick in when we dissociate from our lived (and often traumatic) experiences or from our emotional responses to them. What we are really talking about here is *non-personalisation*, not unnecessarily over-identifying with experiences in ways that are unhelpful for us.

  For more about depersonalisation, see: Lennie, S.-J., Crozier Sarah, E. and Sutton, A. (2019) 'Robocop – the depersonalisation of police officers and their emotions: a diary study of emotional labor and burnout in front line British police officers', *International Journal of Law, Crime and Justice*, [online] Available from: https://researchcommons.waikato.ac.nz/handle/10289/13269 [Last accessed 28/10/21].

25 Hanson, R. (2020). *Neurodharma: New Science, Ancient Wisdom and Seven Practices of the Highest Happiness*, New York: Harmony.

26 Brewer, J.A., Worhunsky, P.D., Gray, J.R., Tang, Y.Y., Weber, J. and Kober, H. (2011) 'Meditation experience is associated with differences in default mode network activity and connectivity', *Proceedings of the National Academy of Sciences*, 108(50): 20254–20259

Farb, N.A., Segal, Z.V., Mayberg, H., Bean, J., McKeon, D., Fatima, Z. and Anderson, A.K. (2007) 'Attending to the present: mindfulness meditation reveals distinct neural modes of self-reference', *Social Cognitive and Affective Neuroscience*, 2(4): 313–322.

27 This phrase is familiar to the Buddhist tradition and a form of it originates from the *Anatta-lakkhana Sutta: The Discourse on the Not-self Characteristic* (SN 22.59), translated from the Pali by N.K.G. Mendis *Access to Insight* (BCBS Edition), 13 June 2010 Available from: http://www.accesstoinsight.org/tipitaka/sn/sn22/sn22.059.mend.html [Last Accessed 160221].

28 Siegel, D.J. (2010) *Mindsight*, Melbourne: Scribe, p 162.

29 Hanson, R. (2020). *Neurodharma: New Science, Ancient Wisdom and Seven Practices of the Highest Happiness*. New York: Harmony, p 127.

30 Rousseau, P.-F., Boukezzi, S., Garcia, R., Chaminade, T. and Khalfa, S. (2020) 'Cracking the EMDR code: Recruitment of sensory, memory and emotional networks during bilateral alternating auditory stimulation', *Australian and New Zealand Journal of Psychiatry*, 54(8): 818–831.

31 Hanson, R. (2020) *Neurodharma: New Science, Ancient Wisdom and Seven Practices of the Highest Happiness*, New York: Harmony, p 184.

It is also worth noting that the lateral eye gaze of horizon scanning on the water may be a factor in the success of the wellbeing and peer support initiative, Surfwell, featured in Chapter 2 by Devon and Cornwall Police with University of Exeter. See: https://whatworks.college.police.uk/Research/Research-Map/Pages/ResearchProject.aspx?projectid=815 [Last accessed 27/12/20].

Tourky, M., Harvey, W. and Badger, L. (2021) *Quick Wins to Long-Term Outcomes: An Evaluation of Surfwell for Promoting the Health and Wellbeing of Police Officers*, Exeter: Exeter University Business School, [online] Available from: https://ore.exeter.ac.uk/repository/bitstream/handle/10871/125398/Surfwell%20Report%20%28March%2c%202021%29.pdf?sequence=1&isAllowed=y [Last accessed 23/07/21].

32 Kirk, U., Wieghorst, A., Nielsen, C.M. and Staiano, W. (2019) 'On-the-spot binaural beats and mindfulness reduces behavioral markers of mind wandering', *Journal of Cognitive Enhancement*, 3: 186–192.

Garcia-Argibay, M., Santed, M.A. and Reales, J.M. (2019) Efficacy of binaural auditory beats in cognition, anxiety, and pain perception: a meta-analysis. *Psychological Research*, 83(2): 357–372.

33 Sensing the inside of the body is sometimes called *interoception*.

34 Banyai, I. (1995) *Zoom*, London: Puffin.

[35] Trauma Impact Prevention Techniques (TIPT), [online] Available from: https://www.policecare.org.uk/get-informed/trauma-impact-prevention-techniques-tipt/ [Last accessed 15/08/21].

[36] Porges, S. (2011) *The Polyvagal Theory: Neurophysiological Foundations of Emotions, Attachment, Communication, and Self-regulation*, New York: W.W. Norton.

Featured in: Being Well Podcast, Series 3, Episode 107 (2020) Available from: https://www.rickhanson.net/being-well-podcast-polyvagal-theory-with-stephen-porges/ [Last accessed 30/01/2021].

[37] Kosfeld, M., Heinrichs, M., Zak, P., Fischbacher, U. and Fehr, E. (2005) 'Oxytocin increases trust in humans', *Nature*, 435: 673–676.

Fredickson, B.L. (2013) *Love 2.0: Creating Happiness and Health in Moments of Connection*, New York: Plume, p 29.

[38] Brodt S. and Tuchinsky, M. (2000) 'Working together but in opposition: an examination of the "good-cop/bad-cop" negotiating team tactic', *Organizational Behavior and Human Decision Processes*, 81(2): 155–177.

[39] Yuen, A.W.C. and Sander, J.W. (2017) 'Can natural ways to stimulate the vagus nerve improve seizure control?' *Epilepsy and Behaviour* (67): 105–110.

[40] Charman, S. (2017) *'Police Socialisation, Identity and Culture: Becoming Blue'*, London: Palgrave Macmillan.

[41] For example, see: McCaffrey, G. (2015) 'Chapter Two: Idiot Compassion', *Counterpoints* (464): 19–27.

[42] Dando, C., Wilcock, R. and Milne, R. (2009) 'The cognitive interview: the efficacy of a modified mental reinstatement of context procedure for frontline police investigators', *Applied Cognitive Psychology*, 23: 138–147.

Hope, L., Mullis, R. and Gabbert, F. (2013) 'Who? What? When? Using a timeline technique to facilitate recall of a complex event', *Journal of Applied Research in Memory and Cognition*, 2: 20–24.

[43] Beaudoin, M. (2005) 'Agency and choice in the face of trauma: a narrative therapy map', *Journal of Systemic Therapies*, 24(4): 32–50.

[44] Miller, J.K., Peart, A. and Soffia, M. (2020) 'Can police be trained in trauma processing to minimise PTSD symptoms? Feasibility and proof of concept with a newly recruited UK police population', *The Police Journal* 93(4): 310–331.

[45] Maguire, E.A., Woollett, K. and Spiers, H.J. (2006) 'London taxi drivers and bus drivers: a structural MRI and neuropsychological analysis', *Hippocampus*, 16(12): 1091–1101.

[46] Miller, J.K., McDougall, S. Thomas, S. and Wiener, J.M. (2017) 'Impairment in active navigation from trauma and post-traumatic stress disorder', *Neurobiology of Learning and Memory*, 140: 114–123.

Hanson, R. (2020) *Neurodharma: New Science, Ancient Wisdom and Seven Practices of the Highest Happiness*, New York: Harmony, p 192.

[47] Sierk, A., Manthey, A., King, J., Brewin, C.R., Bisby, J.A., Walter, H., Burgess, N. and Daniels, J.K. (2019) 'Allocentric spatial memory

performance predicts intrusive memory severity in posttraumatic stress disorder', *Neurobiology of Learning and Memory*, 166: 107093.

48 Siegel, D.J. (2010) *Mindsight*, Melbourne: Scribe, p 197.

Hanson, R. (2020) *Neurodharma: New Science, Ancient Wisdom and Seven Practices of the Highest Happiness*, New York: Harmony, p 94.

49 Photograph accessed under the Creative Commons license and can be found at: https://www.flickr.com/photos/99688449@N00/24293451/

50 Maguire, E.A., Woollett, K. and Spiers, H.J. (2006) 'London taxi drivers and bus drivers: a structural MRI and neuropsychological analysis', *Hippocampus*, 16(12): 1091–1101.

51 Kessler, H., Holmes, E.A., Blackwell, S.E., Schmidt, A.-C., Schweer, J.M., Býcker, A., Herpertz, S., Axmacher, N. and Kehyayan, A. (2018) 'Reducing intrusive memories of trauma using a visuospatial interference intervention with inpatients with posttraumatic stress disorder (PTSD)', *Journal of Consulting and Clinical Psychology*, 86(12): 1076.

52 This is the neuropsychological notion of 'taking in the good' in Hanson, R. (2013) *Hardwiring Happiness*, New York: Harmony.

Also in Hanson, R. (2020) *Neurodharma: New Science, Ancient Wisdom and Seven Practices of the Highest Happiness*, New York: Harmony.

53 Frankl, V.E. (1946) *Man's Search for Meaning*, Vienna: Beacon Press.

There is much contention about who spoke the original words, but the essence of the sentiment is attributed in the main to Victor Frankl.

54 Killingsworth, M.A. and Gilbert, D.T. (2010) 'A wandering mind is an unhappy mind', *Science*, 330: 932.

55 Killingsworth, M.A. and Gilbert, D.T. (2010) 'A wandering mind is an unhappy mind', *Science*, 330: 932.

56 Raichle, M.E., MacLeod, A.M., Snyder, A.Z., Powers, W.J., Gusnard, D.A. and Shulman, G.L. (2001) 'Inaugural article: a default mode of brain function', *Proceedings of the National Academy of Sciences*, 98(2): 676–682.

57 Hanson, R. (2020) *Neurodharma: New Science, Ancient Wisdom and Seven Practices of the Highest Happiness*, New York: Harmony, p 127.

58 Schwartz, J.M. and Begley, S. (2002) *The Mind and the Brain: Neuroplasticity and the Power of the Mental Force*, New York: HarperCollins Publishers.

Hanson, R. (2020) *Neurodharma: New Science, Ancient Wisdom and Seven Practices of the Highest Happiness*, New York: Harmony.

Davidson, R.J., and McEwen, B. (2012) 'Social influences on neuroplasticity: stress and interventions to promote well-being', *Natural Neuroscience*, 15: 689–695. doi: 10.1038/nn.3093

59 Unpublished data, courtesy of Police Care UK February–December 2018.

60 Andersen, J.P., Papazoglou, K., Koskelainen, M., Nyman, M., Gustafsberg, H. and Arnetz, B.B. (2015) 'Applying Resilience Promotion Training Among Special Forces Police Officers', *SAGE Open*, [online] Available from: https://pubmed.ncbi.nlm.nih.gov/26137394/ [Last accessed 28/10/21].

[61] Institute of HeartMath (2014) *HeartMath Certified Trainer: Leader's Guide*, Boulder Creek, CA: Institute of HeartMath .

McCraty, R. and Atkinson, M. (2012) 'Resilience training program reduces physiological and psychological stress in police officers', *Global Advances in Health and Medicine*, 1(5): 44–66.

Harris, D. (2018) *Meditation for Fidgety Skeptics*, London: Hodder & Stoughton, p 198.

[62] Hanson, R. (2020) *Neurodharma: New Science, Ancient Wisdom and Seven Practices of the Highest Happiness*, New York: Harmony, p 127.

[63] Hanson, R. (2018) *Resilient: Find Your Inner Strength*, London: Penguin.

[64] Courtesy of Tara Brach and freely available from: https://tarabrach.ac-page.com/rain-pdf-download [Last accessed 23/07/21].

[65] Trauma Risk Management (TRiM). Hunt, E., Jones, N., Hastings, V. and Greenberg, N. (2013) 'TRiM: an organizational response to traumatic events in Cumbria Constabulary', *Occupational Medicine*, 63(8): 549–555.

[66] This is a freely available tool online produced by The Wellness Society and is available from: https://thewellnesssociety.org/how-to-stop-overreacting-to-the-small-stuff-with-the-stop-technique/ [Last accessed 23/07/21].

[67] McMullen, J., Barnes-Holmes, D., Barnes-Holmes, Y., Stewart, I., Luciano, C. and Cochrane, A. (2008) 'Acceptance versus distraction: brief instructions, metaphors and exercises in increasing tolerance for self-delivered electric shocks', *Behaviour Research and Therapy*, 46(1): 122–129.

[68] Those who meditate extensively show less anticipation of (and emotional response to) pain and recover quicker, see: Goleman, D. and Davidson, R.J. (2017) *The Science of Meditation: How to Change Your Brain, Mind and Body*, St Ives: Penguin Random House, p 240.

[69] Fredrickson, B.L. (2013) *Love 2.0: Creating Happiness and Health in Moments of Connection*, New York: Plume, p 13.

[70] Hanson, R. (2020) *Neurodharma: New Science, Ancient Wisdom and Seven Practices of the Highest Happiness*, New York: Harmony, p 51.

[71] Wimberger, L. (2017) 'Using Neuroscience to Find Healing and Happiness' Neuroscience Training Summit, published by Sounds True, Inc., [online] Available from: https://neuroscience-training-summit-2017-sfm.soundstrue.com/?sq=1 [Last accessed 28/10/21].

[72] It perhaps goes without saying that this practice is not to be done when you are using any form of equipment any more sophisticated than a fork or a hair brush and is not to be used on operational duties!

[73] Denson, T.F., DeWall, C.N., Finkel, E.J. (2012) 'Self-Control and aggression', *Current Directions in Psychological Science*, 21(1): 20.

[74] Gayadeen, S.M. and Phillips, S.W. (2016) 'Donut time: the use of humor across the police work environment', *Journal of Organizational Ethnography*, 5(1): 44–59.

[75] Foley J., Hassett, A., Williams, E. (2021) ' "Getting on with the job": A systematised literature review of secondary trauma and post-traumatic stress disorder (PTSD) in policing within the United Kingdom (UK)', *The Police*

Journal, [online] Available from: https://journals.sagepub.com/doi/full/10.1177/0032258X21990412 [Last accessed 28/10/21].

Charman, S. (2013) 'Sharing a laugh: the role of humour in relationships between police officers and ambulance staff', *International Journal of Sociology and Social Policy*, 33(3): 152–166.

76 Charman, S. (2017) *Police Socialisation, Identity and Culture: Becoming Blue*, London: Palgrave Macmillan.

77 Mobbs D., Greicius M.D., Abdel-Azim E., Menon V. and Reiss A.L. (2003) 'Humor modulates the mesolimbic reward centers', *Neuron*, 40(5): 1041–1048.

78 Quoted in Harris, D. (2018) *Meditation for Fidgety Skeptics*, London: Hodder & Stoughton, p 1.

79 Tseng, J. and Poppenk, J. (2020) 'Brain meta-state transitions demarcate thoughts across task contexts exposing the mental noise of trait neuroticism', *Nature Communications*, 11: 3480.

Lorenz-Spreen, P., Mørch Mønsted, B., Hövel, P. and Lehmann, S. (2019) 'Accelerating dynamics of collective attention', *Nature Communications*, 10(1).

Kowalczyk, D.K. and Hansen, L.K. (2020) 'The complexity of social media response: statistical evidence for one-dimensional engagement signal in Twitter', *Conference: 12th International Conference on Agents and Artificial Intelligence*, [online] January, Available from: DOI: 10.5220/0009169709180925 [Last accessed 28/10/21].

80 College of Policing 'Public Order Tactical Options', [online] Available from: https://www.app.college.police.uk/app-content/public-order/planning-and-deployment/tactical-options/#cordons-and-intercepts-considerations [Last accessed 28/03/21].

81 Goleman, D. and Davidson, R.J. (2017) *The Science of Meditation: How to Change Your Brain, Mind and Body*, St Ives: Penguin Random House, p 277.

82 CNN (Cable News Network). Harris, D. (2018) *Meditation for Fidgety Skeptics*, London: Hodder & Stoughton, p 196.

83 CNN (Cable News Network). Harris, D. (2018) *Meditation for Fidgety Skeptics*, London: Hodder & Stoughton, p 196.

84 Grupe, D.W., McGehee, C., Smith, C., Francis, A.D., Mumford, J.A. and Davidson, R.J. (2021) 'Mindfulness training reduces PTSD symptoms and improves stress-related health outcomes in police officers', *Journal of Police and Criminal Psychology*, 36(1): 72–85.

85 This first-of-a-kind dialogue with the Dalai Lama was co-organised by Dr Kumanga Andrahennadi of the Centre for the Advanced Learning of Mindfulness in partnership with the London Metropolitan Police. Available from: https://www.dalailama.com/videos/in-conversation-with-the-metropolitan-police [Last accessed 230721]. Also see: www.CalmMindfulness.org.

86 Miller, J.K., Soffia, M., Brewin, C.B. and Burchell, B. (2020) *Policing: The Job and the Life Survey 2018 Summary Report*, Police Care UK.

Harris, D. (2018) *Meditation for Fidgety Skeptics,* London: Hodder & Stoughton, p 196.

[87] Miller, J.K., Soffia, M., Brewin, C.B. and Burchell, B. (2020) *Policing: The Job and the Life Survey 2018 Summary Report,* Police Care UK, [online] Available from: https://www.policecare.org.uk/wp-content/uploads/PoliceCareUK_TJTL-Report-.pdf [Last accessed 01/12/20].

[88] Goleman, D. and Davidson, R.J. (2017) *The Science of Meditation: How to Change Your Brain, Mind and Body,* St Ives: Penguin Random House, p 52.

[89] Harris, D. (2018) *Meditation for Fidgety Skeptics,* London: Hodder & Stoughton, p 198.

[90] Kowalczyk, D.K. and Hansen, L.K. (2020) 'The complexity of social media response: statistical evidence for one-dimensional engagement signal in Twitter', *Conference: 12th International Conference on Agents and Artificial Intelligence,* [online] January, Available from: DOI: 10.5220/0009169709180925 [Last accessed 28/10/21].

[91] Desbordes, G., Negi, L.T., Pace, T.W.W., Wallace, B.A., Raison, C.L. and Schwartz, E.L. (2012) 'Effects of mindful-attention and compassion meditation training on amygdala response to emotional stimuli in an ordinary, non-meditative state', *Frontiers in Human Neuroscience,* 1 November.

Goleman, D. and Davidson, R.J. (2017) *The Science of Meditation: How to Change Your Brain, Mind and Body,* St Ives: Penguin Random House, p 138.

[92] It is important to note here that all brains are different and for some with Attention Deficit Disorder, attention can be even more of a challenge. Fortunately, practising with attention can be really helpful for those with attention deficit, see: Gabriely, R., Tarrasch, R., Velicki, M. and Ovadia-Blachman, Z. (2020) 'The influence of mindfulness meditation on inattention and physiological markers of stress on students with learning disabilities and/or attention deficit hyperactivity disorder', *Research in Developmental Disabilities,* 100: 103630.

[93] Jacobs, T.L., Epel, E.S., Lin, J., Blackburn, E.H., Wolkowitz, O.M., Bridwell, D.A., et al (2011) 'Intensive meditation training, immune cell telomerase activity, and psychological mediators', *Psychoneuroendocrinology,* 36(5): 664–681.

Goleman, D. and Davidson, R.J. (2017) *The Science of Meditation: How to Change Your Brain, Mind and Body,* St Ives: Penguin Random House, p 87.

[94] Siegel, D.J. (2010) *Mindsight,* Melbourne: Scribe, p 40.

[95] Guzmán, M. and Blâzquez, C. (2004) 'Ketone body synthesis in the brain: possible neuroprotective effects', *Prostaglandins Leukotrienes and Essential Fatty Acids,* 70: 287–292.

Hsu, T.M., Konanur, V.R., Taing, L., Usui, R., Kayser, B.D., Goran, M.I. and Kanoski, S.E. (2015) 'Effects of sucrose and high fructose corn syrup consumption on spatial memory function and hippocampal neuroinflammation in adolescent rats', *Hippocampus,* 25: 227–239.

Linard, B., Ferrandon, A., Koning, E., Nehlig, A. and Raffo, E. (2010) 'Ketogenic diet exhibits neuroprotective effects in hippocampus but fails to prevent epileptogenesis in the lithium-pilocarpine model of mesial temporal lobe epilepsy in adult rats', *Epilepsia* 51: 1829–1836.

Miller, J.K., McDougall, S., Thomas, S. and Wiener, J. (2017) 'The impact of the brain-derived neurotrophic factor gene on trauma and spatial processing', *Journal of Clinical Medicine*, 6: 108.

96 Guzmân, M. and Blâzquez, C. (2004) 'Ketone body synthesis in the brain: possible neuroprotective effects', *Prostaglandins Leukotrienes and Essential Fatty Acids*, 70: 287–292.

97 Aerobic exercise and a ketogenic diet is not for everybody: please consult your GP before making dietary or physical changes to your lifestyle.

98 Jacobs, T.L., Epel, E.S., Lin, J., Blackburn, E.H., Wolkowitz, O.M., Bridwell, D.A., et al (2011) 'Intensive meditation training, immune cell telomerase activity, and psychological mediators', *Psychoneuroendocrinology*, 36(5): 664–681.

Goleman, D. and Davidson, R.J. (2017) *The Science of Meditation: How to Change Your Brain, Mind and Body*, St Ives: Penguin Random House, p 57.

99 Stroebaek, P.S. (2013) 'Let's have a cup of coffee! Coffee and coping communities at work', *Symbolic Interaction*, 36: 381–397.

100 Jacobs, T.L., Epel, E.S., Lin, J., Blackburn, E.H., Wolkowitz, O.M., Bridwell, D.A., et al (2011) 'Intensive meditation training, immune cell telomerase activity, and psychological mediators', *Psychoneuroendocrinology*, 36(5): 664–681.

Goleman, D. and Davidson, R.J. (2017) *The Science of Meditation: How to Change Your Brain, Mind and Body*, St Ives: Penguin Random House, pp 95–98.

101 Creswell, J.D., Taren, A., Lindsay, E.K., Greco, C.M., Gianaros, P.J., Fairgrieve, A., Marsland, A.L., Brown, K.W., Way, B.M., Rosen, R.K. and Ferris, J.L. (2016) 'Alterations in resting state functional connectivity link mindfulness meditation with reduced interleukin-6: a randomized controlled trial', *Biological Psychiatry*, 80: 53–61, p 156.

Goleman, D. and Davidson, R.J. (2017) *The Science of Meditation: How to Change Your Brain, Mind and Body*, St Ives: Penguin Random House.

102 PS If you just got freaked out seeing the word 'meditation', hang on in there for Chapter 5 – we get it!

103 Radiohead frontman, Thom Yorke, has described the song 'Karma Police' as 'not entirely serious' offering the listener the freedom to interpret any irony as they see fit. Here, we choose to do this in terms of the policing brain and its resilience. See: Footman, T. (2007) *Radiohead: Welcome to the Machine: OK Computer and the Deat Classic Album*, New Malden: Chrome Dreams, p 78.

104 Merzenich, M., Nahum, M. and Van Vleet, T. (2013) 'Changing Brains', *Progress in Brain Research* (Vol 2, 1st ed), Oxford: Elsevier.

See also: https://www.rickhanson.net/get-started/ [Last accessed 31/01/21].

[105] Fitzgibbon, B.M., Kirkovski, M., Fornito, A., Paton, B., Fitzgerald, P.B. and Enticott, P.G. (2016) 'Emotion processing fails to modulate putative mirror neuron response to trained visuomotor associations', *Neuropsychologia*, 84: 7e13.

Chapter 5

[1] In 1933 at his presidential inauguration, Franklin D. Roosevelt is quoted to have said: 'So, first of all, let me assert my firm belief that the only thing we have to fear is ... fear itself', Available from: https://en.wikipedia.org/wiki/First_inauguration_of_Franklin_D._Roosevelt#Inaugural_speech [Last accessed 08/04/21].

[2] The notion of 'post-traumatic growth' can sound very 'fluffy' to those in the midst of dealing with trauma on the front line, but the research is unequivocal that genuine personal development can come out of the most adverse of circumstances, sometimes depending on the directness of the exposure and personal relationships. See: Chopko, B.A., Palmieri, P.A., and Adams, R.E. (2018) 'Relationships among traumatic experiences, PTSD, and posttraumatic growth for police officers: a path analysis', *Psychological Trauma: Theory, Research, Practice, and Policy*, 10(2): 183–189.

[3] One reason for this could be that those with trauma exposure were better practised in applying vital hippocampal contextualisation to make sense of difficult incidents. See: Miller, J.K. (2016) 'Lost in trauma: post-traumatic stress disorder, spatial processing and the brain – derived neurotrophic factor gene', thesis, Bournemouth University, [eprint] Available from: http://eprints.bournemouth.ac.uk/25012/1/MILLER%2C%20Jessica%20Katherine_Ph.D._2016.pdf [Last accessed 08/04/21].

With thanks to Prof Jan Wiener, Prof Sine McDougall and Dr Sarah Thomas of Bournemouth University in the analysis of the data on trauma and navigation self-assessment.

[4] Miller, J.K., Brewin, C.R., Burchell, B.J., Soffia, M., Elliot-Davies and Peart, A. (2021) 'The development of a UK Police Traumatic Events Checklist', *The Police Journal*, April.

[5] Miller, J.K., Soffia, M., Brewin, C.B. and Burchell, B. (2020) *Policing: The Job and the Life Survey 2018 Summary Report*, Police Care UK, [online] Available from: https://www.policecare.org.uk/wp- [Last accessed 28/10/21].

[6] Other variables (such as the extent of urbanisation, local crime rates or the ratio of resource to force size) may also be influential factors on trauma management. Nonetheless, these factors are mediated by decisions at force level, so force level decision-making remains integral to trauma resilience across the UK.

[7] The differentiation between pain and suffering is a helpful one to make in terms of resilience and is reflected in the 'second punch' practice in Chapter 4.

[8] Manuscript in preparation at the time of writing July 2021.

9   University of Cambridge and Police Care UK (2019) *Policing: The Job and the Life*, unpublished data, with permission from Police Care UK.

10 Solving unforeseen problems on your own is known to be a protective factor for wellbeing in the wider labour market, but shows up as being a negative factor for policing. This is perhaps due to the impact of single crewing on trauma resilience and of being first on scene to high-risk incidents.

11 Dolan, P., Hallsworth, M., Halpern, D., King, D. and Vlav, I. (2020) *Mindspace: Influencing Behaviour through Public Policy Discussion Document*, London: Cabinet Office and The Institute for Government, [online] Available from: https://www.bi.team/wp-content/uploads/2015/07/MINDSPACE.pdf [Last accessed 19/03/21].

12 Dolan, P., Hallsworth, M., Halpern, D., King, D. and Vlav, I. (2020) *Mindspace: Influencing Behaviour Through Public Policy Discussion Document*, London: Cabinet Office and The Institute for Government, [online] Available from: https://www.bi.team/wp-content/uploads/2015/07/MINDSPACE.pdf [Last accessed 19/03/21]

13 Greenberg, N. and Tracy, D. (2020) 'What healthcare leaders need to do to protect the psychological well-being of frontline staff in the COVID-19 pandemic', *British Medical Journal Leader*, [online] Available from: https://bmjleader.bmj.com/content/leader/early/2020/05/17/leader-2020-000273.full.pdf [Last accessed 08/04/21].

14 Fear

15 Brewin, C.R., Miller, J.K., Soffia, M., Peart, A. and Burchell, B. (2020) 'Posttraumatic stress disorder and complex posttraumatic stress disorder in UK police officers', *Psychological Medicine*, 1–9.

16 Hornby, N. (1992) *Fever Pitch*, London: Victor Gollancz.

17 Bullock, K., Garland, J. and Coupar, F. (2019) 'Police officer transitions to retirement in the United Kingdom: social identity, social support, and (in)justice', *Policing & Society*: 1–15.

18 There were only two studies found which directly related to authentic leadership in policing and neither's full texts were available, see: Pardede, C.D. and Soeling, P.D. (2020) 'The effect of authentic leadership and organizational culture on employee engagement with internal communication as mediator variable in millennial generation of Polri (Indonesian National Police)', *Advances in Social Sciences Research Journal*, 7(7).

    Jackson, J.D. (2016) *Police Supervisors' Authentic Leadership Influence on Employee Work Engagement: A Phenomenological Examination*. Dissertation, Available from: https://www.proquest.com/openview/3ea4c10c3c2f0c862f2ee6f2ed851d4a/1.pdf?pq-origsite=gscholar&cbl=18750&diss=y [Last accessed 28/10/21].

19 Baron, L. and Parent, Ç. (2015) 'Developing authentic leadership within a training context: three phenomena supporting the individual development process', *Journal of Leadership & Organizational Studies*, 22(1): 37–53.

20 Miller, J.K., Soffia, M., Brewin, C.B. and Burchell, B. (2020) *Policing: The Job and the Life Survey 2018 Summary Report*, Police Care UK, [online]

Available from: https://www.policecare.org.uk/wp-content/uploads/PoliceCareUK_TJTL-Report-.pdf [Last accessed 01/12/20].

[21] If humour helps you to remember this approach, the traditional British folk dance 'The Hokey Cokey' can be a nice gentle nudge when you feel yourself contracting around 'being police and only police'. Just remember the last verse: 'You put your whole self in'.

[22] Williamson, C. (2016) "'We are mothers, fathers, you': Police Federation launch hard-hitting campaign showing human side of policing', *Belfast Telegraph*, [online] Available from: https://www.belfasttelegraph.co.uk/news/northern-ireland/we-are-mothers-fathers-you-police-federation-launch-hard-hitting-campaign-showing-human-side-of-policing-34502110.html [Last accessed 18/04/21].

[23] An organisation is something author Yuval Noah Harari describes as a 'figment of the collective imagination' anyway, a legal fiction, not a physical entity that can be pointed at.
See: Harari, Y.N. (2011) *Sapiens: A Brief History of Humankind*, London: Vintage. p 32.

[24] Charman, S. (2017) *Police Socialisation, Identity and Culture: Becoming Blue*, London: Palgrave Macmillan.

[25] Hodgson, S., Watts, I., Fraser, S., Roderick, P. and Dambha-Miller, H. (2020) 'Loneliness, social isolation, cardiovascular disease and mortality: a synthesis of the literature and conceptual framework', *Journal of the Royal Society of Medicine*, 113(5): 185–192.

[26] For example, the need for safeguarding offenders in child sexual exploitation roles is a known risk of the role, but one that is not always openly discussed during recruitment, limiting individuals' chances to prepare their resilience for the impact it can have.

[27] Examples include the International Trauma Questionnaire: Cloitre, M., Shevlin M., Brewin, C.R., Bisson, J.I., Roberts, N.P., Maercker, A., Karatzias, T. and Hyland, P. (2019) 'The International Trauma Questionnaire: development of a self-report measure of ICD-11 PTSD and complex PTSD', *Acta Psychiatrica Scandinavica*, 138(6): 536–546.
The Police Traumatic Events Checklist: Miller, J.K., Brewin, C.R., Burchell, B.J., Soffia, M., Elliot-Davies and Peart, A. (2021) 'The development of a UK police traumatic events checklist', *The Police Journal*, April.

[28] National Crime Agency.

[29] General Data Protection Regulation.

[30] See: Papazoglou, K. and Tuttle, B.M. (2018) 'Fighting police trauma: practical approaches to addressing psychological needs of officers', *SAGE Open*, [online] Available from: doi:10.1177/2158244018794794 [last accessed 28/10/21].

[31] National Health Service and Royal National Lifeboat Institution.

[32] Sharp, M.L., Harrison, V., Solomon, N., Fear, N., King, H. and Pike, G. (2020) 'Assessing the mental health and wellbeing of the Emergency

Responder community in the UK', *Open Research Online*, Open University, The Royal Foundation and King's College London (King's Centre for Military Health Research, KCMHR), [online] Available from: https://kcmhr. org/erreport2020-mentalhealth-wellbeing/ [Last accessed 27/10/21].

33 At the time of writing in 2021, the Bristol riots against the policing bill were gaining momentum, resulting in confused headlines of protestors calling for society to 'Kill the Bill' – a phrase that for many unfamiliar with the detail of the protest may confuse with a call to action to directly harm police.

Available from: https://www.independent.co.uk/news/uk/home-news/policing-bill-protests-latest-bristol-b1820309.html https://www.belfasttelegraph.co.uk/news/northern-ireland/ni-political-leaders-call-for-calm-as-15-psni-officers-injured-in-belfast-rioting-40269592.html [Last accessed 09/04/21].

Index

References to figures appear in *italic* type;
those in **bold** type refer to tables. References to endnotes show both the
page number and the note number (199n56).